Imagining tomorrow

Imagining tomorrow

Adult education
for transformation

Marjorie Mayo

NIACE
THE NATIONAL ORGANISATION
FOR ADULT LEARNING

Published by the National Institute of Adult Continuing Education
(England and Wales)
21 De Montfort Street, Leicester, LE1 7GE
Company registration no. 2603322
Charity registration no. 1002775

First published 1997
©NIACE

CATALOGUING IN PUBLICATION DATA
A CIP record for this title is available from the British Library
ISBN 1 86201 006 4

Typeset by Midlands Book Typesetters
Text design by Virman Man
Cover design by Sue Storey
Printed in Great Britain by Antony Rowe, Chippenham

Contents

Dedication

To the memory of my parents, who both valued education so highly, and to the memory of my sister, who was going to teach.

Acknowledgements

My special thanks are due to the organisations and individuals who have participated in educational programmes at Ruskin College, Oxford, and Southern African Development Education Programme (SADEP), University of the Western Cape, South Africa. They have raised so many of the questions which feature in this book. I should also like to thank my colleagues at Ruskin and SADEP, together with colleagues at the William Temple Foundation, with whom we have collaborated and shared ideas on developing education for transformation.

My grateful thanks to a number of organisations and individuals who provided materials which I have referred to, including Cuba Solidarity Campaign and Marx Memorial Library, Julie Batten, Brian Denny, Ian Harford, Tom Lovett, Jim Mortimer, Andrew Murray, Peter Shenahan, Tom Steele, Richard Taylor and Kevin Ward.

In addition, a number of individuals very kindly read chapters, in draft, and provided me with comments. These included Richard Bryant, Christopher Feeney, Mayerlene Frow, Ian Harford, Katherine Hughes, Keith Jackson, Jim Mortimer, Ines Newman, Jane Thompson and Stephen Yeo. I am extremely grateful for their constructive criticisms. Any remaining errors and misinterpretations are, of course, my own.

My grateful thanks to Gillian Macfarlane, who provided assistance in wordprocessing and ensured that I saved my drafts with her excellent back-up support. Christopher Feeney has been consistently supportive and constructive in his feedback, and I have benefited immensely from his editorial advice; my thanks to him. Many thanks too, to Virman Man, who concluded the editorial work at NIACE, and to Alan Tuckett – the title emerged from Alan's creative suggestions.

I should like to thank Jessica Sacret for the expert way in which she enabled me to work at a number of questions, and to tackle some blocks, whilst I was writing this; my thanks and deep appreciation for her help.

Finally, my special thanks to my son and daughter, Clyde and Scarlet Harris, who, as always, kept me going, and kept raising questions.

Introduction

As the twenty-first century approaches, both community and workplace adult education can have continuing potential for contributing to strategies for transformation. And this potential may even be enhanced, it will be suggested, in the contemporary context. Whilst key to the argument and overall purpose of this book, this may seem to be an extraordinarily unwarrantable claim to make in a period of such remarkable change and uncertainty, not just in Britain, but on a global scale.

The century which is drawing to a close has been characterised as an 'Age of Extremes'. As the eighties passed into the nineties, the historian Hobsbawm has argued, 'it became evident that the world crisis was not only general in an economic sense, but equally general in politics' (Hobsbawm, 1994: 10). And this was accompanied by an even more obvious social and moral crisis, a 'crisis of the beliefs and assumptions on which modern society had been founded' and of the 'historic structures of human relations' (*ibid*, p.11). It was not, he argued, 'a crisis of one form of organising societies, but of all forms', affecting both East and West, North and South (*ibid*).

The world had become incomparably richer, with vastly advanced technology and communications. Humanity was far better educated, with far higher levels of literacy, at least in terms of official statistics. But it was also a world of increasing polarisation and poverty, which had seen an unparalleled scale of human catastrophes, from the greatest famines in history to systematic genocide and regression to the standards of barbarism. Earlier assumptions about progress, whether this was defined in terms of material progress or social, political, intellectual and moral progress, had been succeeded, Hobsbawm suggested, by a climate of questioning and a mood of uncertainty and unease.

Concluding his introductory 'Bird's Eye View' of the century, he pointed to the shift from a Eurocentric world, at the beginning of the twentieth century, to a globe which had become far more of a single operational unit. But there were fundamental tensions between this 'accelerating process of globalization and the inability of both public institutions and the collective behaviour of human beings to come to terms with it' (*ibid*, p.15). In this developing 'global village' old patterns of human relationships were disintegrating, he argued. And this process of disintegration was being reinforced by the 'erosion of traditional societies and religions, as well as by the destruction, or autodestruction, of the societies of "real socialism" ' (p.15).

'At the end of this century it has become possible to see what a world may be like in which the past, including the past in the present, has lost its role, in which the old maps and charts which guided human beings, singly and collectively, through life no longer represent the landscape through which we move, the sea on which we sail. In which we do not know where our journey is taking us, or even ought to take us' (Hobsbawm, 1994: 16).

In face of such fundamental questioning and uncertainty, how can the continuing potential of any type of contribution to strategies for transformation be argued and established, let alone the specific potential of community and workplace adult education? To respond with certainty would be to invite characterisations in terms of arrogance, perhaps, if not of idiocy.

But the converse, the reverse side of the coin of these losses of the former certainties, may be precisely that there can still be alternatives and options. If the grand narratives of modernisation as progress, and the rationalist and humanist assumptions shared (as Hobsbawm has also pointed out) by liberal capitalism and communism, are no longer so generally taken as given, then that still raises more questions than answers (as he himself has recognised). And if neither free-market *laissez-faire* capitalism nor deterministic, structuralist versions (caricatures, as I shall argue) of Marxism remain plausible, in terms of offering automatically incontrovertible predictions of future patterns of development, then that still leaves vital questions about the scope both for individual human agency and for collective action. (These are questions which can be pursued, I shall argue, via a less caricatured application of Marxist insights.)

This is absolutely not to suggest, of course, that in the increasingly fragmented yet globalised scenario of the late twentieth century such scope for both individual and collective action is unlimited. On the contrary, as Chapter One argues in more detail, men – and women – do still make history, but as Marx earlier commented 'they do not make it just as they please; they do not make it under circumstances chosen by themselves, but under circumstances directly encountered, given and transmitted from the past' ('The Eighteenth Brumaire of Louis Bonaparte', in Marx and Engels, *Selected Works*, 1968: 98). Different theoretical perspectives have offered competing frameworks for analysing the extent and the scope for individual and collective action, the limits as well as the possibilities for shaping history, affecting the course of economic and social development, and political and cultural change.

These differences in theoretical perspective have vital implications, both in terms of the scale of the possibilities, and, of course, in terms of the potential alternative directions for such developments and change. At one end of the theoretical spectrum, neo-liberal, New Right debates focus upon the scope for individual entrepreneurs for maximising profits, despite global recession and restructuring. Meanwhile, at the other end of the theoretical spectrum, debates focus upon the possibilities for both individual and collective action to promote forms of economic and social development which are effectively geared towards combatting poverty and deprivation and towards the enhancement of social justice and equal opportunities. This is the agenda for social 'transformation', the central theme which will be explored in the chapters which follow. This agenda for social 'transformation' will be contrasted with the neo-liberal, New Right agenda, both in theory (in terms of the battles between competing ideas and the relationship between social consciousness and social change) and in terms of practice and practical outcomes, for adult education in the community and in the workplace.

These fundamental differences of perspective and approach are vitally important. As Chapter One argues in more detail, the loss of confidence in old certainties absolutely does not need to entail a post-modernist style agnosticism about all theories, let alone the denial of the possibility of making any judgements at all about the validity and implications of different approaches.

The point which is being made here is simply that there is room for renewed debate about the potential for human action in an uncertain world, for exploring possibilities and opportunities as well as understanding structural constraints. And that, almost by definition, conscious action and the development of strategies for development and change of any type, let alone conscious strategies for development for transformation and social justice, require women and men with critical consciousness.

If a 'crisis' is to be understood, in the terms of the *Oxford Dictionary* definition of crisis, as 'a turning point', 'a state of affairs in which a decisive change for better is possible as well as a decisive change for the worse (*Shorter Oxford Dictionary*) then women and men need to be able to produce their own critical analyses of social, political and economic contradictions. In the terminology of the late Paulo Freire, one of the most influential twentieth century thinkers on adult education as a social and political weapon, they need 'conscientisation' (the development of critical consciousness) in order to take collective action for liberating forms of change. They need to be able to analyse the possibilities and the potential for alternatives to the *status quo*, as well as understanding the structural constraints, if they are to develop effective strategies for transformation.

As Chapter One will also argue, though, Freire's approach entails problems of its own, problems which need to be further unwrapped and explored. On the one hand, the case for adult education to promote Freire's goal of conscientisation or critical consciousness implies the need for adult educators who can work with the oppressed to unmask the myths which cloak reality, myths which 'deceive us and help to maintain the oppressing dehumanising structures' of the *status quo* (Freire, quoted in Youngman, 1986: 76). On the other hand, Freire's approach has been based upon rejecting traditional educators' views of their students as passive recipients of the received wisdom, empty vessels, or blank sheets, to be filled up with knowledge by experts, even if this were to be 'politically correct' knowledge, to replace their 'false consciousness'.

The notion of 'false consciousness' is itself inherently problematic, in any case. The exploited and oppressed are often only too well aware of their exploitation and oppression. As Bina Agarwal, for example, has argued, from attending meetings with rural Indian women, 'At these meetings I learnt more than any single book on feminist theory could teach me. In particular I learnt about peasant women's numerous and ingenious ways of resisting gender oppression that disprove the assumption that women suffer from false consciousness . . . Even the most outwardly compliant women often resist covertly . . . From these interactions I thus learnt that for poor women's empowerment, what is needed is less the raising of consciousness and more the strengthening of their ability to overtly protest and mobilise for change' (Agarwal, 1994: 254).

This, then, poses further questions about the relationships between consciousness and material circumstances. Chapter One explores some of these questions and dilemmas, along with further questions about theories (including competing theories) and practice. And Chapter One also poses questions about the potential contribution of adult and community education, in relation to different levels of consciousness, the development of critical consciousness and the connections between different forms of exploitation and oppression.

Having explored alternative theoretical approaches, models and strategies for adult education and their potential relevance for strategies for transformation, the book goes back, in Chapter Two, to compare and contrast a range of different historical approaches. This is despite Hobsbawm's comments about the prospects of a world in which the past has lost its role, along with the old maps and charts of previously accepted models and assumptions. But the point of reviewing past approaches and experiences is absolutely not to evoke any previous 'golden ages' or to imply that previously successful models either could or should be revived and re-applied in the fundamentally altered and rapidly changing context of the present and immediate future. The quip that 'nostalgia is not what it used to be' may have particular purchase in this specific *fin de siècle*. Uncertainty and questioning would seem to be more in keeping with the contemporary mood than any simplistic appeals to former certainties, let alone to attempt to re-enact the past.

Rather, the point of reviewing a range of different historical approaches is to re-appraise their positive contributions as well as their limitations, within their particular contexts and constraints. What theoretical frameworks and analytical tools were most useful, and why, and how did these approaches relate to the construction of effective strategies for development and change? How were these strategies reviewed, and how did individuals and their organisations learn from their experiences, their mistakes as well as their achievements? This may have relevance in returning to the contemporary context, and reviewing the questions of alternatives and options.

One of the key features of this contemporary context, as it has been suggested, has been the accelerating process of globalisation. The extent to which the world now operates as a single unit has vital implications, in terms of the potential for economic development, let alone for economic development which meets the needs of the poorest and most excluded groups in any society. Globalisation has vital social and political implications, too, as international pressures and constraints, including those applied by international agencies such as the World Bank and the International Monetary Fund, impact upon welfare and the possibilities for social development in particular areas. And globalisation has vital implications in terms of ideology, culture and identities. On the one hand, this has been described in terms of the development of the homogenised 'global village', the world of E-mail, Internet and McDonald's. But this 'global village' is also characterised by an increasing emphasis on diversity and difference, a world of complex multiple identities, and a world characterised by racist national identities and the exclusion of minorities.

Globalisation is not, of course, a brand new phenomenon. Writing in the mid-nineteenth century, Marx and Engels analysed the global implications of the development of capitalism. 'The need of a constantly expanding market for its products chases the bourgeoisie over the whole surface of the globe' they argued, in the Manifesto of the Communist Party, in 1848. The bourgeoisie 'must nestle everywhere, settle everywhere, establish connections everywhere. The bourgeoisie has through its exploitation of the world-market given a cosmopolitan character to production and consumption in every country. To the great chagrin of Reactionists, it has drawn from under the feet of industry the national ground on which it stood.' Old national industries are 'dislodged by new industries, whose introduction becomes a life and death question for all civilized nations, by industries that no longer work up indigenous raw material, but raw material drawn from the remotest zones; industries whose products are consumed, not only at home, but in every quarter of the globe. In place of the old wants, satisfied by the productions of the country, we find new wants, requiring for their satisfaction the products of distant lands and climes ... And as in material, so also in intellectual production. The intellectual creations of individual nations become common property .... [The bourgeoisie] compels all nations, on pain of extinction, to adopt the bourgeois mode of production: it compels them to introduce what it calls civilization into their midst, ie, to become bourgeois themselves. In one word, it creates a world after its own image' (Marx and Engels, 1968 edition: 38–39).

The concept of globalisation has its own history, then, in the critical analysis of capitalist development. And parallels between the impact in terms of social inequalities both within and between North and South have been drawn historically, too. Writing in 1890, for example, William Booth explained the title of his book on the slums, *In Darkest England*, as follows: 'As there is a darkest Africa, is there not also a darkest England? containing, within a stone's throw of our cathedrals and palaces, similar horrors to those which Stanley has found existing in the great Equatorial forest?'

Similar parallels were drawn by Jack London, for instance, when, in 1902, he went into the 'under-world of London with an attitude of mind which I may best liken to that of an explorer' to discover the lives of *The People of the Abyss* (London, 1977: Preface). What is being suggested here, then, is not that globalisation is a late-twentieth century phenomenon, but rather that the form and extent of globalisation has changed dramatically, and that this more evident shift from an apparently Eurocentric world to a globe which has become more of a single operational unit has had vital implications, economically, politically, socially and culturally. More specifically too, it will be argued that this has had key importance for strategies for development for transformation.

In particular, it will be argued that, as Rogers amongst others has demonstrated, globalisation has also meant that models and experiences of adult education for development and transformation, whether in the workplace or the community, can more usefully than ever be compared and contrasted, between North and South, across First and Third Worlds (Rogers, 1992). And in place of the more Eurocentric approaches of the past, approaches to cross-national exchanges of experience can become potentially more reciprocal, as the First World becomes more aware of the relevance and importance of some of the experiences of the Third World, in the more evidently global context of the late twentieth century. Chapter Three focuses upon some of the key implications of experiences of community adult education for transformation in the South, in Third World countries, including experiences in Cuba, India, Nicaragua and Tanzania.

Whilst the overall focus of the book is upon community-based approaches and strategies, Chapter Four is more directly concerned with economic and employment issues. This sets the scene for exploring and evaluating different approaches to education and training to support both community and workplace-based responses to economic restructuring, rising unemployment, increasing casualisation, low pay and the particular exploitation of the most vulnerable sections of the workforce, including women and members of minority ethnic communities. The key point to emphasise here, in developing alternative strategies, is that the starting point needs to be a holistic view of development; local economic development needs to be evaluated in terms of its contribution to development to meet social needs and to promote social justice. And it needs to be evaluated in terms of the quality of the employment which is to be generated and/or safeguarded. Such 'quality' criteria include levels of pay, conditions and security of employment and training, and criteria relating to access, in terms of equal opportunities. In addition, this holistic approach involves evaluating the extent to which local economic development strategies can be integrated as part of regional and national strategies for development for transformation. Adult education has a particularly relevant role to play, here, to enable local communities and workforces to explore the possibilities for local econqmic development and training, as well as to analyse the wider constraints. Education can help to develop communities' critical understanding of these constraints, as the prerequisite for effective campaigning at regional and national levels, and beyond, in the context of the global economy.

This focus upon economic and employment issues in Chapter Four sets the scene for the discussion of community adult education in response to changing and intensifying social needs in Chapter Five. The links between economic restructuring on a global scale, and increasing social polarisation, deprivation, poverty and social exclusion, need to be explored, in terms of at least three related dimensions. First, economic restructuring has resulted in increasing unemployment, with at least three, if not more nearly four million unemployed in Britain, in the context of upward of twenty million people out of work in Europe. The sheer numbers, together with the proportions are, of course, far more dramatic, in Third World contexts, in the South. The social consequences of unemployment are well documented both in terms of material poverty and ill health as well as in terms of social and psychological stress, including depression, isolation and family break-up (eg, Gallie *et al*, 1994; Fryer, 1992).

And as if that were not enough, economic restructuring has also been associated with the deterioration of the quality of so much of the employment that remains. This can be measured in terms of worsening pay and conditions and particularly in terms of increasing job insecurity, in the more 'flexible' labour market conditions of the eighties and nineties. This has been a particular feature in Britain, where government policies have specifically aimed to enhance Britain's competitiveness, in the global economy, by deregulation. Policies have set out to give market mechanisms freer rein, holding down wages and removing protective employment legislation. As a result, Britain's economy has been described as the least regulated in the European Union (OECD, 1994 *Economic Outlook*, July). This characteristic has also been linked with the particularly marked growth of polarisation and poverty in Britain, over the same period of the eighties and early nineties. (As the Rowntree Study on Income and Wealth demonstrated, income inequality grew more rapidly in UK, in the eighties, than in any of the developed countries listed, apart from New Zealand.) Being in and out of low-paid casual work, on the margins, has been a major factor in the rise of poverty and social exclusion. Once again, this characteristic has been especially marked in Britain, although it has also been only too prevalent in Third World contexts, in the South, as well as in the North.

Adult education for transformation has a potentially vital role to play here, in promoting greater awareness and understanding. This includes understanding the connections between these different aspects, between unemployment and low-paid casualised employment, between the workplace and the community, and between the causes of marginalisation and social exclusion in First and Third World contexts, in the North and in the South.

The third aspect of economic restructuring, with particular importance for adult education for transformation, has been the impact on government welfare strategies. The New Right Neo-Liberal agenda has been committed to containing public expenditure on welfare, including education in general and adult education more specifically, as part of strategies to shift resources towards the private sector, and to promote the 'enterprise culture'. This has been key to the New Right project for promoting profitability through market mechanisms. Once again, this has been particularly marked in Britain, together with the US in the Reagan years, although once again, there are powerful international parallels. Specifically, international agencies including the IMF and the World Bank have promoted such market-led strategies through Structural Adjustment programmes as part of their conditions for loans to indebted Third World countries in the South (Christian Aid, 1994).

This sets the background for a critical understanding of the restructuring of the welfare state, and the promotion of the mixed economy of welfare, in general. More specifically, this has led to an enhanced emphasis upon the role of the voluntary sector and community participation, as an accompaniment to this retreat from the public sector. For example, in Britain there has been increasing emphasis upon community participation in urban regeneration (as in the Single Regeneration Budgets, for example) as well as in tenant participation and tenant management co-operatives, local management of schools and community care policies for the elderly, the mentally ill and those with physical disabilities or learning disabilities.

Both in Britain, and more widely, on a global scale, a widespread apparent consensus has been developing about this enhanced importance of the voluntary sector, non-governmental agencies (NGOs) and community-based organisations. This apparent consensus has been endorsed by international agencies such as the World Bank itself, as well as by governments of varying complexions, in the South as well as the North, and by NGOs and people's movements themselves (Korten, 1990; Wignaraja, 1993). Chapter Five explores some of the different and competing interests and perspectives which lie behind such apparent consensus. And the chapter then goes on to explore some of the very important positive potential which this increased emphasis upon community participation can entail, in terms of community-based approaches to adult education for transformation; for social as well as for economic development, within local, as well as regional contexts and beyond.

Chapter Six moves on to focus upon the political aspects of strategies for transformation. How can communities analyse and evaluate the implications of differing power structures? Who are the key figures and the key organisations, locally, and what are the bases of their power? And what are the underlying bases for local power struggles between competing groups within communities? These questions have featured in community adult education programmes, in different contexts (including, for example, the Highlander programmes in the USA). Analysing these questions has been essential, as the prerequisite for building realistic and effective strategies for change, identifying the real nature and extent of the powerful interests which have to be challenged, and unravelling the sources of conflict and competition within communities.

Community action strategies for change have similarly involved this type of critical analysis. There has been a focus upon targeting the powerful, who need to be challenged or at least to be neutralised or even convinced of the case for change. And on the other hand, there has also been a focus upon identifying common interests, and the potential for alliances amongst hitherto competing groups within communities. In the US context, Alinsky, for example, developed some of the most well-known and controversial models for analysing the sources of power, as part of developing strategies for effective community action for change (Alinsky, 1971). Alinsky's work has continued to be read and debated, on an international scale.

Alternatively, in the context of Northern Ireland, Lovett, for instance, has developed models of community education through the Ulster People's College. These programmes have provided opportunities for local communities to explore the issues which divided them. This has been the prerequisite for developing alliances to pursue effective campaigns in relation to the pressing issues which have been affecting working class communities, in common, across the sectarian divide (Lovett *et al*, 1994). Whilst these types of approach have been particularly key, in the context of the conflicts within and between communities in Northern Ireland, there have been comparisons, as well as contrasts, in a number of other contexts, including Somalia, South Africa and the West Bank (Bradbury, 1994).

In the globalised scenario of the late twentieth century, the critical analysis of the political landscape takes on an added dimension. Because it has become more obviously vital to explore the connections and the conflicts between local power bases and wider sources of power, at regional, national and even international levels. Local communities need to clarify both the competing sources and the different levels of power and decision making. 'Think global, act local' has become a slogan of particular relevance. Community-based economic regeneration strategies, for example, entail the identification of the potential for locally relevant projects, as well as a clear understanding of the constraints imposed by competing interests, regionally and beyond, including, of course, the particular interests of transnational capital.

In Britain, debates on citizenship, and the citizen's charters, have included some discussion of the importance of education for citizenship. This type of political education has been identified as essential, if individual citizens are to understand both their rights and responsibilities within the mixed economy of welfare (Speaker of the House of Commons, 1990). However vital this form of individual form of political education, in itself it would still be inadequate in the globalised context of the late twentieth century. In contrast, the type of political education which is explored in Chapter Six starts from collective approaches to adult education, connecting the analysis of underlying power structures and interests with the development of strategies for community action and for community development for transformation.

The analysis of competing power bases and interests in Chapter Six lays the way for the discussion of the potential as well as the limits to developing alliances for transformation in Chapter Seven. Local communities need to be able to clarify the varying bases upon which different groups and interests within and between communities can collaborate, whether this collaboration is limited to particular projects or programmes or whether collaboration can be constructed on a broader and more continuing basis. But in either case, this requires mutual respect, based upon shared understanding, which can be facilitated through adult community education.

This brings the discussion in Chapter Seven to the very specific consideration of diversity and difference. This is within the context of adult community education strategies for combating discrimination and oppression in terms of race and gender, as well as in terms of class, and caste, and in terms of age, disability and sexuality. Adult community education has a long history of addressing discrimination and educational deprivation, in terms of social class. Working class involvement in adult education, to develop critical understanding in order to promote social change has, as Simon for instance has demonstrated, 'a history as long as that of the working-class itself'. Quoting a group of mechanics who formed the Sheffield Corresponding Society in the early 1790s, he showed how they explained the purpose of their meetings: 'To enlighten the people, to show the people the reason, the ground of all their complaints and sufferings' (Simon, 1992: 9). This was a key part of the wider working class movement and struggles for emancipation – a stimulus, in Tawney's words, 'to constructive thought and an inspiration to action' (Simon, 1992: 276).

More recently, there has been increasing focus upon addressing other forms of oppression and discrimination too, as the Women's Liberation Movement and movements for racial equality have placed these issues firmly on the adult community education agenda. Thompson, amongst others, has analysed the contributions of feminism to adult and continuing education, both historically, and more recently, with the re-emergence of the Women's Movement (Thompson, 1995). The basis of knowledge itself was questioned, along with the curriculum. This, it has been argued,

was pervasively malestream within the WEA and Extra-Mural traditions, whilst effectively domesticating and conformist (French cookery,
dress making and flower arranging, for instance) in the leisure-related
liberal education classes provided by local authorities.

From the late sixties and seventies, feminists challenged the basis
and the relevance of what was taught, demanding a new relevance,
based upon 'validating women's experience and challenging the imposi-
tion of ideas and conditions which worked to oppress women as a
group' (Thompson, 1995). Alongside these challenges, a range of new
types of courses and new forms of access for women were developed
(for example, New Opportunities for Women, Second Chance, Fresh
Start, Training in Non-Traditional Skills and Women's Studies
programmes). And whilst these programmes were being developed in
Britain, issues of gender and development (including gender and education for development, and women's transformatory potential) were being
firmly lodged on the international agenda (Young, 1993). Chapter Seven
explores some of these initiatives, their limitations and their strengths,
in terms of their implications for challenging women's oppression, and
developing personal politics, through adult community education for
transformation.

In the globalised economy of the late twentieth century, combatting
racial discrimination and oppression is more vitally important than ever.
There are parallels in the development of black studies, within adult
community education, as part of black people's struggles to recover
their histories, and cultures and to analyse their experiences, within the
framework of the colonial past, and the new imperialist present.

As Fryer, for instance, has argued, the challenge which this type of
approach to adult community education poses is vitally important, not
only for black people and their understanding of themselves and the
sources of their oppression, but also to the development of white working class consciousness. How can the analysis of race and racism be
understood, in relation to the analysis of capital and class relations?
And how can these different dimensions of exploitation and oppression
be understood in relation to gender (Fryer, 1992)?

Chapter Seven is concerned to explore the role of adult community
education, in facilitating understanding of the inter-relationships
between these different forms of exploitation and oppression. Without
understanding these inter-relationships, oppressed groups can so easily
be set up to be in competition with each other; the logic of the strategies
for divide and rule, which were such a prominent feature of the British
approach to social control in the colonies. More recent versions of these
forms of 'divide and rule' include approaches based upon notions of
'hierarchies of oppression'. In these 'hierarchies of oppression' different
groups are ranked, and their needs prioritised, in terms of the severity
of their oppressions. Race before gender, or *vice versa*, gender before
race, whichever way the hierarchies of oppression are set out, there are
risks of ignoring the inter-relationships between them (the specific

oppression of black working class women, in this case). And there are major risks here, in terms of provoking competition between different oppressed groups, chasing scarce resources, rather than challenging the sources of their oppression, and joining forces to press for more adequate resources to meet their varying needs.

Whilst debates from the late sixties focused particularly upon race and gender, with increasing focus upon the inter-relationships between the two, from the eighties the focus has been widened. There has been increasing emphasis upon discrimination in terms of disability, sexuality and age, whether this involves discrimination against older people, or discrimination against younger people.

This last aspect, discrimination against younger people, has raised increasing concern, because of the potential implications for the future, if so many of the next generation suffer exclusion from the world of paid employment, and from related forms of association and organisation. (This form of exclusion, and the need to address it, raises, in turn, the increasing importance of the contributions to be made by youth and community work, and community-based education and training for young people.) In Britain, the labour market position of young people (especially those with few qualifications) has deteriorated rapidly, both in terms of rising levels of unemployment, and in terms of relatively lower wages and deteriorating conditions, for those who are in and out of casualised work (Rowntree Foundation, 1995). These are trends which have been affecting young people more widely. The involvement of young people has become more evidently central, within the broader framework of community education strategies to explore the inter-relationships between different forms of exploitation and oppression.

This focus upon questions of unity and diversity, solidarity and respect for difference, brings the discussion to the questions which are raised in the final chapter. Having argued for the importance of respecting diversity and difference as the basis for building alliances for transformation (the focus of Chapter Seven) Chapter Eight moves on to explore issues of culture, changing consciousness and identity.

This starts from a dual definition of culture – culture in terms of shared values and beliefs, and culture in terms of the expression of these values and beliefs, through the arts and the media. There are key issues for adult community education here, as adult community education engages with and promotes a range of initiatives from community theatre, film and video, music, poetry and other forms of creative writing, through to language classes, to preserve and revive minority ethnic languages. One of the metaphors which has been applied here is the metaphor of the orchestra; the musical totality being so much more creative, potentially, than the sum of the parts of the different instruments.

In contrast, processes of globalisation, as it has already been suggested, have been associated with contradictory tendencies. In terms of culture, globalisation has been seen in terms of its homogenising effects.

Western mass culture has been increasingly marketed worldwide; the 'global village'. And conversely globalisation has also been seen in terms of alternative responses, creative responses from the margins, including the reassertion of roots and the construction of new identities. Stuart Hall has developed this type of analysis, for example, in exploring the development of black cultural movements in this global context (Hall, 1991). Cultural movements can promote positive identities and cultures of resistance, then, just as cultural movements can be backward-looking, inward-looking, exclusive, chauvinistic and even racist. Projects to promote local communities' 'culture' can lead to the production of exotic artefacts, souvenirs and spectacles for the international tourist market. And alternatively, cultural projects and programmes can contribute to the development of collective identities and self-esteem, based upon shared understandings of communities' histories, values and beliefs.

This brings the discussion back to some of the questions which were raised at the outset, questions which are also pursued in the next chapter. These are underlying questions about the nature of changing identities and changing consciousness. As Wallerstein has argued, culture has 'always been a weapon of the powerful' (Wallerstein, 1991: 99) who use it to gain legitimacy. But as Wallerstein has also argued, culture can also be a weapon of the weak, who can and do use culture as a means of resistance.

In certain circumstances, cultures of resistance have involved agitation and propaganda, to put across particular messages, and to mobilise for specific campaigns. But cultures of resistance have absolutely not been confined to 'agitprop' of this type. More broadly, on the contrary, cultures of resistance form part of wider movements for adult community education to promote critical awareness and understanding. And cultures of resistance can contribute to building self-esteem and self-confidence in the possibility as well as the necessity for social transformation.

References

Agarwal, B. (1994) 'Positioning the western feminist agenda: a comment', *Indian Journal of Gender Studies*, Vol. 1, No. 2, pp. 248–55.

Alinsky, S. (1971) *Rules for Radicals*, Vintage.

Bradbury, M. (1994) 'The case of the yellow settee: experience of doing development in post-war Somalia' *Community Development Journal*, Vol. 29, No. 2, pp. 113–22.

Christian Aid (1994) *Who Runs the World?*, Christian Aid.

Freire, P. (1972) *Pedagogy of the Oppressed*, Penguin Books.

Freire, P. (1976) *Pedagogy in Process*, Writers and Readers Publishing Cooperative.

Fryer, B. (1992) 'The challenge to working-class education', in B. Simon (ed.) *The Search for Enlightenment: The working class and education in the twentieth century*, NIACE, pp. 276–319.

Fryer, D. (1992) 'Psychological or material deprivation: why does unemployment have mental health consequences?', in E. McLaughlin (ed.) *Understanding Unemployment*, Routledge.

Gallie, D. and Marsh, C. (1994) 'The experience of unemployment', in D. Gallie and

C. Vogler (eds) *Social Change and the Experience of Unemployment*, Oxford University Press.

Hall, S. (1991) 'The local and the global: globalization and ethnicity' and 'Old and new identities, old and new ethnicities', in A. King (ed.) *Culture, Globalization and the World-System*, Macmillan.

Hobsbawm, E. (1994) *Age of Extremes: The Short Twentieth Century*, Michael Joseph.

Korten, D. (1989) *Getting to the Twenty First Century*, Kumarian Press, West Hartford, USA.

London, J. (1977) *The People of the Abyss*, The Journeyman Press.

Longland, T. (1994) 'The occupied territories', *Community Development Journal*, Vol. 19, No. 2 pp. 132–40.

Lovett, T., Gunn, D. and Robson, T. (1994) 'Education, conflict and community development in Northern Ireland', *Community Development Journal*, Vol. 29, No. 2, pp. 177–86.

Marx, K. and Engels, F. *Selected Works*, (1968 edition) Lawrence and Wishart.

OECD (1994) *Economic Outlook*, July.

Rogers, A. (1992) *Adults Learning for Development*, Cassell.

Rowntree Foundation, 1995 Rowntree Foundation (1995) *Inquiry into Income and Wealth*, Joseph Rowntree Foundation, York.

Simon, B. (1992) 'The struggle for hegemony, 1920–1926', in B. Simon (ed.) *The Search for Enlightenment: The working class and education in the twentieth century*, NIACE, pp. 17–70.

Speaker of the House of Commons (1990) *Encouraging Citizenship: Report of the Commission on Citizenship*, HMSO.

Taylor, V. (1994) 'Social reconstruction and community development in the face of violence and conflict in South Africa', *Community Development Journal*, Vol. 29, No. 2, pp. 123–31.

Thompson, J. (1995) in M. Mayo and J. Thompson (eds) *Adult Learning, Critical Intelligence and Social Change*, NIACE.

Wallerstein, I. (1991) *Geopolitics and Geoculture: Essays on the Changing World-System*, Cambridge University Press.

Wignaraja, P. (1993) *New Social Movements in the South*, Zed Books.

Young, K. (1993) *Planning Development With Women*, Macmillan.

Youngman, F. (1986) *Adult Education and Socialist Pedagogy*, Croom Helm.

Chapter One

Competing perspectives

This book started from the proposition that community and workplace adult education has potential for contributing to strategies for transformation. And this potential contribution may even be considered to be expanding, in the contemporary context. This might seem an ambitious claim, yet there seems to be a range of evidence to support it.

The promotion of 'Lifelong Learning' appears to command widespread enthusiasm, as a strategy for developing the creativity and productivity of the workforce. This emerged as a major theme, for example, in the Report of the Commission on Social Justice. By investing in skills, the Report argued, 'we raise people's capacity to add value to the economy, to take charge of their own lives, and to contribute to their families and communities' (Report of the Commission on Social Justice, 1994, p.120). 'Lifelong Learning', the Commission on Social Justice went on to claim, 'is at the heart of our vision of a better society'. 'Only lifelong learning can win us the prize of economic success' as well as contributing to social justice, social improvement and citizen empowerment. 'Our aspiration,' the Report emphasised, 'is nothing less than the creation of a learning society' (*ibid*, p. 141).

The Commission on Social Justice was set up at the instigation of John Smith, who was leader of the Labour Party at that time (1992), although the Commission itself was independent. But its emphasis upon the importance of creating a 'Learning Society' has been shared far more widely across the political spectrum. It was not only the Opposition, but also the Conservative Government, which had been placing increasing emphasis on the need to invest in people, through lifelong education and training (especially training). By the beginning of the nineties, it has been suggested, 'Every major commentator agrees that the British workforce is under-skilled, under-educated and under-trained, and that increasingly international markets, shorter job-life, and skills shortages in key economic sectors make adult training and education a major imperative' (Tuckett, 1991: 32).

In line with this perspective, in 1995, the Economic and Social Research Council launched a research programme on 'The Learning Society' (focusing upon post-compulsory education and training and continuing education, in all their forms) as a timely response to what was identified as 'the growing national consensus that the UK needs a paradigm shift in its thinking and practice in relation to education and training if it is to survive as a major economic power. This programme (of research) seeks to harness the best ideas in the social sciences to enable the UK to make steady progress towards becoming a learning society' (ESRC, undated).

So there did indeed seem to be very widespread agreement that adult education and training were key ingredients in recipes for economic revival, in Britain. And the development of the 'Learning Society' was also supported, because of the potential benefits, in terms of social improvement and empowerment, for individuals, their families and their communities. But beneath this apparent consensus, there were also deep underlying differences, based upon competing diagnoses of the problems and alternative models of how best to address these. Key terms have been used in different ways, with varying meanings.

This chapter sets out to explore these differences. Firstly, it examines two different and competing perspectives on economic and social development. The market-led approach which increasingly dominated public policy, on a global scale, from the late seventies, is contrasted with alternative perspectives for economic and social transformation, alternatives which are based upon fundamental criticisms of the market-led model. In particular, the chapter focuses on the contributions of Gramsci, Freire and Gelpi, in developing alternative perspectives for adult education for transformation, within an international framework. The chapter then moves on to focus upon the differing implications of these competing perspectives, in terms of policies for adult education and training, to promote the 'Learning Society', however this is defined.

Finally, the chapter concludes by looking at the question of competing perspectives, as an issue in its own right. If adult education is to be geared towards transformation in the 'Learning Society', then adult learners need to be enabled to identify competing perspectives, together with their differing policy implications, so that they can evaluate these critically. Only then will they be in a position to make fully conscious choices about alternative futures. This, it will be argued, is an essential component of education for empowerment. But this approach is also problematic, posing further questions, rather than providing simple solutions. This includes questioning the relationship between theory and practice/experiential learning and the role of the educator in participant-centred adult learning. And this relates to wider debates about the relationship between the world of ideas (and contests between competing ideologies) on the one hand, and the material world (and contests between competing interests, structured by material constraints) on the other.

But before coming on to these questions about some of the implications of competing perspectives for adult learning, the perspectives themselves need to be summarised. Readers who are already familiar with the market-led approach, and with alternative approaches for transformation, may prefer to move on to the final section of the chapter.

Or alternatively, they may prefer to skim the next sections, simply to check the particular ways in which these approaches are being set out, and the ways in which terms are being defined, for the purposes of this book.

Market-led perspectives

In summary, the 'market-led' approach is precisely that; an approach which emphasises the key role of the free market, as the co-ordinator of the economy and the dynamic of economic development. This free market operates through the decisions of individuals, buying and selling. When market mechanisms operate effectively, economic growth is facilitated, and the benefits of that growth can 'trickle down', to benefit all sections, from the entrepreneurs who have produced the wealth, through to the poorer and more disadvantaged groups in society.

Once the free market economy is functioning effectively, the benefits of economic growth can also be used for a degree of social spending. But social spending must never be allowed to hamper the essential needs of the economy, or to divert disproportionate resources away from productive investment. In particular, public expenditure must be kept firmly in check, and government intervention must be strictly contained, so that market mechanisms do not suffer from undue interference: constraining market mechanisms would, it is argued, jeopardise economic growth, killing the goose which lays the golden egg of wealth creation.

In summary, then, the free market is argued to be the most efficient and dynamic system, capable of producing rapid economic growth. The free market has also been seen as capable of reducing the extent of inequality (through the 'trickle down' effect) (Friedman, 1962) and promoting social development. Most importantly too, the free market has been linked to individual freedom and political democracy. Market-led approaches are based upon this view of the free market.

This is a very crude summary. Others have written more eloquently and persuasively of the advantages of market-led approaches in a free society. And this emphasis on the benefits of market-led approaches has been an increasingly dominant theme, not only in Britain, but more widely, on a global scale, in recent years. Market-led approaches have been exported and reinforced in a number of ways, including reinforcement through the policies of international development organisations such as the World Bank and the International Monetary Fund. (Typically, World Bank/IMF loans to developing countries in the South are conditional upon the adoption of market-led development strategies, through Structural Adjustment Programmes.) In particular, since the collapse of the former socialist governments in Eastern and Central Europe, from 1989, it has been widely argued that there is no longer any effective alternative to the free market; a view which has been expressed in such terms as 'the end of ideology', even 'the end of history'.

This, then, became the predominant approach in Britain and beyond. So what are the key criticisms of this, in general (before coming on to some of the implications of this approach for adult learning and the 'Learning Society', more specifically)? In summary, as Hobsbawm argued, in the 'Bird's Eye View' of the twentieth century which was outlined in the Introduction, market-led approaches *did* enjoy a Golden Age, after the Second World War. Hobsbawm described this period, between the end of the Second World War and the early seventies, as an era of extraordinary economic, social and cultural dynamism and change, on an increasingly global scale. But more recently, subsequent decades have been characterised by global recession and crisis, accompanied by increasing questioning. Just as they have been seen to have triumphed on a worldwide scale, market-led approaches have been subjected to processes of fundamental questioning, too. Is this approach necessarily still the most effective strategy for promoting economic growth? And does economic growth necessarily lead to social development and sustainable livelihoods, anyway, let alone to greater equality, social justice, and democratic participation?

In the final decade of the twentieth century, market-led approaches seem to continue to produce dynamic economic growth, at least in parts of the globe, such as the Pacific Rim. Or do they? Whilst the rapidly growing economies of South-East Asia such as South Korea typically proclaim the merits of the market, the reality may be more complex. On the contrary, in fact, it has been argued that the most dynamic of these economies (such as China) have, in practice, been characterised by very considerable degrees of state intervention and planning, to facilitate the workings of the free market.

Meanwhile, in contrast, in states such as Britain, where government policy has been geared towards the reduction of state intervention and planning, the results have been distinctly disappointing. Nor have these criticisms been confined to the Opposition. For example, one of the main theorists behind the market-led strategies of the Thatcher years in the 1980s has gone on record as concluding that this was an experiment which failed *in its own terms* (Gray, 1994).

If market-led approaches have been subjected to criticisms, in terms of necessarily being the most effective way of promoting economic growth, they have been subjected to perhaps even fiercer criticisms, in terms of their capacity to promote social development, let alone social justice. On the contrary, in fact, as a study by UNICEF demonstrated, human welfare had actually declined, in the first half of the 1980s. And the most severe effects had been suffered by the most disadvantaged, in the less developed countries in the South, with children being particularly vulnerable. Despite gaps and inadequacies in the data, overall the findings have pointed consistently in the same direction; with very few exceptions, malnutrition increased amongst children, acutely in some areas, over this period. There was less accessible health care and reduced educational opportunities (Cornia, 1987).

These devastating social consequences persisted, as economic recession continued, and social spending was constrained. By the United Nations World Summit for Social Development, in 1995, the Non-Governmental Organisations (NGOs) were increasingly coming to the conclusion that these problems were inherent in the predominant, market-led approach to development itself. As the Africa Symposium argued, in the paper which they prepared before the Summit, the dominant, market-led model had been disillusioning; there had been widening economic and social divisions, unprecedented wealth on the one hand, and accelerating poverty and human misery on the other. There had been increasing social exclusion, fragmentation and violence; a situation which they described in terms of 'social apartheid'.

The women's network DAWN (Development Alternatives with Women for a New Era) put it in the following terms:

> *The disappointment and disillusionment of people with the development strategies of the past 40 years has led to frustration, cynicism and a sense of helplessness and futility. In spite of phenomenal advances in scientific achievements and technology, the quality of life for millions of people throughout the world has seen a marked deterioration. There is widespread anxiety about the safety of society, increasing social fragmentation and the sense of breakdown that pervades our consciousness*

(DAWN, 1995: 1).

Whilst the focus here was on the urgency of promoting social development in the South, there were parallel debates about the need to address increasing poverty, polarisation and social exclusion in industrialised countries of the North. And this included the USA and Britain (where, as it has already been suggested, social inequality had grown faster than in any other developed country apart from New Zealand, where market-led approaches had also been particularly predominant, Rowntree, 1995). So in place of the market-led approach, there were calls for alternatives, based upon human needs and values, geared towards environmentally-sustainable livelihoods, on the basis of equity, democracy and community participation.

There was fundamental questioning of market-led approaches, then, both in terms of economic growth, and in terms of social development, social justice, social integration and democratic participation. So how have these criticisms applied, more specifically, to debates around adult education and training, and the 'Learning Society'?

In summary, the market-led approach emphasises the importance of individual decisions, on a voluntary-rational-utilitarian basis. Employers each work out, on a voluntary basis, the logic of their employment and training needs, and then develop education and training strategies to meet these. And individual adults similarly reach rational decisions about their own best interests, in terms of improving their employment prospects (and, indeed, enhancing their leisure interests).

The role of the state, in this scenario, is to facilitate these market-led processes. Whilst education (and especially vocational training) is seen in terms of investment, decisions about these investments should be determined, as far as possible, by the needs of employers, and defined as far as possible, by them too (and their representatives on Training and Enterprise Councils, in the British context). With minimum regulation, the state aims to encourage the market in education and training, and to promote the culture of 'enterprise' more generally (Coles and MacDonald, 1993).

In relation to adult education and training, the impact has been problematic, even in the market's own terms. In summary, the focus has been on training to meet employers' needs. Yet leaving training to the market has been increasingly recognised as inadequate. Individual employers do *not* necessarily invest in training, rationally; and the sum total of their investments has been seriously inadequate, giving rise to widespread concern about Britain's skills levels (National Commission on Education, 1993; Keep and Mayhew, 1994; House of Commons, 1994).

Meanwhile, there has been increasing concern that the workforce of the future needs a broad basis of education, as well as job-specific skills, if labour is to be creative and flexible, in a rapidly changing economy (Forrester, Payne and Ward, 1993). But this type of broad-based education, it has been argued, potentially requires more forward planning, in the collective, community interest, backed by more active state intervention.

There are real dilemmas inherent in the market-led approach here, and particular tensions around the increasing focus upon training for very specific, job-related skills, as measured in terms of competences, through the National Vocational Qualifications (NVQ) and Scottish Vocational Qualifications (SVQ) system. Whilst these competences are supposed to be broadly-based and transferable, critics have argued that the reality may be quite otherwise. It has, on the contrary, been argued that the 'competency-based' approach which underpins the NVQ/SVQ system 'necessarily involves a narrowing of educational experiences' (Shaw and Crowther, 1995; see also Alexander and Martin, 1995). This represents a major educational debate in its own right – a debate which will re-emerge in subsequent chapters. The point of raising it here is simply to indicate that market-led approaches have been far from unproblematic, even in their own terms, in relation to adult education and training.

Whilst the market-led approach has raised dilemmas in relation to work-related education and training, and the changing needs of the economy, it has been just as, if not even more, problematic in relation to adult education and training in the community. Bringing the market into adult education involves cutting back public provision and encouraging providers, such as local education authorities and voluntary organisations, to sell their wares like any other leisure/recreational activity. For the most part, the punters are expected to pay for their classes, with public support being concentrated on meeting a limited amount of social priority needs (Tuckett, 1991).

This type of approach fails to give adequate recognition to the links between participating in so-called 'leisure and recreation' classes, and gaining the confidence and skills to progress to more directly job-related education and training. And it most particularly fails to give adequate recognition to the contribution of adult education and training in the community in social terms, whether in terms of involving educationally disadvantaged participants, prolonging the active involvement · and participation of the elderly, or promoting active citizenship and democracy more generally. These types of goals have been key to alternative approaches to development, for social and political goals, as well as for economic goals. In the market-led scenario, however, they tend to be effectively marginalised. This, it might be argued, represents a very limited view of 'Lifelong Education' even in terms of meeting economic goals, let alone social, political and cultural goals.

Which brings the discussion on to the more detailed summary of alternative approaches. Before moving on to this, it is important to emphasise, though, that there have been, and currently are, a number of differing alternative approaches. It is beyond the scope of this book to give them all adequate treatment, ranging from one end of the theoretical spectrum to the other. Rather, the purpose is to summarise those perspectives which have been particularly influential in debates about developing the most fundamental alternatives to market-led approaches. This sets the framework, staking out the ground at either end of the theoretical spectrum. Readers can, of course, fill in some of the intervening positions, in the middle ground, for themselves. As the final section of this chapter will argue, the key issue here is how far readers, and adult learners more generally, are enabled to identify the range of different approaches for themselves, and to appraise their differing policy implications critically.

Alternative approaches

In contrast with market-led perspectives, approaches from the other end of the theoretical spectrum start from the view that market-led economic growth is not the be-all and end-all of development. On the contrary, development should be measured, it is argued, in terms of a society's success in meeting the basic needs of all its people, including their needs for education and for health, on the basis of environmentally sound, sustainable livelihoods. Development, from this viewpoint, should be measured in terms of:

> social justice, giving priority 'in the use of the earth's natural resources to assuring all people the opportunity for a decent human existence'
> sustainability, using 'the earth's resources in ways that will assure

sustainable benefits for our children' inclusiveness, recognising the right of everyone to be a 'respected contributor to family, community and society'

(Korten, 1989, p.4).

It should be based upon active community participation and empowerment; bottom-up, 'People-Centred Development' as this has also been termed. This emphasis upon inclusive participation and empowerment is particularly central, because 'people-centred development', by definition, entails active involvement.

Such an approach has been characterised as 'transformational', because this would involve the fundamental *transformation* of economic, social, political (including personal) and cultural relations in society. Existing relations, based upon exploitation and oppression, would be 'transformed'. The term 'transformation', together with the terms 'people-centred' and 'sustainable development', have been developed within the context of development debates in the South. In response to increasing concern about the persistence of poverty, deprivation, discrimination and social exclusion in industrialised countries, the terms 'transformation' and 'sustainable', 'people-centred' development have also gained currency, in debates about regeneration, in the North.

In summary, 'transformational' approaches have criticised market-led approaches on a number of grounds. Market-led growth has been criticised as an end in itself, because this fails to take sufficient account of the social aspects of development. And market-led growth has been criticised for failing to reach those in greatest need. Critics have pointed to the failure of 'trickle down' economics and to the rapid increases in poverty and deprivation, both in the North and in the South, over past decades, dominated (as they have been), by market-led approaches.

Market-led approaches have also been criticised for reinforcing, rather than addressing, the sources of discrimination and social exclusion, and for failing to address the critical environmental issues, which pose such vital global challenges in the late twentieth century. As DAWN put this, the increasing predominance of market-led approaches 'for the majority of the people of the South has only meant a sustained and progressive reduction in the standard of living beyond reasonable levels' (DAWN, 1995: 8).

Earlier in the twentieth century, as Hobsbawm's 'Bird's Eye' view explained, socialism (based upon Marxist approaches) represented the key fundamental challenge to capitalism (based on market-led approaches), although there were, of course, significant differences within as well as between the rival perspectives. Since the collapse of the USSR, in 1989, there has been even less coherence than before. There is certainly no clear consensus about the continuing relevance or irrelevance of Marxist approaches amongst those who support 'transformational' approaches. In some of these debates, socialist ideas in general, and Marxist ideas more specifically, have been more notable for their absences; the great unmentionables. But some of the theorists who have made particularly significant contributions to developing 'transformational' approaches clearly have been influenced by Marxist analyses. This has certainly been the case in relation to debates about adult education and training for transformation. For the purposes of this book, the three key contributors to be outlined here in this context are Gramsci, Freire and Gelpi.

Gramsci, the Italian intellectual and revolutionary, developed his thinking at the beginning of the twentieth century on the basis of Marx's analysis of capitalism. Amongst his contributions, Gramsci brought to the Italian socialist and communist movements a critical analysis of the role of ideas and ideology in general. And, more specifically, after the First World War, Gramsci also contributed to experiments in workers' education, through the Factory Council movement. The aim was to enable the workers to gain the intellectual tools which they needed to develop their own alternatives for workers' control, as a major step towards socialism.

Everyone was a 'philosopher', Gramsci argued, even if unconsciously, in the sense that people accept given sets of ideas as uncontested – as common-sense – and these ideas influence their views and their actions. In capitalist society, these ideas (the taken-for-granted common-sense ideas of everyday life) are dominated by capitalist/ruling class assumptions. For example, it has been largely (although by no means entirely) taken for granted that the free market is the most effective system for ensuring not only economic growth, but also for guaranteeing individual freedom and democracy.

But potentially, Gramsci argued, everyone could develop the critical awareness, not simply to question these dominant ideas, but to go on to envisage alternatives. This was key to social change, Gramsci believed, because without the capacity to envisage (socialist) alternatives, the movement would be limited to demanding only partial reforms, within the *status quo*, without the capacity to work towards more fundamental transformation (Gramsci, *The Modern Prince*, 1968 edition).

Gramsci was absolutely not an economic determinist. He firmly rejected fatalistic interpretations of Marxism, fatalistic approaches which explained change only in terms of the underlying economic contradictions between classes. In contrast, Gramsci argued that class struggles also involved battles of ideas between competing ideologies. The ruling class maintained control over subordinate classes, not simply by force, through the state, Gramsci argued, but because the *status quo* was seen as having legitimacy in the eyes of the dominated. The ruling class exercised 'hegemony' or dominance in the sphere of ideas, ideas which were reproduced, through social and cultural institutions, including educational institutions.

In contrast to this state of affairs, alternative ideas were key to the process of social transformation; the dominant hegemonic ideology had to be challenged with counter-hegemonic ideas. This was why Gramsci was so concerned that the short-term struggles of the socialist and communist movements should be linked into longer-term analyses and strategies for transformation.

Gramsci argued for the importance of the battle of ideas, then, and so for the importance of education, in the movement. And he, himself, played an active role in promoting workers' political education, including education for workers' control, in the Factory Council movement, for these reasons. But he was absolutely not suggesting that societies can be transformed just by changing peoples' ideas, without also addressing the economic, social and political dimensions of transformation. On the contrary, in fact, Gramsci was clear that ideas and material class interests interconnect and inter-relate. This is an important point, in relation to subsequent debates about the inter-relationships between the material world and the world of ideas.

Gramsci was also clear about the importance of relating theory to practice; and developing dialogues between intellectuals and activists. In one account, a young university lecturer visited Gramsci, saying that he intended to 'instruct the workers'. The writer who provided this account described the young man as arrogant, giving the impression that he considered himself as having a 'monopoly on knowledge'. He demonstrated no awareness of the fact that the workers had knowledge and ideas too, including ideas about their own struggles and about the goals which they were already working for. 'From the beginning,' the informant reported, 'Gramsci fumed in silence; he kept taking off and putting on his spectacles. I saw that he was about to lose his patience'; but in the event, Gramsci calmed down and advised the young lecturer to consider whether he, himself, might also need to learn from the workers, if he really wanted to make a valuable contribution to workers' education for change (Introduction to *The Modern Prince and Other Writings*, 1968 edition, p.15).

For Gramsci, rigorous theoretical work was essential, and intellectuals had a potentially vital role to play. But they needed to be clearly aligned to the movement ('organic' intellectuals, in Gramsci's terminology) and engaged in dialogue with activists: worker-educators working with worker-learners (P. Mayo, 1994). Once again, this relates to subsequent debates, both debates on socialism in general, and debates on adult learning, more specifically.

Both of these themes, the inter-relationship between the world of ideas and the material world to be transformed, on the one hand, and the relationship between theory and practice, intellectuals and activists, educators and learners, on the other, also appear in the work of Freire. Freire has perhaps been the most influential theorist and practitioner of critical approaches to adult education, in the South and in the North. And as a proponent of adult education for the development of critical consciousness (conscientisation) he has been key to debates on adult education for transformation. Whilst Freire has drawn on a range of intellectual traditions, including Christian Liberation Theology, he has certainly also acknowledged a debt to Marxist analyses, including the work of Gramsci. Key aspects of Freire's writings which need to be summarised, for the purposes of this book, include his overall approach to 'conscientisation' to enable the oppressed to gain critical consciousness. The oppressed need this critical consciousness in order to challenge the dominant oppressor's ideas. They need to be able to 'problematise' – to question fundamentally ideas and situations which have previously been taken for granted or accepted as unproblematic. And they need to be able to question the root causes of their oppression.*

Freire's approach has been described in terms of the 'problem-posing' approach, exploring the root causes, rather than focusing upon the symptoms of problems, in order to plan action strategies to address them. As the oppressed gain this critical consciousness they can more fully perceive, interpret, criticise and finally transform the world about them. This is the process which Freire describes in terms of 'praxis', 'reflection and action upon the world in order to change it' (Freire, 1972: 28). It is a process which the oppressed, themselves, must actively engage with because liberation has to come from the oppressed themselves, acting collectively. Liberation cannot be handed down from the top; it has to come from the bottom up.

More specifically, this chapter will also summarise Freire's views on the relationship between conscientisation, cultural action and the battle of ideas, on the one hand, and the material, economic, social and political factors which produce exploitation and oppression, on the other. And the chapter will summarise Freire's approach to processes of adult learning, based upon dialogue, problem-posing and active learning (rather than upon filling people's heads with information and ideas, even 'politically correct' ideas). This also relates to debates on the role of the educator and the learner, and debates on the relationship between theory and practice, more generally.

Paulo Freire came to develop his educational theories through his own experiences of witnessing (and to some extent experiencing) poverty and deprivation in north-east Brazil, in the inter-war Depression. He built upon these experiences, through his work in educational philosophy, in Brazil, and then through his work in adult educational practice in Chile and Geneva (as Special Consultant to the World Council of Churches).

Through these experiences, Freire developed strategies for tackling

---

* 'Oppression' is used, here, to cover the range of ways in which people suffer from poverty, inequality, deprivation and discrimination, including discrimination on the grounds of race, ethnicity, gender, sexuality, age, and disability. This is in contrast with the term 'exploitation', which, in the Marxist usage, covers the more specific 'exploitation' which workers experience when they produce profits for capital.

the phenomenon which he described as the 'culture of silence', the apparent apathy and resignation which can submerge the dispossessed. He developed alternative approaches, based upon the belief that every human being, however oppressed and submerged in this culture of silence, *is* capable of challenging the root causes of his or her oppression, capable of 'looking critically at his (*sic*) world in a dialogical encounter with others. Provided with the proper tools for such an encounter, he can gradually perceive his personal and social reality as well as the contradictions in it, become conscious of his own perception of that reality, and deal critically with it' (Shaull, Foreword to *Pedagogy of the Oppressed*, 1972: 12). And this process involves not just individual men – and women – but communities, working together for transformation.

As Freire himself explained, his theoretical work did not come from study alone, but was 'rooted in concrete situations and describes the reactions of workers (peasant or urban) and of the members of the middle-class whom I have observed directly or indirectly during the course of my educative work' (Freire, 1972: 16). Through his novel approaches to teaching literacy, he developed a wider theoretical approach to adult education for liberation and transformation. In this way, he argued, the oppressed can gain the tools to develop critical consciousness, to replace the images of the oppressor, which they have internalised, and acquire autonomy, responsibility and fuller humanity. Through acquiring critical consciousness, then, the oppressed can challenge the oppressors' definitions of reality and overcome their own self-deprecation. Instead of internalising the oppressors' views of them (as incapable of learning, lazy and unproductive, for instance, stereotypes which the oppressed had been internalising, in some of the Latin American contexts with which he was familiar) the oppressed can come to see themselves, afresh, as inherently capable and creative – although currently exploited. These self-deprecating definitions, which the oppressed need to challenge, can be broadly related to Gramsci's accounts of the dominant, hegemonic ideology, too. As it has already been suggested, Gramsci also argued that the dominant 'common-sense' definitions of reality can paralyse the oppressed into believing that there are no realistic alternatives.

While Freire focused upon the role of adult education, as a tool of conscientisation, or the development of critical consciousness, he was not suggesting that liberation and transformation could be achieved by changing consciousness alone. 'The oppressed can overcome the contradiction in which they are caught only when this perception enlists them in the struggle to free themselves' (Freire, 1972: 26). He argued that 'the concrete situation which begets oppression must be transformed' (Freire, 1972: 27).

This is an important point, because, as was suggested in the Introduction, some of Freire's critics have pointed to the focus upon consciousness, rather than material and structural factors, especially in his earlier work (Youngman, 1986). Since the early seventies, however,

Freire provided more explicit analyses of the relationships between education and consciousness, on the one hand, and material, structural factors on the other. This brought his analysis closer to Marxist approaches (although clearly not to the full satisfaction of all his critics). As it has already been suggested, debates about the nature of these relationships, between consciousness and its material basis, between competing ideas and class struggles, between cultural action and political action, re-emerge, in different forms, in subsequent chapters.

And so do debates about critical adult learning as a process. Freire, himself, had been extremely critical of what he had termed the 'banking' approach to adult education. Education of the 'banking' type involves acts of 'depositing' information into students, acting as 'receptacles'. According to Freire 'the scope of action allowed to the students extends only as far as receiving, filing and storing the deposits' (Freire, 1972: 46). This reduces the learners to an essentially passive role. In contrast, Freire argued, if people are to be truly human, then they need to become actively engaged in critical inquiry, and in related and reflective action or praxis, linking theory and practice to transform their situations. The role of the educator, or the 'animator', here, is based on partnership and critical dialogue. The teacher also becomes a student, and the students become teachers. Working together on the basis of problem posing, 'they become jointly responsible for a process in which all grow' (Freire, 1972: 53).

In Freire's later work, he considered as well some of the dilemmas involved in putting this into practice. Clearly, educators and learners do not start on an equal footing, and educators do start from the basis of their critical understanding of competing theories, as well as their already existing access to relevant information. Freire accepted that these differences are important. He even went so far as to accept that in some situations, where learners are only accustomed to 'banking'-style approaches to education, educators cannot move straight into alternative styles, based upon dialogue (Freire, in Horton and Freire, 1990). But he did continue to emphasise that the role of the educator does not need to entail authoritarianism. The prevailing spirit should be democratic.

Once again, there are parallels with the views of Gramsci, who also emphasised the importance of dialogue between educators and learners, intellectuals and activists. But he was clear, too, that the movement needed theory as well as practice. And this necessitated gaining a critical understanding of the dominant theories, culture and ideology, otherwise the exploited and oppressed would remain at the margins of political life, without the tools to challenge the dominant ideology, let alone the tools to develop effective challenges and coherent alternatives for transformation. As it has already been suggested, some of these dilemmas re-emerge in subsequent chapters – how to develop democratic dialogues between educators and learners, avoiding 'banking' approaches to education, on the one hand, whilst providing the tools of critical theory for transformational praxis, on the other.

This brings the discussion to the third key influence in the development of alternative perspectives and approaches, Gelpi. As chief of the Unesco Lifelong Education Unit, Gelpi has developed a global perspective on lifelong education which draws upon his analysis of the links between oppression in both the industrialised North and the less-developed South. Educators need to start from a critical understanding of the sources of exploitation and oppression on a global scale. This involves understanding 'the oppression of one social class by another, the conflicts between rural and urban regions, the subordination of pre-industrial societies by industrialised societies' rooted in the global development of capitalism and the international division of labour. For Gelpi, this also means that the world of production is key for adult educators. This is vital if they are to understand the context for their work, and to develop adult education for transformation, both for those in employment and for those outside employment or on the margins of employment, the under-employed, as well as the unemployed, in both North and South.

Gelpi emphasises the potential which lifelong education can have for transformation. His view of lifelong education's potential here is dialectic; lifelong education cannot provide solutions to the material sources of oppression and exploitation, on a global scale. But lifelong education can contribute towards such solutions, according to Gelpi, based upon alternative approaches. He rejects the view that, because lifelong education has been taken up and promoted from a market-led perspective, to meet employers' changing labour requirements, this means that lifelong education is necessarily a negative force. Lifelong education does not have to represent a new form of manipulation, an aspect of social control, to tame the workers of the world, even if some employers would like to see it in such terms.

Gelpi is only too well aware that lifelong education can be used precisely to manipulate and tame, providing what has been characterised as 'useful knowledge' in the sense that employers find it useful for their workers to have the knowledge in question – the new vocationalism.* And lifelong education can be used to perpetuate divisions between different categories of workers, with more or less access to education and training, and divisions between those in regular work and those outside it. But lifelong education can also be transformational.

Gelpi's focus upon the world of work and relations of production are key to his underlying analysis. This sets the context too, for his discussion of lifelong education in terms of those outside the formal

---

* This notion of 'useful knowledge', and the contrasted notion of 'really useful knowledge' which is useful in terms of its transformational potential, has a long history, which is explored in more detail in the following chapter.

workforce, the unemployed, and the under- or marginally-employed, the young as well as older people and migrants. He includes women in terms of these categories and women more generally, too, women demanding new roles. These groups will, he argues, continue to provoke new educational strategies, and these groups will be key to wider struggles for transformation (Griffin, 1987). Indeed, their importance in both educational terms, and in terms of wider struggles for transformation, can be expected to increase relatively, as the processes of deregulation, casualisation and social exclusion proceed on a global scale. This analysis is key for the purposes of this book. Because, although the major emphasis will be upon community-based education and training for transformation, this will be rooted in the importance of the interconnections with the world of the workplace, and the productive sphere.

Competing perspectives: A key issue in adult education and training for transformation?

At the outset of this chapter, the question of competing perspectives was posed as a key issue in its own right. Adult education and training for transformation need to start from respecting the knowledge and skills which adults bring, based upon their life experiences. As the Introduction suggested, adults, even the most oppressed and exploited adults, are not necessarily ignorant at all, or suffering from what intellectuals might describe as 'false consciousness'. This point was made, for example, by Agarwal, who pointed to rural Indian women's numerous and ingenious ways of resisting gender oppression that disprove the assumption that they suffer from false consciousness (Agarwal, 1994). On the contrary, she argued, they were only too well aware of their oppression; what they needed strengthening was not so much their consciousness as their ability to protest overtly and effectively, to mobilise for change.

This book starts from the position that consciousness does not exist in a vacuum, and that changing consciousness, alone, is insufficient to transform society. Nor will oppressed and exploited people become empowered through 'banking' type approaches to education, even if this claims to be education and training for transformation, with 'right-on' educators putting them straight about their oppressive and exploitative situations and how to transform them. Freire's view was that 'education' of this 'banking' type was 'domesticating'; and that when the Left operates in this way, giving people received truths in the name of liberation, this can lead to profoundly unliberating consequences. Revolutionary regimes can 'harden into a "dominating" bureaucracy, the humanist dimension of the struggle is lost and it is no longer possible to speak of liberation' (Freire, 1972: 33). In the aftermath of 1989, and the rethinking which has followed the collapse of the USSR, these dangers from bureaucracy and from the lack of socialist democracy are not to be lightly dismissed.

But conversely, as Freire had also acknowledged, following Gramsci, unless the oppressed and exploited do have the tools to challenge dominant ideas, they risk remaining trapped in the present, unable to conceive of the possibility of alternatives for the future. The language of critique links with the language of possibility, he has argued; education for liberation is about opening up people's abilities to reflect critically on their situation, in order to see the possibilities for acting to transform it. As the previous section has argued, Gramsci, Gelpi and, to some extent, Freire have all addressed these dilemmas, in developing alternative approaches to education and training for transformation. The oppressed and exploited do need a critical understanding of competing perspectives and approaches, in order to challenge the dominant approaches, and in order to develop alternatives. Without this, they may continue to accept the dominant explanations; they may even continue to accept and to internalise dominant ideological accounts of themselves, and their cultures, as being the problem; the oppressors' values, inside their own heads. This undermines people's sense of their own identity and worth, and their capacity to envisage the possibility of transformation.

But the oppressed and exploited also need educators committed to processes of dialogue, between theoretical learning and experiential learning, between theory and reflective practice. And they need a critical understanding of the inter-relationships between ideological struggles, and material, economic, social, political and cultural struggles for transformation. These have also represented dilemmas within debates on alternative approaches, as the previous section has suggested.

These issues re-emerge in subsequent chapters. The point is absolutely not to suggest that there is consensus within alternative approaches, or that key dilemmas have now been resolved; only that these debates represent key issues for education and training for transformation. There continue to be significant differences, as well as points in common, amongst those who broadly agree on the necessity and the importance of education and training for transformation. These include disagreements on each of these aspects. They include broader differences of emphasis between those who are closer to a social democratic approach, on the one hand, and an approach which is more closely informed by a Marxist analysis, on the other. And other perspectives, including environmental perspectives, cut across each of these categories.

This makes it all the more essential that adult learners are critically aware of these issues and debates, just as it is essential for them to be critically aware of issues and debates within market-led perspectives. Without this critical understanding, they are not in a position to come to their own views about the *status quo*, let alone to opt for transformation for the future.

References

Agarwal, B. (1994) 'Positioning the Western feminist agenda: a comment', *Indian Journal of Gender Studies*, 1, 2, pp. 249–56.

Alexander, D. and Martin, I. (1995) 'Competence, curriculum and democracy', in M. Mayo and J. Thompson (eds), *Adult Learning, Critical Intelligence and Social Change*, NIACE.

Coles, B. and MacDonald, R. (1993) 'From new vocationalism to the culture of enterprise', in R. Edwards *et al.* (eds) *Adult Learners, Education and Training*, Routledge.

Cornia, G. (1987) 'Economic decline and human welfare in the first half of the 1980s', in G. Cornia *et al.* (eds) *Adjustment with a Human Face*, Clarendon Press.

DAWN (1995) *DAWN Informs 2/95, Social Development: DAWN's Perspectives*, Women and Development Unit, University of the West Indies, Barbados.

DAWN (1995) 'Challenging the Given: DAWN's Perspectives on Social Development', DAWN paper prepared for the World Summit for Social Development, Copenhagen, March, 1995, UN, New York.

Economic and Social Research Council (undated) Research Specification for the ESRC Learning Society, ESRC, Swindon.

Forrester, K., Payne, J. and Ward, K. (1995) *Workplace Learning: Perspectives on education, training and work*, Avebury.

Friedman, M. (1962) *Capitalism and Freedom*, Chicago University Press, Chicago.

Freire, P. (1972) *Pedagogy of the Oppressed*, Penguin Books, Harmonsdworth.

Gelpi, E. (1979) *A Future for Lifelong Education*, Department of Adult and Higher Education, University of Manchester.

Gray, J. (1994) *Beyond the New Right*, Routledge.

Gramsci, A. (1968) *The Modern Prince and Other Writings*, International Publishers, New York.

Griffin, C. (1983) *Curriculum Theory in Lifelong Education*, Croom Helm.

Griffin, C. (1987) 'Ettore Gelpi', in P. Jarvis (ed.) *Thinkers in Twentieth Century Adult Education*, Croom Helm, pp. 280–98.

Hobsbawm, E. (1994) *Age of Extremes*, Michael Joseph.

Horton, M. and Freire, P. (1990) *We Make the Road by Walking: Conversations on Education and Social Change*, Temple University Press, USA.

House of Commons (1994) *Competitiveness of UK Manufacturing Industry, Trade and Industry's Second Report*, HMSO.

Ireland, T. (1978) *Gelpi's View of Lifelong Education*, Department of Adult and Higher Education, University of Manchester.

Keep, E. and Mayhew, K. (1994) 'The changing structure of training provision', in T. Buxton *et al.* (eds) *Britain's Economic Performance*, Routledge, pp. 308–41.

Korten, D. (1989) *Getting to the Twenty First Century*, Kumarian Press, West Hartford, USA.

Mayo, P. (1994) 'Synthesizing Gramsci and Freire: possibilities for a theory of radical adult education', in *International Journal of Lifelong Education*, 11, 2, pp. 125–48.

National Commission on Education (1993) *Learning to Succeed: A Radical Look at Education Today and a Strategy for the Future*, Report of the Paul Hamlyn Foundation, Heinemann.

Report of the Commission on Social Justice (1994) *Social Justice: Strategies for National Renewal*, Vintage.

Shanahan, P. (forthcoming).

Shaw, M. and Crowther, J. (1995) 'Beyond subversion', in M. Mayo and J. Thompson (eds), *Adult Learning, Critical Intelligence and Social Change*, NIACE.

Tuckett, A. (1991) 'Counting the cost: managerialism, the market and the education of adults in the 1980s and beyond', in S. Westwood and J. Thomas (eds) *Radical Agendas?: The Politics of Adult Education*, NIACE, pp. 21–43.

Youngman, F. (1986) *Adult Education and Socialist Pedagogy*, Croom Helm.

Chapter Two

Comparing and contrasting histories of adult education for transformation

In the previous chapter, the notions of 'useful knowledge' and 'really useful knowledge' were introduced. Although these notions have a long history rooted in debates in the very different context of early nineteenth century Britain, there are also parallels with aspects of more recent debates. 'Useful knowledge' was to be provided to working class men in the first Mechanics' Institute, set up in 1823 by Lord Brougham, a leading aristocrat and philanthropist, who 'sought to increase men's scientific knowledge in the belief that such learning would contribute to new inventions, and to serve as a safety valve offering a controlled context for debate in order to deter more politically motivated attacks on the *status quo*' (Wolfe, 1993, p.7). Perhaps unsurprisingly, the Institutes did not succeed in attracting large numbers of unskilled labourers to attend these evening lectures and discussions at the end of their long shifts in the factories of newly industrialising Britain (although they did attract more skilled workers and lower middle class students.)

But they attracted criticism, not only from the reactionary right, which feared any expansion of knowledge amongst the lower orders, but from progressives, such as the Chartists, who saw the Institutes as being too geared towards providing knowledge in the interests of the *status quo*, to meet the changing skill requirements of employers. By restricting the range of books available and the topics covered (eg, excluding revolutionary political literature, such as Tom Paine's *Treatise on the Rights of Man*) such education would help to 'domesticate' (using Freire's twentieth-century terminology) rather than to liberate the labouring classes, it was argued. There are parallels, here, with criticisms of market-led approaches and the new vocationalism, in the contemporary context.

In contrast, early British socialists established their own meeting places (including residential centres), organising lectures and classes as part of a strategy to Educate, Agitate and Organise. The notion of 'really useful knowledge' implied knowledge which was not controlled by the interests of the *status quo* (the plaque over the door of the Working Men's College in London read, 'Under the control of nobody'). On the contrary, in fact, 'really useful knowledge' was knowledge for empowerment and social change. This, in turn, has parallels with alternative contemporary approaches, geared towards education for liberation and transformation.

As the Introduction suggested, there are important caveats about drawing parallels with previous debates and experiences, rooted as these were in very different historical contexts. In the contemporary context of such rapid and fundamental change, Hobsbawm has questioned whether the past was losing its role, more profoundly, as the 'old maps and charts which guided human beings singly and collectively through life no longer represent the landscape through which we move, the sea on which we sail' (Hobsbawm, p.16). Clearly, romantic accounts of past experiences are unhelpful as models for contemporary practice, in very different contemporary circumstances. Commenting upon the relevance of previous approaches to adult education, Steele has reflected that 'instead of uncritically attempting to reproduce old models we need to understand (their) strengths and weaknesses and how they might apply to the new formations and to grasp reflexively what our point for leverage is within the dominant order' (Steele, 1987, p.124). More generally, too, this chapter will suggest, previous experiences can also provide examples of what could be achieved, as well as the limitations of what could be achieved, and what was achieved, often with very limited resources. This final point relates, in turn, to the theme which was raised in the previous chapter: the language of possibilities, for transformation, as well as the language of structural constraints.

This chapter summarises a number of past examples which have relevance for contemporary debates on adult education for transformation. The focus is primarily geared towards experiences and practice, although there are references to the contributions of 'great men' educators (and they were mostly men, for a number of reasons relating to women's disadvantaged position). These include examples from Britain, together with examples from Scandinavia, and from Canada and the US. Clearly, in the space of one chapter it will not be possible to provide anything approaching an adequate account of relevant experiences; these examples are offered merely for the purposes of illustration. Experiences from the South are explored, on a similar basis, in Chapter Three.

Although the focus in selecting examples is upon the relevance for adult education for transformation, and the examples all share some common criticisms of dominant approaches, there are also significant differences between them, ranging as they do from religious-based traditions of varying types, through social democratic to more explicitly Marxist-based approaches. There are also differences of emphasis, in terms of the content, on the one hand, and the processes of alternative education, on the other. For the purposes of this chapter, both of these need to be examined critically (and the findings are by no means all predictable – progressive content not being necessarily linked with progressive processes and pedagogies; and *vice versa*).

British experiences

As has already been suggested, British experiences have included examples of competing approaches. There have been examples of competing approaches and processes co-existing as well as competing within some institutions, as well as examples of competition between institutions and programmes. There were Christian examples and Socialist examples and there were Christian Socialist examples, including Christian Sunday schools, and Socialist Sunday schools in nineteenth century Britain. Through the Settlements and through the University Extension Movement, the universities also played a major role in providing adult education to women (then barred from the mainstream of university life) as well as to men, including working class men, who were effectively excluded from mainstream provision in the universities at that time. Although these programmes tended to attract middle class students, it has been estimated that there were some 15,000 working class students, around a quarter of the total enrolled in university extension programmes, at the end of the century. This was the context in which Mansbridge, a Christian Socialist, founded the Workers' Educational Association (WEA) in 1903, based upon tutorial groups and summer schools, which together would constitute a workers' university, to bring the benefits of the university more effectively to the working class. For Mansbridge, as a Christian, the purpose was spiritual, and as a socialist, the purpose was for social service for the common good (Alfred, 1987).

Both the university extension movement and the Workers' Educational Association have been criticised from the Left for being too closely linked with the dominant interests in society, too broad an alliance (the WEA for example being described as politically safe according to one account: Jennings, 1973) although these criticisms have also been contested. Similar differences of view emerged in the debates over the future of Ruskin College, Oxford, which had been set up in 1899 to provide opportunities for working class people to study in a residential setting. There were major differences over the extent of co-operation with the university, to extend mainstream provision, on the one hand, versus the need to concentrate upon alternative approaches, based upon Marxist analyses, on the other.

Within Ruskin, 'The key issue for many students at the college', as Simon has summarised it, 'lay in the teaching of economics. Was this to be based on what the students regarded as capitalist apologetics, or on Marxist analyses?' This particular debate, in turn, related to the underlying question: 'Was it (the main purpose of the college) to equip its students to challenge the existing social order and work to transform it, or to prepare students to function within the limitations set by existing social relations?' (Simon, 1992: 19). In the event, following a student strike and the dismissal of the principal in 1909, the college split, with the predominantly Marxist 'Plebs League' setting up the rival Central Labour College (Craik, 1964; Pollins, 1984; Simon, 1992).

The differences between these two positions have been characterised in terms of competing approaches to adult education, differences which persisted in terms of competition between rival traditions. In his history of Ruskin, Pollins describes these differences as follows; 'The National Council of Labour Colleges (1923-64), an offshoot of the Central Labour College, regarded the Workers' Educational Association – with which it included Ruskin in a minor role – as supporting the existing economic and social system in the guise of "neutral" education'. In contrast, 'the WEA dismissed the NCLC's teaching as mere class-war propaganda and not education at all' (Pollins, 1984: 19).

Does this mean, then, that the WEA-type tradition was effectively no more 'neutral' than the so-called 'neutral' approaches which Freire has criticised for effectively supporting the *status quo*; education for 'domestication', rather than for transformation? And conversely, does this leave the National Council of Labour Colleges (NCLCs) as the bearers of alternative education for transformation, at least until their demise, when they disappeared within the education provision of the Trade Union Congress in 1964? The reality is less straightforward.

In practice, both the NCLC and the WEA made very significant contributions, both in terms of the numbers of students taught, and in terms of the education provided, and they both, in their different ways, provided examples of education based upon alternative approaches. Both, incidentally, also fed students into full-time residential education at Ruskin.

Despite its achievements, like the WEA, the NCLC tradition has also been seen as problematic in terms of providing education for transformation, both in terms of the content of the courses, and in terms of the educational processes involved. Simon, for instance, has criticised this tradition for pursuing its much-valued independence to the point of becoming effectively somewhat isolated from political and industrial struggles, and so from the working class, as a whole. (Simon, 1992). This isolation was, he argued, compounded when the Communist Party was formed in 1920, developing a strong focus upon education which was directly linked with political understanding and action. Some of the Communist Party's influence on education emerges later in this chapter in the discussion of the role of Marx House, in the 1930s and 40s in particular.

The NCLC tradition enjoyed what Simon described as a 'heroic' period up to the General Strike in 1926 (and the subsequent difficulties which beset the movement, following the defeat of the General Strike). Kelly put this as follows: 'The period of the most rapid advance came in the 20s especially in the years centring on the General Strike. The number of classes, 529 in 1922-23, jumped to a peak of 1,234 in 1925-26; the number of students in classes reached a peak of 31,635 in the following year' (Kelly, 1970: 283). Subsequently, though, the NCLC became, in Simon's view, 'the voice of the more extreme right-wing in the labour movement'. By the 1940s and 50s, he argued, 'it is probably true to say that there was more Marxism being discussed and studied in the WEA (and in the university extra-mural departments) than in the NCLC' (Simon, 1992: 63-4). In practice, however, others have argued that the NCLC could not simply be identified with the right-wing of the Labour movement. The reality was more complex, and there continued to be strong progressive influences, including Marxist influences, whatever the positions taken by particular key figures (Mortimer, 1995).

Quite apart from the question of the content of NCLC courses, however, there were also criticisms of the educational processes employed. NCLC courses were criticised for being geared towards eliciting 'right answers' rather than encouraging students to think out their conclusions for themselves, on the basis of the critical analysis of competing perspectives. Or so the critics argued, at least.

Nevertheless, the NCLC was a major force, with a strong base, especially within particular geographical areas and within particular trade unions. The NCLC was especially renowned for its correspondence courses, through which many thousands of workers were introduced to alternative ideas, including basic Marxist ideas. In the late 1950s, shortly before it was absorbed within the TUC, the NCLC had almost 15,000 students enrolled on correspondence courses (Corfield, 1969; Mortimer, 1995).

Meanwhile, the WEA tradition clearly included not only 'safe', but also more transformational experiences, and this was the case in relation to the content of courses and in relation to the processes involved. From the outset, in fact, the WEA had been based upon Mansbridge's strong commitment to democracy, both in general and in adult education more specifically. This meant that it must be WEA members who should say 'how, why, what or when they wish to study' (Mansbridge, 1920: xvii-xviii, quoted in Alfred, 1987: 25). In setting out his approach to educational methods, Mansbridge quoted an Arabian proverb, 'The lecture is one, the discussion is one thousand'. This underlying democracy within the WEA's approach meant that there clearly was space for critical and problem-posing forms of education. Mansbridge has even been described as 'the most dangerous man in England' because 'he taught the working people to think for themselves' (quoted in Alfred, 1987: 32).

Within the WEA there was certainly scope for alternative approaches. One of the most renowned WEA tutors was RH Tawney, who has been described as the 'patron saint of adult education', a charismatic teacher, and WEA President, who was deeply committed to adult education for citizenship, equality of opportunity and social justice. In his later life, Tawney was critical of any falling off in what he viewed as the WEA's mission in terms of education for citizenship and for socialism, based upon the highest intellectual standards, coupled with the active participation of students through the tutorial class (Elsey, 1987). In addition to Tawney, a number of other progressives and radicals, including Marxists, worked as tutors for the WEA in different areas over the years.

The WEA developed into a major force in working class adult education, with over 20,000 individual members just after the First World War. As the major provider of trade union education, the organisation also worked to establish the Workers' Education Trade Union Committee (WETUC) in 1919 to take forward trade union education (Corfield, 1969). The WETUC was a key player in this field; by the late 1950s, before the re-organisation of trade union education into the TUC, the WEA and the WETUC were providing classes for some 84,000 trade unionists, together with some 250 one-day schools and 276 weekend schools, catering for some 6,000 and 9,000 trade unionists respectively (Corfield, 1969). From the early days, the aims included the promotion of 'efficient, intelligent loyalty in the trade-union movement', together with the wider aims of enabling workers 'to answer the questions and solve the problems that arise from and are due to their social and industrial conditions' (quoted in Corfield, 1969: 31). As Corfield pointed out, this related to a wider interest in industrial democracy and the transformation of economic and social relations, through workers' control.

As Steele has argued, the apparently mutually exclusive dichotomy between the NCLC's conception of the WEA as an instrument of social and ideological control over the working-class movement, and the diametrically opposite view of the WEA which was held by more sympathetic social-democratic and liberal intellectuals has obscured the reality. In fact, 'the WEA's actual practices were plural, differing widely throughout its twenty-one districts' (Steele, 1987: 109).

This argument can be illustrated as follows. Through the study of the work of George Thompson, in Yorkshire, in the inter-war period, Steele has analysed experiences of working class adult education which were firmly committed to social change, with the tutorial class as an 'instrument of social regeneration' (Steele, 1987: 114).

Thompson has been described as seeing adult education's purpose in terms of the social and industrial emancipation of the working classes. In his view, the core curriculum should consist of what he termed the 'controversial' subjects like economics, social and political history, political philosophy and social history (although other subjects, including the arts, were taught, these were secondary). The success of the district's work was measured not only in terms of the numbers of students attracted and the quality of study, but also in terms of the influence of the work, on the labour and progressive movement, on those taking part in public life (including local councillors and MPs) and in the general spread of culture in the area.

As Steele demonstrates, Thompson was clear that the aim was not propaganda (which, he argued, was what the NCLC called education). Whilst he felt that propaganda had its place, the role of the WEA was to promote deep and sustained study, in classes taught by the most highly qualified tutors, to provide the movement with the theoretical basis for effective social renewal. Education of this type was, he believed, a decisive instrument in creating class-consciousness. He argued that

'workers will only achieve emancipation when they are capable of thinking out issues for themselves and have the capacity and sufficient toler-
ance to achieve the ends collectively' (quoted in Steele, 1987: 116). He
was particularly critical of the NCLC for the ways in which he thought
that they taught Marxism – as dogma, rather than as an approach which
needed to be evaluated in relation to the issue under consideration.
Working class education, in contrast, needed to link the abstract with
the concrete experiences of the students in question, he believed.

Whilst emphasising the importance of making working class education relevant, however, he was not unappreciative of the importance of
theory. And he was convinced of the importance of the contribution of
intellectuals such as Tawney and GDH Cole, for instance – but only as
long as working people could exercise control over the process.
Unsurprisingly, in the event, though, Thompson was criticised from all
sides, from the universities and from the mainstream of the WEA, as
well as from the NCLC.

Without romanticising his contribution, Steele nevertheless
concludes that Thompson's work had much to celebrate and defend,
even if his approach to working class adult education was significantly
stronger in terms of class than gender (Steele concludes by describing
him as a patriarchal tyrant). Since then, others within the WEA have
provided examples of adult education which has been more specifically
focused upon social transformation, in terms of race and gender relations, as well as in terms of class relations.

Just to take one example of more recent practice, the WEA North
Western District published a report on the work of the Trade Union and
Basic Education Project, summarising 10 years of community education
in the inner city. This covered trade union education, political education, which included courses on racism and combatting racism, black
history, culture and politics, and black and third world women, and
health education (an example of work which was specifically geared
towards the women's health movement). The model of trade union and
community education which was developed was based upon working
with community groups, aiming to 'foster the process of consciousness-
raising by which communities – especially black communities – can
begin to address the circumstances of their own lives'. The educational
process was 'political in the widest sense of the term, that of encouraging people actively to take up those issues which directly affect them as
individuals and as a community' (NW WEA, 1989: 5). Some of these
experiences are discussed more fully in Chapter Five.

There are parallels, here, incidentally, with some of the subsequent
debates which took place about the way forward for Ruskin and the
other residential colleges, as the context for the Labour and progressive
movement underwent major changes, in response to restructuring and
recession, from the mid-1970s. In a collection of essays on residential
adult education, Jackson put the case for the importance of widening
student recruitment to offer more opportunities for women (including

women outside paid employment), as well as unemployed men, with more focus upon addressing community-based issues in addition to workplace issues (Jackson, in ed. Houlton, 1978). This was the model for Northern College, which was being established as a new adult residential college at the time.

More recently, Fryer, the Principal of Northern College, reflected upon the importance of these new and wider horizons, when summarising the college's work with black and minority ethnic communities and with pensioners, as well as with women (both in and outside paid work) and with the unemployed, alongside the more traditional constituency of trade unionists. Whilst the constituency had widened, taking account of underlying processes of social change and social exclusion, the purpose of working-class adult education was still to be defined in terms set out by RH Tawney, Fryer argued. Knowledge, in these terms, was, he argued, quoting Tawney's words, 'but a stimulus to constructive thought and an inspiration to action', a tool for transformation (Fryer, 1992: 311).

Some of these contemporary debates re-emerge in subsequent chapters. Meanwhile, for the purposes of this chapter, the discussion returns to another strand, in alternative approaches, the case of Marx House in the Thirties and Forties. Compared with the mass scale of adult education and trade union education which was carried out through the WEA and the NCLC, the significance of Marx House should not be over-estimated. Nor do these examples begin to cover the range of varied educational activities which were taking place at this period. Other examples include factory-based discussion groups and discussion groups linked to the flourishing Left Book Club. Many hundreds of these latter groups were active, at this period, and their activities were publicised through the Left Book Club's journal (Mortimer, 1995). Another significant source of working class education was the Co-operative Movement. In particular, the Co-op Women's Guilds had a history of introducing working class women to education, a history which goes back to an earlier period. The following comments on Marx House are included to illustrate examples from a period when transformative approaches were relatively flourishing.

The example of Marx House

Cohen has entitled her account of Marx House *Revolutionary Education Revived: The Communist Challenge to the Labour Colleges, 1933-1945* (Cohen, 1992). As she explains, in 1933 the NCLC faced a new challenge, when the Communists set up the Marx House Schools in London and Manchester. In the previous year, to commemorate the fiftieth anniversary of Marx' death, the Marx Memorial Library and a workers' school had been established to provide a centre for working class education. Whilst the project was clearly committed to study based upon Marxist approaches, the supporters included Labour Party and

Independent Labour Party members and trade unionist delegates, as well as Communist Party representatives. This was to be workers' education for the broad movement. Non-Marxist books were included in the library, as well as Marxist books, and tutors included non-Party members (although the majority of tutors were Communists). Marx House opened in 1933, in Clerkenwell Green, London, in a property which had been used by progressive organisations in the past. (Lenin had had his office in the building, when *Iskra* was printed in London, from 1902-3. Lenin's office can still be seen by visitors to the Library in the original building and classes continue to be organised in Marx House.)

Student numbers grew, demonstrating that there was very considerable interest. There were lectures and classes, Sunday lectures, discussion circles, correspondence courses and summer schools. By 1935, for example, over 300 workers attended the three-week summer school, studying a range of topics including trade unionism, fascism and war (not surprisingly a popular topic at the time), and socialism. Similarly, the Sunday lectures in 1935 included the topic of fascism and war, as well as current economic and political problems, and art (Marx House Bulletins, 1934-5). By 1936, there were 1,533 individual members, and apart from those who attended the classes, there were 67 discussion circles (Cohen, 1992). This is a significant indication of interest in political education, even if it is small indeed, compared with the enrolments achieved by the WEA, the WETUC and the correspondence courses of the NCLC. Affiliations of organisations took longer to build up, and tended to be Communist Party branches, although some trade union and Co-operative organisations did also affiliate.

The Second World War caused disruption; the entire programme for the winter of 1940-1 had to be cancelled because of the London Blitz. But a limited service was maintained. And educational materials were produced to meet the educational needs of those who could not get to Marx House. These included not only Communist Party branches, but also factory branches with non-Communist activists (political education through factory branches is another story, with its own significance, in reaching both Communists and non-Communist activists). Members of the forces also used the materials, which were even said to have been used in army education (unofficially), which was ironic, given that army education had been promoted to improve morale, in terms of a somewhat more Establishment perspective.

This latter aspect had particular importance, both at the time and in the immediate post-war period, when the influence of progressive adult education in the forces was seen as a significant factor in the widespread support which developed for progressive programmes for post-war reconstruction, including support for the Labour election victory in 1945 and support for post-war nationalisations and for the development of the Welfare State. The Tory Cabinet Minister RA Butler wrote, 'the forces vote in particular had been virtually won over by the left wing influence of ABCA' (Army Bureau for Current Affairs).* RA Butler, amongst many others, may have actually exaggerated the impact of the Left in army education in terms of the specifics of the vote for Labour in 1945. Denny points to some of the other factors which also need to be taken into account. But progressives certainly had operated within the context of forces education, and raised political awareness.

Denny quotes, for example, from the memoirs of one such progressive, Fred Westacott, a Communist who had organised lively, and very critical discussion sessions in Italy at this period. 'A straw poll of O[ther R[ank]'s in my unit revealed almost 100 per cent support for Labour,' Westacott commented. 'The lads were not going to tolerate going back to the Britain of before the war. There was a clear understanding of how things could be changed.' During the election campaign itself, Westacott was not invited to give any of his usual education sessions, although, in fact, he commented, 'Of course, there was plenty of discussion'. In Westacott's view, the war 'was not just against Fascism. But against the conditions which had spawned Fascism, the world of mass unemployment, homelessness, poverty and extreme class divisions'. And political education had played a role in promoting discussions of the alternatives; education for transformation, drawing upon experiences of progressive education in the pre-war period.

Syllabuses of class courses were sold in large numbers throughout the war years. For example, in 1941, 5,000 copies of *Scientific Socialism* sold out within two months and had to be reprinted. *The Economics of Capitalism*, published in 1943, sold 12,500 copies in 12 months. Other topics included *Introduction to Political Economy, Socialism in Practice, Problems of Trade Unionism, Marxism and War, Women in Industry, Imperialism and the People, India*, and specifically for particular industries, *Railways and Railwaymen in the UK*, and *Problems of the Building Industry*, with *What You Need to Know about Local Government* for those involved with local councils. The syllabuses were very cheap and accessible, giving a brief guide to the topic in question, together with further reading suggestions. Tutors' notes encouraged tutors to use these as the basis for question-and-answer discussion, to stimulate critical understanding.

Cohen has argued that Marx House fell short in developing outreach work and in training tutors. These limitations affected the growth of study circles, nationally. Cohen has also suggested that although Marx House did welcome women alongside men, overall insufficient account was taken 'of women's additional inequalities' (Cohen, 1992: 150) and not enough was done to challenge these. But overall there were significant achievements. In the 1930s, Marx House did provide a prestigious and successful school, which attracted well-known lecturers,

---

* (Quoted in *Present and Correct*, B. Denny, unpublished dissertation, Ruskin College, Oxford).

she concluded. And Marx House reached a significant number of activists, both Marxists and non-Marxists, and provided them with a challenging political education. In the war years, she argued, the printed educational materials had a wide impact, too, and this affected both labour and progressive movement activists, and those involved in the forces education. So does this fit within the alternative approaches which were discussed in the previous chapter? What is the evidence, in terms of the educational materials which were developed, and the ways in which these were supposed to be used?

The materials covered a range of topics, from Marxist theory and political economy through to issues in science and the arts. And they certainly focused upon the links between critical theory on the one hand, and issues in practical politics on the other, how to work for change, on the basis of critical analysis. So, for example, the pamphlet for new members (price 1d, or old penny) provided the basics of Marxist analysis, under headings such as 'The Kind of World We Live In' and 'How That World Can be Changed' and 'The Force That Can Change It'. Other pamphlets tackled issues in the British Labour Movement (*Socialism and the British Labour Movement*, for example, and *Social Democracy and the Fight for Working Class Unity*). There were pamphlets on women's issues (*Women in the British Labour and Democratic Movement*) and there were pamphlets which tackled global issues, including aspects of imperialism (both in theory and in relation to the practice of British imperialism, in India, for example; as in Palme Dutt's *Syllabus for a Course of five Study Classes on India Today*).

And these educational materials included some very specific questions, linking the material to strategies for action for change. For example, the Indian syllabus included questions about the last days of British rule; what kind of free India will it be, and what are the politics of reconstruction? Similarly, the pamphlet on *What Every Worker Wants to Know* combined the basics of political economy with more specific questions about the implications for recent debates in the movement, such as how to explain the defeat of the General Strike, and what the objective of workers' control in industry might actually mean.

The pamphlets on the *Problems of the Building Industry* and *What You Need to Know on Local Government* were very specific examples of educational materials designed to link theoretical analysis with concrete strategies for change in the post-war period. Having provided a historical analysis of the industry from the Industrial Revolution through to more recent technological changes, the pamphlet on the building industry put forward the arguments for progressive policies for reconstruction in the future, bringing together the skills of the workforce and the related professionals and technicians. It was not just a question of defending wages and conditions, it was argued, but of developing the consciousness of the workers on 'all questions affecting the industry, relations with the State, the relation of construction to the social needs of the people, etc. Only by working out and fighting for a positive policy on these issues can the workers fit themselves for ultimate control of the industry' (*Problems of the Building Industry*, published for the Marx Memorial Library and Workers' School, p.35). Similarly, the pamphlet on Local Government was specifically designed to give a broad outline to the mass of questions which were to be thrown up in the post-war period, when it was argued, 'the scope for enlarging local government is enormous, and the mass of people feel the need for radical change' (p.5). These educational materials were to provide the tools for critical analysis, as the basis for strategic progressive action.

In terms of the educational methods employed, there was emphasis, too, upon active participation. Educational materials included sets of questions and exercises, to prompt the tutors into involving the students in dialogue. As the pamphlet on Local Government explained, for example, 'To help tutors, a number of questions intended to stimulate discussion, are given at the end of each section . . . Tutors should, as far as possible, add local examples to those given in the text and develop their own questions, too, so that the general information is closely related to local experience' (M. Shapiro, *What You Need to Know on Local Government*, p.5).

The Marx House Bulletin was very clear in its emphasis on active learning. For example, tips were provided for tutors, as follows. Planned discussion could 'stimulate interest' and help participants to 'develop their powers of exposition'. The class would not be a success if 'it simply results in a catechism; the tutor merely stringing off a series of questions and pushing them round the class until he gets (or himself supplies) an approximately correct answer'. Careful preparation was essential for success, starting with arguments and examples to explain the theoretical aspects, and backing this up with local material, for illustration. This would then be followed by carefully thought-out questions.

At this point, the *Tips for Tutors* referred to the example of Lenin's approach to teaching Marxism. He used to sit the workers in a circle, apparently, and present the subject, before encouraging the workers 'to raise objections to the points he raised and provoked disputes among the students, encouraging us to defend our points of view against one another'. Thus, the former student, Babuskin, explained, 'our studies were always interesting and lively and at the same time effective in training us as speakers' (quoted in *Some Tips for Tutors* Alick West, Marx House). Which all sounds familiar to those who have been schooled in participative approaches to adult learning. Similar points were made, too, in another issue, in relation to the teaching style employed by Marx himself. Soon after his exile in London began, in 1850 and 1851, Marx gave a course of lectures on political economy to crowded meetings in the Lecture Hall of the Communist Workers' Educational League. Marx is described as having explained the topic, very carefully, and then called upon the listeners to put questions, to engage the audience in discussion and deepen their understanding.

If this all sounds too right-on to be true, the sceptical reader may reflect that, in another issue of the Bulletin, in the early forties, Stalin was described in somewhat similar terms. 'One of the outstanding qualities in the work of Stalin, setting a model for all active workers, is the way in which he consistently combines practical political leadership with Marxist education of the workers.' And when leading a study circle, Stalin, too, is credited with 'at the same time having learned much from the workers' through these dialogues. Indeed, he is quoted as saying that 'my first teachers were the workers of Tiflis'. Was this what Gramsci had in mind, when he emphasised the importance of learning from the workers, the sceptic might wonder? Or maybe the workers of Tiflis could have done without being described as Stalin's teachers? Alternatively, of course, it might be argued that the point at issue is not so much Comrade Stalin's approach to workers' education, but what this all says about the importance which Marx House placed on encouraging participative approaches amongst their tutors.

After the war, Marx House was re-opened, and still functions as a specialist library, the Marx Memorial Library, which includes copies of the pamphlets and educational materials which have been referred to in this chapter. There are series of lectures, too, at Marx House, although on a different scale in comparison with the thirties and forties. The Communist Party of Great Britain also continued to produce educational materials (although on a different scale too) until it wound itself up, in the aftermath of the events of 1989 in the former USSR and other former socialist countries in Eastern and Central Europe.* There are also copies of these materials, in the Marx Memorial Library.

Examples of these more recent educational packs include some of the relatively familiar themes, such as *British Capitalism Today*, from the sixties, covering Marxist political economy as applied to the British context. In addition, from the seventies and beyond, there are examples of applying political economy to the development of alternative strategies for the labour and progressive movement, the Alternative Economic Strategy; *The Road from Thatcherism*. The Alternative Economic Strategy (AES) was a key factor in uniting progressive forces within the labour and trade union movement around a set of demands, within the framework of a longer-term strategy for transformation.

And there are packs on *Introduction to Feminism* and on *Power and Prejudice = Racism*, to address sexism and racism within the movement, as well as within the wider society. The pack on *Approaches to Feminism*, for example, also illustrated the continuance of the tradition of questions and discussion, including a number of questions to tease out sexism, and tackle this; basic practical questions like who does which jobs in the home, and what provision does the branch make for children

---

* To be re-established as the Communist Party of Britain.

when parents attend meetings? And what needs to be done about this? These educational packs were for use in Party education schools, and in branch educational meetings, which were a regular feature of branch life within local communities as well as within workplace branches.

The tradition of the summer school continued too, for a time, with the Communist University of London, which, in its heyday in the seventies, attracted hundreds of students, and others, to what the prospectus for 1970 described as 'Nine Days of Intensive Courses in the World's most Explosive Ideology: Marxism Leninism'. In the aftermath of the student strikes and demonstrations in the late sixties (including the events of May 1968 in France) these summer schools tapped into a new interest in Marxism, amongst students and other young people – an interest which has shown some, albeit modest, signs of revival in the nineties. Communists, together with Labour Party activists, have again started to organise successful weekend schools aimed primarily at young people, drawing upon the long tradition of summer schools and weekend schools which were such a prominent aspect of political education, in the past. In addition, the Socialist Workers Party has organised large highly successful summer schools primarily directed at students and other young people, with over 7,000 participants taking part in the summer school in 1995, for example.

So much, then, in summary, for some examples of alternative approaches in Britain. As it was suggested at the outset of the chapter, this was no more than the most cursory, thumbnail sketch, rather than a full and balanced account, to illustrate the simple point that Britain has a long and varied history in this respect. This is not to romanticise this history, though, or to suggest that such a history either could or should be repeated, in the present. But although this present context differs, neither has it arisen in a vacuum, unaffected by the ideas or the experiences of the past. And these ideas and experiences have, of course, included influences from beyond Britain, too.

The examples of Scandinavian Folk High Schools

The Scandinavian Folk High School has been one such key influence, both in Britain and beyond. The Danish experience has been particularly formative, with a powerful and continuing tradition of adult education as 'popular enlightenment'; out of a total population of some five million, at least 30 per cent of the adults are engaged in some way, at any one time. The Folk High Schools which have been central to this were developed in Denmark, deeply influenced by the work of Grundtvig, a nineteenth century poet, clergyman and educational thinker. The Folk High School approach was also adopted in a number of other countries, including Germany and the rest of Scandinavia. In Britain, three residential adult colleges, Coleg Harlech in Wales, Fircroft in Birmingham, and Newbattle Abbey in Scotland, were developed on this model.

Grundtvig started from his rejection of traditional forms of academic education, in Denmark, on the grounds that these promoted rote learning, which was profoundly alienating and divorced from life. In contrast, he set out to develop alternative approaches, targeted at those who were excluded or felt alienated from traditional, formal academic learning, especially young people in the rural areas. His objective was to promote forms of education which would assist people in improving their situations; schools for life. And this would include education for citizenship and democracy.

The Folk High Schools which were established from the mid-nineteenth century provided residential education during the winter months for men (when there was less agricultural work to be done). Some of the Schools were mixed, but others took women students when the men were back at work in the summer. The content of the courses emphasised Danish culture and education for citizenship, rather than vocational training, with a strong emphasis upon democracy and co-operation, in both the content and the organisation of the learning. Teachers came from the same backgrounds as the students (Campbell, 1928). Group meetings were key to the decision-making process; staff in some would take part in domestic chores (Lieven, 1988).

The notion of 'popular enlightenment', it has been argued, was centrally linked to the view that 'the initiative and focus are in the people themselves, not in the state or other authorities' (Jacobsen, 1992, p.278). (The schools started on the basis of voluntary rather than state support, although state subsidies subsequently became available.) The process of people's enlightenment was to start when people come together, and people's movements have had central value for democratic change. This emphasis upon democracy, collectivity and social commitment has parallels, it has been suggested, with the work of Freire (Jacobsen, 1992).

The Folk High Schools spread; by 1870 there were 52 schools and by 1890 this total had grown to 75 (Jacobsen, 1992). Meanwhile, the model has diversified. There are still around a hundred residential schools in Denmark, together with day and evening schools. The day schools have been particularly geared towards meeting the needs of the unemployed, who have grown in number in Denmark, as elsewhere. The Folk High Schools include a range of different perspectives, although the predominant perspective has been social democratic, and this has also been the case in the trade union high schools. (Similar connections have been identified, too, between Study Circles, in Sweden, for instance, and the social democratic party.) And whilst cultural subjects still retain popularity, other subjects include Marxism, development and ecology (Rordam, 1980). Although the Folk High Schools have been criticised from the Marxist Left, they have also been seen as having valuable contributions to make in supporting education for citizenship and for democratic social change.

The Folk High Schools have also provided examples of education for change in terms of challenging gender inequalities in society. For instance, Wainwright has provided an account of a feminist Women's Folk High School, founded in 1985, in Gothenburg, Sweden (Wainwright, 1994). She visited the school in 1990, and found the one hundred or so students positive about its achievements. The school was run on the basis of democratic structures and decision-making, and this was a central value, part of the commitment to running the school by women for women, on the basis of 'women's values'. And the school shared the wider Folk High School aim of 'developing a critical sense, independence and a capacity for co-operation' and of 'increasing the student's awareness of his or her own circumstances and those of the world at large' (Wainwright, 1994, p. 129). Wainwright acknowledged some of the problems which had been experienced in the Women's Folk High School, including difficulties with funding, and difficulties in making less formal structures work effectively and democratically. But she concluded that the critical ways in which the women engaged with these problems, and grappled with them, was indicative of the potential for further innovation and creativity.

North American examples: the Antigonish Movement and the Highlander Folk School

As it has been suggested, the Folk High Schools have had influence beyond Scandinavia, in Germany and Britain, for example. This influence also extended to North America, where alternative approaches were being developed, too (Campbell, 1928). Historically, there had been parallels as well as differences in the development of adult education, more generally, in North America. For example, nineteenth century settlement houses were developed in US cities, as well as in Britain. Parallels have also been drawn, for example, between the National Council of Labour Colleges, in Britain and the American Labour College Movement. And some of the key thinkers in the development of approaches to student-centred lifelong learning were North American. These included Dewey, who is mainly associated with his educational work on children, but the logic of his concern with growth had vital implications for lifelong education – democratically-based, active learning, rooted in awareness, analysis and problem-solving for life (Cross-Durrant, 1987).

Lindeman was also a precursor of lifelong learning, with a strong commitment to experiential learning, with adults working in democratically organised small groups to analyse their situations, as the basis for taking action to shape their own lives. In addition to focusing upon issues in political economy, Lindeman considered that key issues included 'what is to be done about our deep-seated habits of racial discrimination, how we are to democratize our vast educational equipment, how we are to play an appropriate role in world affairs' (Lindeman, 1945, quoted in Brookfield, 1987, p.133). Reflecting upon Lindeman's contribution, Brookfield has drawn parallels with the work of Freire (although Lindeman, as an advocate of the mixed economy, was, perhaps, less critical of existing economic structures).

For the purposes of this chapter, however, the focus is less upon these individual contributions, and more upon the ways in which alternative approaches were developed in practice. Here there are two particular examples to summarise: the Antigonish Movement in Nova Scotia, Canada (which drew upon influences elsewhere, including the WEA and the Folk High Schools) and the Highlander Folk School, Tennessee, which also drew upon the experiences of the Danish Folk High Schools (as well as the writings of Dewey, Lindeman and others). Brookfield has drawn comparisons between the Antigonish movement and the WEA, in the sense that 'both are cited by present day analysts as examples of a fine heritage of social commitment in the field of adult education within a democratic (rather than revolutionary) tradition' (Brookfield, 1984), in the past, if perhaps less so in the present.

The Antigonish Movement was rooted in the work of Catholic Action, based at Saint Francis Xavier University Extension Department in the twenties. Father Hopkins, and his nephew, Moses Coady, who became director of the Extension Department in 1928, set out to 'bridge the gap between book learning and real life, and to put knowledge into a form that the ordinary people could understand and use' (quoted in Brookfield, 1984). The specific context for this project was a depressed area, where the three main sources of livelihoods – fishing, mining and agriculture – were all suffering. Coady set out to provide the type of adult education which would support the development of co-operatives, including credit unions, as part of a strategy for community-based renewal. By 1939, nearly 20,000 people were enrolled in study clubs and over 300 credit unions had been established.

Brookfield quotes Coady to summarise key guiding principles: 'We hold, therefore, as a fundamental principle, that an adult education programme, to produce results and affect the lives of the people must result, in the first instance, in economic action on their part . . . this is good pedagogy. We must take the learner where he is. We build upon the interests which are uppermost in his mind' (Coady, 1979, quoted in Brookfield, 1984). This was to be achieved through group work, study circles run democratically, to stimulate discussion and reflection, followed by collective action, for community development. Although Coady was a reformist, in the social democratic tradition, rather than being committed to more fundamental forms of social change, as Lovett has commented, his work in the Antigonish movement linked adult education to social action 'with methods and techniques which even today (1980) would be regarded as too radical for many educational institutions' (Lovett, 1980: 160). Since the death of Coady, the Antigonish Movement has developed its global influence. Coady himself was advocating the application of this approach to adult education for co-operative development in the South before the war, although it was somewhat later before Antigonish was 'discovered' in terms of its relevance for Third World development. Visitors came from Asia, Latin America, the Caribbean and Africa in the post-war period. And just after Coady's death, in 1959, the Coady International Institute was established to train people from the South to apply these approaches in their own contexts (Crane, 1987).

The second North American example of alternative approaches comes from the Highlander Folk School, which was set up in 1932 as part of attempts to respond to the problems of the depression in inter-war Tennessee. The catalyst for the particular development of this educational project was a strike by non-unionised miners, which led to appeals for community support for the strikers in the form of food and clothing. The Highlander students and teachers became radicalised by the strike, and union workers became involved in what came to be a programme geared towards social change.

In addition to the trade union and workplace-related work at Highlander, the school became involved in the Civil Rights Movement in the fifties, challenging racial discrimination in the US. This involvement at Highlander included the establishment of a Citizenship school providing literacy skills to support black people in taking the voter registration test then required. It has been estimated that nearly 100,000 black people learned to read and write through these programmes (Adams, 1972, quoted in Brookfield, 1984).

Highlander has been committed to working with social movements for change. This is on the basis of democratic education and decision-making, with an emphasis upon working in groups, with active participation. Short residential workshops have been a feature of this approach, to support group problem-solving.

Highlander has been characterised as being both 'an idea and a process. It is the idea that people have within themselves the potential to solve their own problems. It is the process by which individuals come to realise that their problems are shared by others, that problems can be solved collectively, that their individual problems are not solved until the common problem is eradicated for all' (Conti, 1977: 38-9, quoted in Brookfield, 1987). Although the processes are democratic, Highlander has also recognised some of the problems inherent in social democratic approaches; at least in the sense that Highlander has recognised the importance of underlying conflicts of interest in society, conflicts of interest which have to be addressed in radical ways (in contrast with the Antigonish analysis, which has been more consensual).

The Highlander Centre is alive, having been reorganised as the Highlander Research and Education Centre (following attacks by the Ku-Klux-Klan, and then having its charter revoked by the State of Tennessee in 1961). The rechartered Highlander Research and Education Centre continues to promote radical community development. The focus is still on tackling poverty and inequality, both in the workplace and community, which reflect the maldistribution of power in society. And the democratic, participative, educational approach is central to this commitment to adult education for transformation.

Reflecting upon Highlander's recent work, promoting Participatory Action-Research, Gaventa has commented, 'In our work at the Highlander Center, we have found that this process of people gaining control over knowledge and skills, normally considered to be the monopoly of experts, is an empowering one that produces much more than just the information in question' (Gaventa, 1991: 124). Through Participatory Action Research (PAR) people continue to question and to pursue contradictions, leading to further action (as in the case which he quoted, when miners in West Virginia discovered that their breathing problems really did come from the mines, as they had suspected, and not from inherent asthma, as had been claimed by the employers, anxious to disclaim responsibilities which might involve changing production methods and/or compensation claims). Gaventa related this approach of PAR to the ideas of Gramsci, and in particular to the notion that every person has the capacity 'to be an intellectual, and to develop a popular, organic knowledge that converts spontaneous common sense into "good sense" ' (Gaventa, 1991: 127).

As has already been suggested, the point is not to replicate Highlander elsewhere, or at least not necessarily. But the Highlander experiences, along with the other examples which have been summarised, do illustrate some of the ways in which adult education has been and can still be a force for transformation, even on the basis of often very limited resources. These examples do also provide some illustrations of the ways in which projects and programmes have learned from each other, and been inspired by each other, taking ideas and practices and applying relevant aspects, in different ways, in a range of contexts, both in the North and in the South.

References

Alfred, D. (1987) 'Albert Mansbridge', in P. Jarvis (ed.) *Twentieth Century Thinkers in Adult Education*, Croom Helm, pp. 17–37.

Brookfield, S. (1993) *Adult Learners, Adult Education and Community*, Open University Press.

Brookfield, S. (1987) 'Eduard Lindeman', in P. Jarvis (ed.) *Twentieth Century Thinkers in Adult Education*, Croom Helm, pp. 119–43.

Campbell, O. (1928) *The Danish Folk High School*, Macmillan, New York

Cohen, M. (1992) 'Revolutionary education revived: the Communist challenge to the Labour Colleges, 1925–1944', in B. Simon (ed.) *The Search for Enlightenment*, NIACE, Leicester, pp. 137–52.

Corfield, A. (1969) *Epoch in Workers' Education: A History of the Workers' Educational Trade Union Committee*, The Workers' Educational Association.

Craik W. (1964) *The Central Labour College*, Lawrence and Wishart.

Crane, J. (1987) 'Moses Coady and Antigonish', in P. Jarvis (ed.) *Twentieth Century Thinkers in Adult Education*, Croom Helm, pp. 217–42.

Cross-Durrant A. (1987) 'John Dewey and lifelong education', in P. Jarvis (ed.) *Twentieth Century Thinkers in Adult Education*, Croom Helm, pp. 79–97.

Denny, B. (1994) 'Present and Correct: Radicalism in the Armed Forces in World War Two', unpublished dissertation, Ruskin College Library, Oxford.

Elsey, B. (1987) 'R. H. Tawney: patron saint of adult education', in P. Jarvis (ed.) *Twentieth Century Thinkers in Adult Education*, Croom Helm, pp. 62–76.

Fryer, B. (1992) 'The challenge to working-class education', in B. Simon (ed.) *The Search for Enlightenment*, NIACE, Leicester, pp. 276–319.

Gaventa, J. (1991) 'Towards a knowledge democracy: viewpoints on participatory research in North America', in O. Fals-Borda and M. Rahman (eds) (1991) *Action and Knowledge*, Intermediate Technology Publications.

Hobsbawm, E. (1994) *Age of Extremes*, Michael Joseph.

Jackson, J. (1978) 'What sort of experience: what kind of activism?', in B. Houlton (ed.) *Residential Adult Education*, Society of Industrial Tutors, pp. 49–58.

Jacobsen, B. (1992) 'Denmark', in P. Jarvis (ed.) *Perspectives on Adult Education and Training in Europe*, NIACE, pp. 278–86.

Jennings, B. (1973) *Albert Mansbridge*, Leeds University Press.

Johnson, R. (1988) 'Really useful knowledge: 1790–1850', in T. Lovett (ed.) *Radical Approaches to Adult Education*, Routledge.

Kelly, T. (1970) *A History of Adult Education in Great Britain*, 2nd ed, Liverpool University Press.

Lieven, M. (1988) 'Authority in an educational institution', *Studies in the Education of Adults*, 20, 2, pp. 124–34.

Lovett, T. (ed.) (1988) 'Introduction', in *Radical Approaches to Adult Education*, Routledge, pp. xv–xxii.

Marx House Bulletins, Marx Memorial Library, 37a Clerkenwell Green, London.

Mortimer, J. (1995) Personal communication to the author.

Peters, J. and Bell, B. (1987) 'Horton of Highlander', in P. Jarvis (ed.) *Twentieth Century Thinkers in Adult Education*, Croom Helm, pp. 243–64.

Pollins, H. (1984) *The History of Ruskin College*, Ruskin College Library, Oxford.

Rordam, T. (1980) *The Danish Folk High School*, Det Danske Selskab, Copenhagen.

Simon, B. (1992) 'The struggle for hegemony, 1920–1926', in B. Simon (ed.) *The Search for Enlightenment*, NIACE, pp. 15–70.

Steele, T. (1987) 'From class-consciousness to cultural studies: George Thompson and the WEA in Yorkshire', *Studies in the Education of Adults*, 19,2, pp. 109–26.

Wainwright, H. (1994) *Arguments for a New Left*, Blackwell, Oxford.

WEA North Western District (1989) *Ten Years of Community Education in the Inner City*, WEA, Manchester.

Wolfe, M. (1993) *Adult Basic Education in Nineteenth Century Britain* (study unit), YMCA, London.

Chapter Three

Learning from experiences of adult education for transformation in the South

In the increasingly globalised context of the late twentieth century, those concerned with adult education for development have 'much to learn from the insights and experiences of the Third World', Rogers has argued (1992: 3). Similar arguments have been put by others; for example Bown has argued that in recent times, 'our own circumstances are becoming closer to those prevailing in developing countries. We, like them, face the problems of poverty and great unevenness in access to formal education. We still have unemployment levels much lower than theirs, but they are still dislocatory and destructive of human dignity. Thus we too are forced to consider adult education in relation to economic and social development ... Since some of our human and social problems are not dissimilar, there would seem to be real value in the broad vision and innovatory approaches which we can gain from the Third World' (Bown, 1983: 47-8).

This growing focus upon the importance of mutual learning and the cross-fertilisation of ideas and approaches, to and fro between North and South, has already emerged as a theme in the previous chapter. This chapter looks at some examples of adult education in the Third World in the South, and particularly at examples with key relevance for debates about adult education for transformation. But before coming to these examples, in the relatively recent post-war period, the scene needs some setting in terms of alternative perspectives rooted in alternative approaches and competing interests from the past.

To summarise, 'adult education for development' has taken on different meanings in the past: differences which continue in the current context. 'Development' itself has different meanings, depending upon the user's perspective, as Chapter One showed in summary. The definition of development which underpins McGivney and Murray's *Adult Education in Development* comes from the 1990 *UN Human Development Report*. 'Human development is a process of enlarging people's choices. The most critical of these wide-ranging choices are to live a long and healthy life, to be educated and to have access to resources needed for a decent standard of living. Additional choices include political freedom, guaranteed human rights and personal self-respect' (UNDP, 1990, *Human Development Report*, quoted in McGivney and Murray, 1991: 7). This positive definition is consistent with the approach to development in terms of transformation as set out in the previous chapter. This was the approach which was adopted, for example, by the DAWN women's network. But DAWN and others at the 1995 UN World Summit for Social Development in Copenhagen agreed on the importance of challenging predominant approaches to development precisely because they were *not* consistent with this approach. On the contrary, in fact, the critics at Copenhagen emphasised the importance of challenging predominant definitions, because these were so dominated by market-led approaches to economic growth. The critics were concerned that there was so little concern for the social, political and cultural aspects of development.

There are parallels and points of comparison as well as points of contrast between these contemporary differences of approach, and differences of approach towards development, including adult education for development, in the past. Early international debates on adult education were, as Bown has demonstrated, heavily dominated by Europe. Even in the immediate post-war period, Unesco's first international conference on adult education in 1949 was attended by only five Third World delegates, out of a total of some hundred. It was only in the seventies, she has argued, that Unesco conferences began to focus upon adult education in terms of 'social, economic and cultural development, as part of a global scheme for lifelong education and training' (Bown, 1983: 41, referring to the conclusions of the 1976 Unesco General Assembly in Nairobi).

The British, as colonisers, had already worked on their own approaches to adult education for development, linking informal adult education with social and community development. And there were similarities with the approaches which were developed elsewhere in the South, because the British were not the only imperialists to adopt these types of strategies.

During and after the Second World War, the British Colonial Office developed policies for 'Mass Education' (1944) and for 'Social Development in the British Colonial Territories' (1948), as part of strategies to prepare for approaching self-government. Adult education programmes were to promote the development of democratic political institutions, to encourage a smooth transition to independence, without the fear of threatening alternatives (at this time, there were particular fears that Communism would spread, in the newly-independent countries in the Third World in the South, just as there were fears that Communism would spread in post-war Europe). As a colonial administrator commented at the time, there were fears about what would become of the returned soldier (which links back to some of the points which were made in the previous chapter about the politicisation which had been linked to army education). Would the returned soldier 'explode

and become either a fervent reformer or red-hot enemy of all government or a violent and dangerous criminal?' The answer, according to
this source, lay in a balanced programme to promote reconstruction. 'A
comprehensive programme of economic and social betterment that kept
everyone busy, body and mind, would do more than anything else to
ease the solution of the constitutional problem' (Brayne, 1944, quoted in
Mayo, 1975: 131). Adult education for community development would
be key to this.

And adult education and community development could also
contribute, more directly, to colonial efforts to defeat Communism. In
Malaya, for example, by 1953, there were 450 new community development villages, as a result of the resettlement of half a million people, as
part of military operations against Communist insurgents. There are
some comparisons to be drawn here between British approaches and
United States programmes for informal education and community
development. As Brokensha and Hodge commented, at the end of the
sixties (at the time of the Vietnam War) 'by far the greatest American
expenditures on community development occur in those countries
(Vietnam, Thailand, Laos) considered to be most threatened by communism' (quoted in Mayo, 1975: 132).

In addition to these political objectives, adult education and community development programmes had economic objectives. During and
after the Second World War, Britain arranged with the United States to
make repayments on war loans in the form of raw materials from the
colonies; the key materials here were rubber from Malaya and cocoa
from West Africa. Altogether, in this and other ways, the colonies made
a significant economic contribution to the war effort and its aftermath.
So British colonial policy was geared towards facilitating the growth
and export of these raw materials. Adult education, especially informal
education and community development, played a role here, with education for literacy and informal education through agricultural extension,
to improve cocoa farming in what is now Ghana, for example (du Sautoy,
1958).

The British Colonial Office, and its US equivalents, promoted adult
education for development/community development, then, in ways
which accorded with their *own* economic and political objectives. Similar
points have been made about workers' education, and particularly about
trade union education, geared towards technical training and social
integration, rather than towards wider processes of questioning and the
analysis of underlying conflicts of interest in Third World countries.
This relates back to the NCLC view of such forms of 'education' for
domestication more generally – approaches to the economy and trade
union issues which have been described as 'filleted economics', being
'without bones of contention' (Hopkins, 1985).

This is not to suggest, of course, that the programmes which resulted
contained no local benefits. On the contrary, as has already been argued
in Chapter One, education in general, and adult informal education and

community development programmes more specifically, have been more complex. Literacy, for example, may indeed be promoted as a tool for 'domestication' in Freire's terminology; but literacy can also be a powerful weapon for change and transformation, as the British found when their efforts reinforced the mobilisation of independence movements which then went on to develop their own agendas.

And there were of course examples in practice which were actually based upon very different approaches. There are cross-references here with some of the alternative approaches which had been developed in Britain, for example, in the pre-war period and during the Second World War itself. These included the direct links which were developed through the army education programmes, which continued in the immediate post-war period. For instance, Denny quotes from a personal interview with Bert Ramelson, a Communist who was actively involved in education work. In October 1945, Ramelson was in India, where British troops were still stationed, engaging in political debates – 'parliaments'. To illustrate these influences, Ramelson described how, in one such debate, he had put forward a motion calling for Indian independence, which was overwhelmingly passed. As Ramelson wryly commented on this evidence of international solidarity, 'of course the lads supported it, they thought the sooner the British left India the sooner they could go home' (Denny, 1994). But Ramelson was also in close contact with the Indian progressive movement, exchanging ideas.

As the Cold War developed in the post-war period, there were increasing efforts to re-establish control, both within the army and within adult education more generally. This was the period when notable progressives, Communists and 'fellow-traveller' sympathisers, with background experience in the WEA, university extension departments and elsewhere, were subjected to attempts to control their influence (both in Britain and in the colonies). As Fieldhouse has commented, 'Towards the end of 1949, the government (in the form of the Colonial Office) took direct action to break the "Oxford monopoly" in extramural work in Africa because of the anti-colonial and left-wing tendencies of some of its expatriate tutors and TL Hodgkin, the Secretary of the Extramural Delegacy ... Over the next few years the Colonial Office also took steps to prevent other communist or anti-colonialist lecturers, including D Wiseman, J Rex and M Barratt-Brown, from taking up extramural posts in Africa' (Fieldhouse, 1991: 144). Meanwhile, despite these official efforts, many independence and progressive movement leaders were actually developing their political education, through their contacts and experiences in the metropolis, during and just after the war.

In summary, then, although adult education for development gained prominence as an issue within international debates from the sixties and seventies, as Bown has demonstrated, there were previous histories, too, dating from the colonial era. And these histories included a range of views and experiences from different perspectives and approaches to development.

So far, these differences in perspective have been summarised in terms of two ends of a spectrum. At one end, there were colonial approaches, based on a view of development which started from the economic and political agendas of the metropolis. There are some parallels here with the market-led approaches of more recent times. (There are differences too, however; and current approaches cannot simply be reapplied to past debates, in periods when the imperatives of the market were typically presented in more tempered fashions, albeit within the framework of Cold War debates.) And conversely, at the other end of the spectrum, there were alternative approaches, for national liberation and social change. (Once again, however, these alternative approaches cannot simply be equated with contemporary debates, although there are parallels as well as differences.)

But another dimension to these differences of approach is also relevant, and especially so when attempting to make comparisons and contrasts between approaches in the First and Third Worlds, in the North and in the South. Both Bown and Rogers, for example, have characterised these differences in terms of the emphasis on adult education for individual development and self-fulfilment in the North, in contrast with the more collective development focus which became more characteristic in the South. Bown, for instance, has pointed to the importance of Third World approaches which link adult lifelong education with development policies more generally, and with policies to promote positive action for the disadvantaged. These are aspects which she has identified as being increasingly relevant in the First World, in the North.

Rogers has similarly contrasted the individualism of so many First World approaches with the more collective approaches to mass education for change and development in the South. These more collective approaches were becoming, he has also argued, increasingly relevant in the First World in the North. (He clearly identified that there had been exceptions to the individualised approaches and 'free-market' choices which had predominated in the North, however: exceptions which had included the NCLC, for instance, some of the work of the WEA, and recent approaches to adult education and community action, as analysed, for example, by Jackson and Lovett; see Rogers, 1992.)

At this point it might be useful to suggest expanding the previous model, which was summarised in Chapter One, and to identify four different tendencies, rather than simply two tendencies. This 'four tendency' model draws upon the approach which has been developed by Shanahan, in characterising different contemporary approaches to university adult education in various contexts (Shanahan, forthcoming).

Shanahan's four tendencies in university adult education can be summarised as follows:

Tendency 1: 'academic' (in the sense of non-technical/vocational) adult education, for individuals, within the current socio-economic and political context (i.e. this tendency fits into a market-led approach)

Tendency 2: 'training' geared to fitting the individual adult learner into the requirements of the current socio-economic and political context (which also fits into a market-led approach)

Tendency 3: 'professional education/training, to train professionals to act as change agents, acting on other people's environments (i.e. accepting the need for change, but for change as defined by experts, rather than by those directly affected).

Tendency 4: adult education and training for groups and communities, geared towards empowerment and transformation.

Diagrammatically this can be set out in the following way;

	Cut off from life	Integrated with life
Not aimed at changing the socio-cultural and politico-economic environment	**TENDENCY I** 'Academic'	**TENDENCY 2** 'Training'
Aimed at changing the socio-cultural and politico-economic environment	**TENDENCY 3** 'Professional' education	**TENDENCY 4** 'Empowerment'

A modified version of this model would include the following;

Tendency 1: Individualistic, market-led approaches (emphasising individual choices, through market-mechanisms).

Tendency 2: Collective, market-led approaches to training (emphasising the overall importance of market-led approaches to development, and renewal, but recognising the relevance of collective and community-based approaches to reach these ends. This was the case in some of the colonial programmes for adult education to promote market-led development, for example.

Tendency 3: Individualistic approaches to education for transformation. Academic, 'armchair' approaches to political education, and education for transformation, would fit into this category, along with approaches which emphasised the role of the leader, as change agent, to such an extent as to devalue the role of the people directly affected, themselves.

Tendency 4: Collective alternative approaches (emphasising the value of collective, workplace and community-based education for transformation).

Whilst the approaches outlined in the Third Tendency do indeed exist, however, and have exercised powerful influences, historically, the alternative approaches to adult education for transformation, which were summarised in Chapter Two, were not based on such a model. On the contrary, in fact, in their different ways, these alternative approaches emphasised the importance of collective approaches, and of continuing dialogues between action and reflection, theory and practice.

In reality, of course, there have been considerable differences in theoretical orientations within alternative approaches to adult education for transformation, too. As the previous chapter also pointed out, there have been cleavages between approaches and programmes based upon social democratic policies and perspectives, on the one hand, and perspectives based upon more fundamental criticisms of the *status quo*, drawing more explicitly upon Marxist analyses, on the other. These have represented, and continue to represent, significant areas of disagreement. Without minimising the significance of these differences, however, it is also important to recognise that, in the present context at least, both share common ground, in developing alternatives to the market-led approach which is so predominant, on a global scale.

In practice too, as the history of alternative approaches illustrated in the British context, particular programmes and institutions may be less readily classifiable in terms of these differences between social democratic perspectives, on the one hand, and Marxist based perspectives, on the other. This was the case with the WEA, for instance, and the NCLC. Neither of these fitted into their supposed categories as neatly as some of their critics' characterisations of them might have suggested. This issue emerges too, in categorising some of the examples, which follow, based upon experiences in the Third World, in the South.

Examples from India

The first case summarised here is precisely one that combines different elements, within alternative approaches. Indian experiences in the post-war period drew upon approaches which had been developed in the independence struggles in the pre-war period. And within the independence movement there were differing strands, although these were able to work together, creatively.

A key figure, here, was Gandhi, whose criticisms of Western, bookish, colonial education informed alternative attempts to develop forms of education which would relate to all aspects of life. Character building and spirituality were key objectives, to be achieved through an emphasis upon practical skills for development, especially craft skills for rural development. Education of this type should be conducted, he argued, in the mother tongue, in contrast to the more academic education which was provided in English. Gandhi's approach to 'Basic Education' or 'nai telim' has been described in terms of populism; but this was a populism which emphasised non-violent and spiritual values, in the context of the struggle against colonialism. And Gandhi also emphasised what Steele and Taylor have described as the 'fundamentally humanistic bases of adult education's objectives' together with a firm commitment to the inclusion of the poorest and the untouchables (Steele and Taylor, 1995).

Although Gandhi's contribution to the involvement of the masses was vital in the struggle for independence, this was not the only strand. Nehru represented the more secular strand, coming from a Western-educated, elite background although committed to socialism (of a social democratic rather than a Marxist variety). Gandhi's ideas were not so dominant in adult education, it has been suggested, in the immediate post-independence period. From 1947, the new leadership under Nehru was committed to modernisation. 'In Nehru's vision of a secular, social-ist and prosperous India, vocational training, but not education *per se*, had a key role to play' (Steele and Taylor, 1995).

Adult education did have a role to play, here, in the Five Year Plans from 1951 to 1966. But after the First Five Year Plan there was less emphasis upon literacy and more focus upon community development. This fitted into the overall emphasis upon modernisation and develop-ment. How effective these efforts were was less clear. There were real achievements, including achievements in literacy, despite population growth. Overall, however, the plans for community development became bogged down in the bureaucracy which was a legacy of the British Raj. By the Third Plan, Nehru had become somewhat disillusioned with the failure of education to provide instant answers to the problems of modernisation, and increasingly anxious about the rapaciousness of some sections of the business community, and the persistence of communal violence and religious bigotry (problems which had been central concerns in Gandhi's approach).

These early post-war programmes have been criticised, then, for their relatively limited impact. They were not adequately resourced, it has been suggested, or sufficiently forcefully implemented (Handa, 1984). But the picture was not entirely negative and there were examples of areas where programmes were implemented in progressive ways. Kerala and West Bengal, for instance, have been referred to in this context (and Kerala has been quoted as the State with the highest levels of literacy). Similarly, positive experiences in Maharashtra were valued, and built upon, in the next phase of development at national level.

In response to some of the limitations of the earlier programmes, critics, from the sixties and early seventies, began to focus once again upon the contributions of the great names of the past, such as Gandhi. There was increasing interest in non-formal education, with an emphasis upon social rather than personal development, with priority to address-ing the needs of the poor and oppressed, in relation to social justice and access to resources (Steele and Taylor, 1995). Building upon this, the National Adult Education Programme (NAEP) was launched, to come into operation in 1978.

Writing in the early eighties, Bown has drawn attention to the overall ambitiousness of the programme. Indeed, it has been described as one of the most ambitious and revolutionary adult education programmes to be launched (Steele and Taylor, 1995). NAEP was aimed at 100 million people aged between 14 and 35, with 10 per cent of the education budget allocated to adult education. As Bown pointed out, 'this may seem small, but it is a larger allocation than is made by any other country outside Scandinavia (Bown, 1983: 42).

The programme was based upon three conceptual elements, 'awareness', 'literacy' and 'functionality'. Literacy was to be combined, here, with 'functionality', which included skills to improve economic conditions, health care and family and community welfare and citizenship. And 'awareness' would include awareness of economic, social and political conditions, as the prerequisite for empowerment. In this sense, the development of 'awareness' resembles Freire's concept of conscientisation. The NAEP's objectives, then, combined elements of the traditions of both Gandhi and Nehru, together with some influences from Freire's thinking.

In the event, the Indian NAEP has been subject to a number of criticisms, however, despite its scale and despite the government's overall statements of commitment to mobilisation to tackle poverty and inequality. Commenting upon an evaluation of the programme, as implemented in Tamil Nadu, Duke referred to this as a 'somewhat depressing study' which 'typifies India's scholarship and its community of adult educators: highly professional, deeply committed, often self-critical and critical of failures and disappointments. Given the national and local political and socio-cultural realities of India one cannot but agree with the judgement that the NAEP was naively over-optimistic.'

This was a somewhat depressing conclusion, overall, especially in view of the keen interest in the Indian experience in the non-socialist world: 'The picture which emerges from Tamil Nadu is of failure of nerve: mobilisation of the poor seemed too dangerous; easier, purely literacy objectives were adopted instead'. And 'even in terms of pure literacy success was low', it was argued, in such a top-down programme, which was so inadequately related to local conditions and needs, and inadequately resourced (Duke, 1985: 69–70). Ramakrishnan's analysis provided the evidence for these conclusions; and he also quoted from a nationwide assessment: 'Most of the studies found the achievement of learners in literacy to be very modest; in some projects the achievements appeared extremely low ... The situation with regard to achievements in 'functionality' and 'awareness' by and large appeared still more unsatisfactory' (Ramakrishnan, 1985: 74).

More generally, some of the Left critics, including Marxist critics, doubted whether the powerful in India would permit the effective transfer of power and resources to the oppressed through such a programme. The dominant classes and the state would outweigh the interests of the poor (Shukla, quoted in Steele and Taylor, 1995). Others, whilst recognising these constraints, were also interested in exploring ways of maximising any possible benefits which could be obtained for the poor from such programmes. Although the NAEP was criticised from both the right and from the left, then, it did open up some space for a radical agenda, it has been argued, with priority for the poor and for women within a more participatory framework.

Since then, in 1985 there was a new Indian government focus upon combining literacy and practical vocational training for development with wider awareness and consciousness-raising (in Freire's sense of conscientisation). The India Ministry of Education set out these purposes, to integrate literacy (combined with health education and environmental awareness) with skills training (including agricultural skills, and the skills to develop village industries) with awareness. This latter objective was aimed at 'making learners capable to shape their own future through the inter-linking of learning, reflection and concrete action' (Ministry of Education, India, 1985). Drawing on reflections upon the Cuba experiences of literacy and adult education for transformation, this programme also involved students and other young people. And there was a particular focus upon targeting women and girls and Scheduled Castes and Scheduled Tribes, who had suffered from a legacy of educational as well as other forms of disadvantage.

The voluntary sector was to be more involved too. This had been a feature of the NAEP, and the voluntary/NGO sector had its own histories of developing adult education for transformation, in any case. Srinivasan, for example, has provided an account of such approaches, related to strategies for People Centred Development, drawing upon the approaches developed by Freire and others (Srinivasan, 1992).

The role of popular participation, and people's movements more generally, has also been seen as key to the success of official programmes. Writing of Kerala in this context, Sen has argued that the particular success of the 'Kerala model' in terms of education and health can be explained as follows; 'Kerala's success, therefore, was the outcome of protracted historical processes in which large sections of its population came to participate both in the definition of social needs, and in assuming accountability for meeting those needs' (Sen, 1992: 276). This was due to a combination of responsive state, public awareness and social reform movements (including militant peasant and worker organisations, linked to a strong Communist party). 'Pressures on the state made governments willing to commit themselves to spend money on education and health; public awareness and participation made them effective ... The unusually strong position of women in society ensured that when health and education expenditures were made, they did not exclude women either as workers or as recipients' (Sen, 1992: 277).

Steele and Taylor's critical history of Indian adult education provides case studies of the radicalism of some of these voluntary sector/NGO initiatives in practice, especially from the late seventies and eighties and beyond. For example the Mobile Orientation and Training Team (MOTT) set out to travel round villages training voluntary instructors in political education for peoples power. MOTT's approach was based upon Freire's approach to conscientisation, together with Nyerere's ideas on education for self-reliance and nation-building. Whilst MOTT was committed to participatory methods, this aspect was developed further, in more dialogic and experientially-based approaches to learning in some of the projects which derived from the women's movement. Steele and Taylor refer to a range of projects which developed this type of approach, moving beyond literacy to empower women to tackle the root causes of their oppression.

Within the vast and varied experiences in India, then, there have been a series of government and state initiatives, covering the range of approaches within the 'alternative' spectrum. There have been attempts to link literacy work with programmes to encourage somewhat limited projects to increase participation; but without alarming the powerful, or disturbing the interests of the status quo. And there have been varieties of initiatives, in the voluntary/NGO sector, as well as the state sector, including approaches which have been clearly rooted in strategies to promote conscientisation, to empower the disadvantaged to challenge the power structures which exploit and oppress them.

Whilst there have been a range of examples of approaches which could be described in terms of different positions on the 'alternative' spectrum of approaches in India, however, there have also been powerful pressures from the opposite direction. Rogers, for instance, has pointed to the powerful pressures which have been exerted by aid donors, when Third World countries in the South have been considered to be challenging the interests of the powerful, and the predominantly market-led approach which they have tended to support. For example, to illustrate such pressures, which he characterised as neo-colonialist, Rogers pointed out that 'US Congress cut aid to India for voting against it at the United Nations and for its trade ties with Nicaragua' (Rogers, 1992: 112). The case of Nicaragua, and its approach to adult education for transformation, is considered later in this chapter.

The case of Tanzania

Meanwhile, Tanzania provides another well-known and often-quoted example of alternative approaches to adult education for transformation. Although Tanzania's programmes were also broadly within a social democratic, rather than a Marxist perspective, the state was clearly committed to relatively thorough-going versions of transformation, in the post-independence period at least.

Adult education in newly-independent Tanzania, from the sixties, was increasingly geared towards the promotion of both economic and social development. This was to be based upon active people's participation in the workplace and in the community. At the time of independence, Tanzania was an extremely poor country, with an economy which was based upon agricultural cash crops for export. Explicitly, the programmes were developed as alternatives to colonial approaches in the past, and to neo-colonial pressures, after independence. In contrast, these were to be programmes to contribute not just to development, but to building a democratic socialist form of development.

In 1967, in the Arusha Declaration, President Nyerere set out the goals for this path for democratic socialist development, based on self-reliance and co-operation. Adult education was to be key to these objectives. There was a national literacy campaign. 1970 was the Year of Adult Education, with the focus upon education for development based upon participation. This was to be in contrast with previous approaches which were described as having been essentially more paternalistic; adult education 'to show people the "right" way to live', in the colonial tradition (Hall, 1975: 118). The emphasis, it was argued, had been upon educating people to produce cash crops (such as coffee) more effectively (which was, of course, in the colonisers' interests as well as the interests of local producers), together with a more general emphasis upon self-help. In newly-independent socialist Tanzania, people were to participate, actively, in building socialist development.

Nyerere's own definition of adult education was that this comprised 'learning about anything at all which can help us to understand the environment in which we live and the manner in which we change and use the environment to improve ourselves' (quoted in Hall, 1975: 61). The purpose of education was 'the liberation of Man from the restraints and limitations of ignorance and dependency ... Nothing else can properly be called education. Teaching which induces a slave mentality is not education at all – it is an attack on the minds of men' (Nyerere, quoted in Bown, 1983: 42-3). The goal was to mobilise the people for participation for social and political as well as economic objectives.

Adult education was certainly intended to promote economic development. There was no time to lose, it was argued; the nation could not afford to wait for the effects of improved schooling to percolate through, in terms of a more productive next generation. Adult education was to provide useful knowledge, for example, about crop improvements. Rural Training Centres were a key ingredient here, along with education for co-operative development. Literacy was a vital prerequisite for subsequent education. And residential colleges were set up in 1975 as 'Folk Development Colleges' to provide further education for those who had graduated from the literacy scheme. These colleges drew upon the model of the Swedish Folk High Schools (Bwatra *et al*, 1989). Meanwhile, there were also programmes for workers' education, to increase productivity. And adult education was to provide useful knowledge for social development; for example health education, working with the Union of Women of Tanzania.

Most importantly, adult education was to contribute to combatting passivity and the 'colonial mind' (which relates, of course, to some of the key concerns which Freire addressed, in his work on the development of critical consciousness). In the workplace, adult education included political education, and education for participation (Workers' Councils were to be developed). People were to be made aware of national goals and encouraged to participate in building socialism in Tanzania.

The Institute of Adult Education became more focused upon supporting mass campaigns. Back-up publications were produced and the use of radio was developed. There were close links with the political party which had worked for independence (TANU) and there was a national centre for political education, Kivokoni College. Kivokoni, which was established in 1961, had drawn on the model of Ruskin College, Oxford, as a basis for adult education, with both long-term courses and short courses in the social sciences. These courses had been attended by a range of political (TANU) and trade union leaders. In 1973, Kivokoni was taken over directly by the Central Committee of TANU and expanded. Writing in 1975, Hall reflected that 'nearly every leader in Tanzania has taken part in courses at Kivokoni College' (Hall, 1975: 82). Programmes included party history and socialism, and self-reliance in the context of African development. Whilst providing official support and legitimacy, however, these close ties with TANU meant close links, too, with the limitations of that political party, a point which links to some of the criticisms of the Tanzanian experience.

Reflecting upon the achievements in the mid-seventies, Hall drew parallels with other examples of adult education to promote development and social change, and adult education for transformation, including the Cuban experiences. 'Tanzania has embarked on a unique social experiment . . . At the root of this faith (in adult education for transformation) is a trust in the wisdom and judgment of the people themselves (Hall, 1974: 137).

But although the achievements of the Tanzanian experience had been valued so highly, there were also key problems and limitations. Criticism of the Tanzanian experience has come from the Left, as well as from the Right. Lovett, for example, has argued that the whole strategy of promoting market-socialism through self-help and co-operative development, which Nyerere and TANU pursued, was inherently flawed, and failed to take adequate account of external structural factors (Lovett, 1983). Adult education had come into the centre of the political stage, but the production, itself, was in increasing difficulties, for a number of reasons. From the mid-seventies, and into the eighties and beyond, these difficulties became more and more acute. Wider structural pressures were, in any case, making it increasingly problematic for the very poorest countries in the South, like Tanzania, to pursue independent strategies for transformation, even if they were to retain the political impulse and the ability to keep on trying to do so.

The case of Cuba

Similar points could also be made about the next example, both in terms of the goals, for transformation, and in terms of the increasing pressures and structural constraints on achieving them. Cuba, however, despite increasing pressures from the US blockade, and despite structural changes resulting from the loss of major trading partners in the former socialist countries, has continued to prioritise education, along with other social commitments, especially health.

The Cuban literacy campaign which Fidel Castro announced in 1960 has been described as 'one of the truly great achievements of mankind ... it was a remarkable achievement for many reasons, but principally because it worked' (MacDonald, 1985: 54). At that time, some 25 per cent of Cubans were illiterate; by the end of 1961, after the Year of Education, which involved nearly a million Cubans out of a total population of some ten millions, illiteracy was down to under 5 per cent (compared with a figure of some 12 per cent in the US). Some 100,000 students and some 170,000 adult volunteers took part in teaching literacy to their fellow Cubans.

When Castro announced the literacy campaign at the UN in 1960, the Cuban revolution had not yet defined itself, in terms of Marxist objectives. The goal was less clearly defined – broadly in terms of national liberation and development. At the time, Cuba was still looking to maintain relations with the US and with international companies. Indeed, Coca Cola, for example, even contributed to advertising for the campaign. (A Coca Cola billboard showed the white hand of the lady of a household, with a bottle of coke beside her, guiding the dark and roughened hand of a domestic servant over a line of print. Underneath was written 'Use the Pause that Refreshes while Teaching Someone how to Read'; Fagen, 1969: 51.)

All this was to change, over the period in question, which covered the Bay of Pigs Invasion, in 1961, and the successful Cuban repulse of the US invaders. By 1962, Cuba was clearly and explicitly building socialism, drawing upon Marxist analyses. Literacy, and education more generally, had particular political significance in this context, linked to the development of political consciousness. Castro had earlier commented that 'the most important education is the political education of the people' and that 'revolution and education are the same thing' (quoted in Fagen, 1969: 15).

And conversely, those who opposed the revolution, including the CIA-supported gunmen who murdered some young teachers, demonstrated the fear which the literacy campaign generated. It was argued that the enemy must feel threatened indeed, by the prospect of a literate and better-educated Cuba, if they were prepared to go to the lengths of murdering volunteers and intimidating the illiterates, to prevent them from participating in the campaign. Freedom from illiteracy was seen as linked with freedom from imperialist oppression.

Significantly, the badge which was issued to the volunteers (along with their teaching manuals, boots, clothes, hammocks and lanterns) commemorated an 18-year-old, Conrado Benitez, who had been captured and tortured, before being murdered by a CIA-supported counterrevolutionary band in a remote area, in a pilot project. This badge became the symbol of resistance and determination (MacDonald, 1985).

Literacy was seen as key to economic development, improving the knowledge and skills of the workforce. But literacy was also seen as contributing to political and social goals, part of the Revolution. 'In philosophy, spirit, and organisation it was an integral part of wider change', as Seers expressed it (1964: 199). The illiterate were to gain not only literacy skills, but also the wider self-confidence, and sense of dignity which were key to political participation, becoming agents of transformation.

As one of Cuba's senior educators commented, 'the goal of the campaign was always greater than to teach poor people how to read. The dream was to enable those two portions of the population that had been most instrumental in the process of the revolution from the first, to find a common bond, a common spirit, and a common goal. The peasants discovered the word. The students discovered the poor. Together, they all discovered their own patria' (quoted in MacDonald, 1985: 68–9). As a former brigadista was quoted as saying, 16 years after the event, 'I could never have known that people lived in such conditions. I was the child of an educated, comfortable family . . . It was, for me, the dying of an old life and the start of something absolutely new . . . I did not need to read of this in Marx, in Lenin, in Marti. I did not need to read of what I saw before my eyes, I wrote my mother and father. I was only twelve years old' (quoted in MacDonald, 1985: 69).

Some 70,000 'Conrado Benitez' brigadistas were under 20 years old. These were schoolchildren and students, who went off with their hammocks and lanterns to teach in the rural areas, after only brief training. (The hammocks were needed because they were staying with people who would have no spare beds; indeed the brigadista might be staying in the same room or small hut with the peasant, his family and his fowls; and the lanterns were required, because, in remote rural areas, there was no electricity.) In addition, there were adult volunteers, 'Alfabetizadores Populares' (Popular Alfabetisers) who taught in their spare time (mainly in the towns and cities). Urban workers also went to rural areas, with the 'Patria o Muerte' (Fatherland or Death) brigades, whilst their fellow workers, back in the factories, filled in for them, to keep production going. And there were schoolteacher brigadistas, 'Maestros y Profesores Brigadistas', who mostly provided more technical back up.

Initially, it has been suggested, Castro saw the question of literacy teaching as a straightforward matter of transferring skills. He was, apparently, quickly disabused of the view that it would be this simple, by the experts. But the experts were too pessimistic when they predicted that only qualified teachers would be successful in teaching illiterates. Building relationships with the illiterates, at a personal level, proved to be central to the campaign's success, along with enthusiasm and commitment.

It was impressed on the volunteers that they must not separate themselves from the learners, dispense orders, or set up hierarchical relationships. The volunteer 'was instructed to do everything possible to reflect that they were both learning – from the words and from each other' (MacDonald, 1985: 67). They would start with pictures of particular aspects of daily life in Cuba, and written material relating to these. The learner would be asked what the pictures meant to him or her, and this would then be the basis for working on the core of 'active words' identified as being words which the learner needed to know. Although the brigadista could read the words in question, the learner had a far deeper idea of what the concepts were; which was the basis for each learning from the other. There are, of course, parallels with Freire's approach to literacy teaching for conscientisation.

The literacy campaign illustrated the commitment, determination and enthusiasm of so many Cubans, both as volunteers and as learners. The youngest volunteer was an eight-year-old girl, apparently, and the oldest learner was a black woman 106 years old, who had been a slave. And the campaign also illustrated the importance of the contribution of workplace- and community-based organisations.

Workplace-based organisations organised production, to release urban workers to participate. The Cuban Federation of Women and the Committees for the Defence of the Revolution mobilised volunteers, through their local branches, and encouraged illiterate people to come forward to participate. The Federation of Cuban Women organised literacy committees within neighbourhoods, with volunteers teaching their neighbours to read.

The literacy campaign was followed up in a number of ways. There were technical programmes for workers, and there were continuation classes for the newly literate. There were 'family circles' for those who felt more comfortable in smaller groups, in people's houses. And there were political education programmes. The literacy campaign threw up some very practical needs, too, including the need for spectacles for some 177,000 people, who were provided with these by the government. In pre-revolutionary Cuba, opticians had worked in the private sector only, mainly in the cities, which effectively precluded most poor rural people from eye-care.

Since then, as a result of the impact of the US blockade, compounded by the loss of Cuban trading arrangements with the former socialist countries, the Cuban economy has experienced serious difficulties. Although Cuba has retained a strong commitment to education, along with its commitment to health and welfare more generally, programmes have been affected, and priorities have had to be adjusted to take account of changing pressures and needs. For example, the Cuban Federation of

Women runs classes in cooking and healthy eating, assisting people in learning to use ingredients which may be unfamiliar, and to cope with shortages of familiar ingredients; very practical classes to meet immediate needs, as well as classes providing broader education.

The case of Nicaragua

Nicaragua, in the period of the Sandinista government, has also provided an example of adult education for transformation, including a major five-month mass literacy crusade in 1980, drawing upon the ideas of Freire and the Cuban experiences of developing mass literacy. And like Tanzania, too, Nicaragua suffered from external pressures and constraints, in this case the very particular pressures which resulted from the US trade embargo. Nicaragua also suffered from internal conflicts, in the shape of the war with the Contras, who were supported by the US, as part of US strategies to contain alternative approaches to market-led development in its own 'back-yard' of Latin America. Whilst the Sandinista government was defeated in the elections of 1990 and a war-weary population opted for an end to these internal conflicts, this did not necessarily imply a total rejection of all these experiences. This summary of the Nicaraguan experiences will conclude with the view that, despite the overall reverses, there were some continuing effects from these programmes of adult education for transformation and community development (Plunkett, 1995).

When the Sandinistas defeated the Somoza dictatorship in 1979, they set out to build alternative approaches to development, in contrast with the market-led approaches which had predominated. Adult education and community participation were seen as key elements in strategies for transformation. Commenting on this focus on adult education for transformation, Payne has quoted from a report by a delegate to the conference of the International League for Social Commitment in Adult Education, held in Nicaragua in 1989.

'In this context (ie, of strategies for transformation) education is seen as a part of a comprehensive programme to empower the majority of the population so that they may participate in organisations that represent their interests, and through them, in the equitable development of society . . . In order to participate fully, people must be able to read, to make calculations, to analyse, to criticise, to evaluate and reflect. The creative forces of education are also needed to enable people to survive during the reconstruction of their society – to raise standards of health and nutrition, rates of production, levels of self-sufficiency, and the efficient use and conservation of resources' (Harvey, 1990). This was why education, including popular education, was given such priority (Payne, forthcoming).

In the words of Father Cardenal, the charismatic director of the National Co-ordinating Office, 'the Revolution and Literacy Crusade are one in purpose and mission . . . to transform the nation' (Miller, 1985:

112). 'We believe that in order to create a new nation we have to begin with an education that liberates people. Only through knowing their past and present, only through understanding and analysing their reality, can people choose their future. Only in that process can people fulfil their human destiny as makers of history and commit themselves to transforming that reality' (quoted in Miller, 1985: 114).

Similar points have been made by other commentators. Popular education in Nicaragua, as in India, Tanzania and Cuba, was geared to promote development, in the fullest sense. In Nicaragua, at the outset, this included goals of both improved production and improved well-being. This was to be achieved through health education, for example, and through practical forms of community development, to construct latrines, and improve water supplies, as well as to vaccinate children. Plunkett, for instance, has argued that these achievements were to be based upon popular participation, to give people confidence 'to reflect and act according to their needs. (Plunkett, 1995). But she has also pointed to increasing problems, as the Sandinista government became more and more beleaguered by external pressures, and internal conflicts (with the anti-government Contra fighters being supported by the US). In these circumstances, community participation became squeezed as a priority.

In parallel with the experiences in Kerala, which were considered by Sen, however, the Community Movement in Nicaragua was not totally reliant upon the state (even, in this case, a state which had been committed to popular participation, at least initially). The National Literacy Commission included delegates from workers' associations and citizens' groups. Parallel commissions were formed at local level, and local workers and community-based organisations played key roles; for example, they organised accommodation for the volunteer literacy teachers. (There are parallels, here, too, with the active involvement of workplace and community-based organisations in Cuba.)

Plunkett argues that the Community Movement also had a life of its own, a factor which was key to its determination to survive, and to continue to mobilise against market-led approaches, in the neo-liberal, free-market-dominated policy framework of the government which took over from the Sandinistas in 1990 (policies which were reinforced through the IMF-imposed Structural Adjustment Programme in 1991).

But to go back to the early days of the Sandinista government, there was a strong emphasis upon participation which was built into the programmes, from the start. Drawing upon the Cuban model, the Nicaraguan Literacy Campaign involved some 60,000 high school and university students, over a five-month period. Adults with family responsibilities gave classes in their own areas, whilst young single people went to remoter areas. Illiteracy was reduced from 50 per cent to 12 per cent, over the five months of this campaign. And in addition to developing literacy skills, the campaign also aimed to build solidarity and to give the young a chance to contribute.

The advantages of such an approach were two-fold. Those who gained literacy were empowered. But those who went out to teach also gained in the process. 'Specific goals', as Miller explained, included the goal 'to encourage an integration and understanding between Nicaraguans of different classes and backgrounds' (Miller, 1985: 115). The following comment, made by a farm worker, to the mother of his literacy teacher, illustrates this point. 'Do you know', he said, 'I'm not ignorant anymore? I know how to read now. Not perfectly, you understand, but I know how. And do you know, your son isn't ignorant anymore either. Now he knows how we live, what we eat, how we work. And he knows the life of the mountains. Your son, ma'am, has learned to read from our book' (Hirshon and Butler, 1983: 161). Again, there are parallels with the Cuban experiences.

The methodologies which were developed in the Nicaraguan Literacy Campaign drew upon the work of Freire and experiences of applying his work elsewhere, as well as in Nicaragua itself, in clandestine literacy groups which had been organised by the Sandinistas, when they were operating as a guerrilla movement, before the Somoza dictatorship was overthrown. 'Learning had been based on a process of action and reflection. Lessons had direct, urgent and immediate application to reality' (Miller, 1985: 117). These experiences were applied, in the National Literacy Campaign.

There was an emphasis upon experiential learning, dialogue, group discussion and problem-solving. There was, in addition, emphasis upon drawing, murals, poetry and songs, recovering Nicaraguan folk culture. At the end of workshops, Miller pointed out, 'the walls were covered by summaries of group discussions and popular poetry', cultural action for transformation and growth (Miller, 1985: 119).

Plunkett has described the ways in which the work of the literacy campaign was built upon, particularly in terms of health education and health promotion. The Division of Education and Popular Communication in the Ministry of Health developed materials for use in literacy teaching. Following close consultation with the local organisations (the Sandinista Defence Committees) manuals of health lessons for literacy workers were devised to introduce themes such as inadequate sanitation, lack of clean water and poor nutrition. These were used to stimulate critical discussion and follow-up action. Volunteer health workers were also trained (some 30,000 of them in the first year of the new government). Plunkett considered, however, that the Ministry then came to see these volunteers, increasingly, as their staff, rather than as people's community representatives; there was, she argued a decreasing focus upon community participation, overall. Subsequently, as the Contra war became more serious, it became more and more difficult to sustain and resource these community initiatives, in any case.

Despite all the difficulties of the situation, after the defeat of the Sandinistas in 1990 and the pressures from market-led World Bank and IMF economic policies, there have been attempts to maintain some of the earlier initiatives. Cardenal, the former director of the 1980 National Literacy Crusade, together with others, set up the National Institute for Popular Education and Research, as an independent organisation, to maintain educational work with popular movements and peasant co-operatives. The long-term goal was to work towards sustainable and integrated development. In the short term, realistically, Cardenal pointed out 'our aim is survival' (Cardenal, 1992: 148).

Similarly, Plunkett has argued that the Community Movement refused to lie down and die. Nicaragua is the poorest country in Latin America, with the largest *per capita* debt. Malnutrition is widespread, and access to education and health services has been severely constrained by dramatic spending cuts. Seventy per cent of the population are estimated to live in poverty. But despite all these objective difficulties, she has argued, the Community Movement continued to organise, both to tackle immediate issues, in the community, and to mobilise opposition to the predominant, market-led approach of the UNO government, and its international supporters. She concludes, 'The Community Movement recognises that practical action has come a long way towards developing popular participation in the process of empowerment. Through the experience of working together, people have developed the confidence to protest and demand improvements' (Plunkett, 1995). This is in no way to minimise, of course, the seriousness of the problems, and the significance of the losses which have been experienced in recent years in Nicaragua.

This brings the discussion back to some of the questions which were raised in Chapter One; questions about the connections between ideas and consciousness on the one hand, and structural factors and material constraints, on the other. How far could changes in people's ideas and consciousness strengthen their contributions to processes of transformation? And conversely, to what extent would people's consciousness be constrained by their material circumstances, and by the power structures which were working to reproduce and reinforce their perceptions of these realities – as 'natural', inevitable, or at least as unchangeable? Clearly, each of the examples which has been summarised in this chapter illustrates the key importance of wider structural constraints and the scale of the inherent difficulties when it comes to challenging powerful vested interests. Programmes for social transformation and the adult education and training programmes which were to promote these, whether based upon social democratic or Marxist models, ran into these wider constraints, in terms of global market forces and in terms of pressures from international agencies (such as the World Bank and the IMF) as well as from the US.

But each of these programmes for transformation placed considerable value on adult education and training; as an essential component of transformation; a necessary, if not a sufficient, condition of change. Plunkett, for example, has also suggested that the strength of popular participation, which had been so strongly linked to adult education for transformation in Nicaragua, was key to continuing mobilisation in resistance to the prevailing market-led policies of the new government, after 1990. And in Cuba, popular consciousness has also been key to the continuing resistance to the US blockade, and to Cuban determination not to abandon commitments to social development (including commitments to education and health) or to embrace market-led approaches unreservedly. None of which, of course, is to deny the significance of the changes which have been necessitated, in the current context.

Finally, these experiences, from the South, also relate back to questions which have already been posed in Chapter One, questions about the two-way relationships between theory and practice, reflection and action. How could adult education and training programmes relate to the development of popular participation in strategies for transformation, in practice? This was a vital objective, in each of the examples which was summarised. These questions about the connections between theory and practice, reflection and action emerge as a key theme in subsequent chapters.

One particular aspect of these connections, with relevance for subsequent chapters too, has been set out in terms of 'Participatory Action Research' (PAR). PAR starts from questioning the basis of knowledge; how is knowledge produced, by whom and for whose interests? How does access to and control of existing knowledge relate to the structures of power, in society? And how can the exploited and excluded participate in developing their own knowledge and understanding, collectively, in order to challenge these power structures, and in order to promote alternative approaches to development, for transformation? The roots of PAR have been linked to Marxist analyses, as well as to the specific work of Freire on breaking down traditional distinctions between the subjects and the objects of knowledge. As people participate in gaining and creating knowledge in their own interests, their consciousness can develop, in Freire's view, along with mobilisation for action (Shenahan, forthcoming). PAR also has other roots too, however (including the influence of the Spanish philosopher Ortega y Gasset), and has been the subject of considerable debate (Fals-Borda and Rahman, 1991). PAR has been developed in the South, but it has also been taken up in Northern contexts. For example, Gaventa, of the Highlander Research and Education Centre, Tennessee (discussed in the previous chapter) has written about the experiences of participatory research in the US. PAR has been used in workers' and community-based environmental campaigns against pollution and toxic waste (Gaventa, 1991). PAR, then, provides another illustration of the point which was made at the outset of this chapter, about the growing recognition of the potential for the cross-fertilisation of ideas and experiences, between North and South, the Third World and the First.

References

Bown, L. (1983) 'Adult education in the Third World', in M. Tight (ed.) *Adult Learning and Education*, Croom Helm, pp. 38–49.

Brayne, F. (1944) *Winning the Peace*, Oxford University Press.

Brokensha, D. and Hodge, P. (1969) *Community Development: An interpretation*, Chandler, New York.

Bwatra, Y. *et al.* (eds) (1989) *Adult Education: The Tanzanian experience*, Oxford University Press, Nairobi.

Cardenal, F. (1992) 'Education for what: a letter from Managua', *Adults Learning*, 3,6, pp. 147–8.

Denny, B. (1994) 'Present and Correct; Radicalism in the Armed Forces in World War Two', unpublished dissertation, Ruskin College Library, Oxford.

Duke, C. (ed.) (1985) *Combatting Poverty through Adult Education: National development strategies*, Croom Helm.

Fagen, R. R. (1969) *The Transformation of Political Culture in Cuba*, Stanford University Press.

Fals-Borda, O. and Rahman, M. (eds) (1991) *Action and Knowledge*, Intermediate Technology Publications.

Fieldhouse, R. (1991) 'Conformity and contradiction in English Responsible Body adult education, 1925–1950', in S. Westwood and J. Thomas (eds) *Radical Agendas?: The politics of adult education*, NIACE, Leicester.

Gaventa, J. (1991) 'Towards a knowledge democracy: viewpoints on participatory research in North America', in O. Fals-Borda and M. Rahman (eds) *op. cit.*

Hall, B. (1975) *Adult Education and the Development of Socialism in Tanzania*, East African Literature Bureau, Dar-es-Salaam.

Handa, M. (1984) 'Adult Education and Social Transformation: A Political Economy Analysis of Some of India's National Adult Education Programme (NAEP) 1978–1984', Working Paper, International Council for Adult Education.

Harvey, D. (1990) *The Condition of Postmodernity*, Basil Blackwell.

Hirshon, S. L. with Butler, J. (1983) *And Also Teach Them to Read*, Lawrence Hill.

Hopkins, P. (1985) *Workers' Education: An International Perspective*, Open University Press.

Lovett, T. *et al.* (1983) *Adult Education and Community Action*, Croom Helm.

MacDonald, T. (1985) *Hippocrates in Havana*, Bolivar Books, Mexico.

McGivney, V. and Murray, F. (1991) *Adult Education in Development*, NIACE.

Mayo, M. (1975) 'Community development: a radical alternative?', in R. Bailey and M. Brake (eds) *Radical Social Work*, Edward Arnold, pp. 129–43.

Miller, V. (1985) 'The Nicaraguan Literacy Crusade: education for transformation', in C. Duke (ed.) *op. cit.*

Ministry of Education, Government of India (1985) *Adult Education in India*, New Delhi.

Plunkett, H. (1995) 'The Nicaraguan community movement: in defence of life', in G. Craig and M. Mayo (eds) *Community Empowerment: A reader in participation and development*, Zed Books, pp. 194–205.

Ramakrishnan, K. (1985) 'The Indian Adult Education Programme in Tamil Nadu', in C. Duke (ed.) *op. cit.*, pp. 74–102.

Rogers, A. (1992) *Adults Learning for Development*, Cassell.

Sautoy, P. du (1958) *Community Development in Ghana*, Oxford University Press.

Seers, D. (1964) *Cuba: The Economic and Social Revolution*.

Sen, G. (1992) 'Social needs and public accountability: the case of Kerala', in M. Wuyts *et al.* (eds) *Development Policy and Public Action*, Oxford University Press.

Shanahan, P. forthcoming

Srinivasan, L. (1992) *Options for Educators*, PACT/CDS.

Steele, T. and Taylor, R. (1995) *Learning Independence: A political outline of Indian adult education*, NIACE, Leicester.

United Nations (1990) *Human Development Report*, Oxford University Press.

Chapter Four

Economic restructuring: Developing alternatives

The restructuring of the world of production and the international division of labour has 'For too long been neglected by too many progressive educators', Gelpi has argued (quoted in Griffin, 1987: 288). As Chapter One suggested, from his point of view this concerns not only the world of work itself and workers' education. Global restructuring is also key, Gelpi has argued, to the exclusion and marginalisation of the unemployed, the under-employed and the casually employed, including so many women, ethnic minorities, migrant workers, older people, even children who are forced to work as cheap or unpaid labour. Together these groups have been estimated as exceeding 900 million people, in the late eighties, with the prospect of exceeding 1,500 million people by the turn of the century (Griffin, 1987). In this globalised context, lifelong education can contribute to transformation, he has argued, but 'only if it is not content to be merely a compensatory instrument' (Gelpi, 1979, vol 1: 47). Nor should lifelong education be content to be merely an instrument of 'domestication', to train people to fit into existing economic, social, political and cultural constraints, in the international division of labour.

This chapter focuses upon adult education responses in this context of global economic restructuring. Whilst the chapter includes some discussion of experiences in the workplace, however, the main focus then moves on to explore experiences within the community, which links into the focus of the chapters which follow. And this also relates back to the scale of the problems which global restructuring has been giving rise to, in terms of unemployment and underemployment, exclusion and marginalisation, both in the North and in the South. In the current context of an increasingly globalised economy, the world of production, as Gelpi has emphasised, is so central to adult education for transformation.

After summarising key arguments about the development of workers' education, and some of the conflicting tendencies within workers' education, in the current context of global restructuring, this chapter moves on to summarise debates and experiences in education for unemployed workers. And finally, the chapter focuses upon approaches to addressing production-based issues, through adult education in the community. These approaches include the analysis of local economies, by and for local communities and local workforces, and Participatory Action Research to produce community economic profiles. This type of analysis is the prerequisite, it will be argued, for developing alternative local economic strategies.

These local strategies need to be developed within the framework of alternative development strategies at regional, national and international levels. And these alternative strategies also need to include education and training programmes to support local and regional development policies. The development of co-operatives, community businesses, credit unions and local economic trading schemes, for example, need to be accompanied by local education and training projects, if they are to meet the needs of local people, including the needs of those who have been most marginalised and excluded. As the chapter concludes, such strategies can contribute to the development of alternative perspectives on development, taking development in social as well as economic terms. And such strategies can combine short-term projects to address immediate needs with longer-term projects, which form part of democratically planned strategies for transformation.

But before addressing these questions, this chapter starts by summarising key aspects of debates about the development of workers' education, more generally. And, as Chapters One and Two have already set out, these can be related back to underlying debates between alternative perspectives. On the one hand, workers' education has, in the past, been related to the acquisition of 'useful knowledge', to equip them with the knowledge and skills which employers required for enhanced productivity and economic growth; an approach which, it has been argued, has some parallels with more contemporary, market-led approaches. On the other hand, workers' education has been related to the acquisition of 'really useful knowledge', or critical knowledge to enable the workforce to work out how 'to get out of our present troubles' (in the words of the *Poor Man's Guardian* in 1834), 'to enable men (*sic*) to judge correctly of the real causes of misery and distress so prevalent . . . to consider what remedies will prove most effectual in removing the causes of those evils so that the moral and political influence of the people may be united for the purpose of supporting such measures as are really calculated to improve their condition' (*Poor Man's Guardian*, 1832, quoted in Hughes, 1995). This comment from the nineteenth century has some parallels with adult education and training for transformation, in the twentieth.

Whilst the contrasts between these different types of approaches have been highlighted both in the past and in the current context, previous chapters have also pointed to some of their inherent tensions. And in terms of workers' education, as has already been suggested, there have been particular tensions. Employers' interests have been identified as focusing upon very specific skills training, within the market-led approach. But employers have also shown increasing interest in developing more broadly educated, multi-skilled and hence more flexible workforces. This latter concern can actually lead to a widening of workers' education and training opportunities. This is consistent, of course, with the conclusions which have been drawn by Gelpi and by others, including Gramsci before him, that lifelong education can be viewed in very different ways. Employers may have different and contradictory interests and perceptions, and these may differ again from the interests and the perceptions of their workforces. Lifelong education is potentially both enlarging and transformative, and potentially controlling and domesticating.

In Chapter Two, some of these differences and tensions were summarised, in terms of the history of workers' education in Britain and beyond. More recently, it has been argued, workers' education in Britain has been increasingly dominated by skills-based courses, rather than broader educational provision. And it has been argued that this has applied to trade union education, too (McIlroy, 1992).

Since 1964, when the TUC took over the functions of the NCLC, the focus was further geared to providing very specific training for shop stewards and health and safety representatives, and this, it has been argued, has been at the expense of political education, including education to provide a critical understanding of political economy: 'the triumph of technical training?' (McIlroy 1992, 1995). 'Courses on socialism and economics were eliminated', it has been argued (McIlroy, 1992: 244). At the 1966 TUC a former NCLC veteran summarised the situation as he saw it, and condemned this shift of focus; the more technical courses demonstrated, he argued 'ideological bankruptcy and betrayal' (quoted in McIlroy, 1992: 245).

So despite the expansion of courses and student numbers, and the securing of state funding and statutory rights for paid release for trade union officials, by the end of the seventies, McIlroy has argued, the trade union movement was not adequately prepared for the challenges of the New Right, after the election of the first Thatcher government in 1979. And there was increasing pressure on the TUC and on individual unions to keep away from political or controversial subjects, and confine their educational activities to training, within the context of the new vocational training system if they wanted to retain state funding; despite which, state funding is to be phased out in any case.

So do these experiences of pressure effectively mean that education for critical understanding – 'really useful knowledge' in terms of working for change – has been squeezed out of the picture in the workplace in Britain? The reality is more contradictory. Both trade unions and indeed employers have also found that they have needed to widen the focus, if they are actually to address the implications of restructuring effectively.

For example, trade unions have been faced with major changes in the labour market, with higher unemployment and increasing casualisation, reinforced by privatisation and compulsory competitive tendering and by legislative changes to restrict trade unions. And trade unions have been faced with key changes in industrial relations theory and practice, as Japanese-style Human Resources Management/Total Quality Management methods have spread across Europe and the US, as employers strive to face up to global competition by increasing productivity.

Human Resource Management has been described as the modern approach to personnel management, whose features include increased direct communication between managers and workers. But from the trade union perspective, this may also be manipulative; part of a strategy to undermine collective bargaining, and persuade workers to identify with the company, to the detriment of their own interests. For example, in 1994 shop stewards at Cadbury Limited came across a confidential document entitled *Manufacturing Human Resource Strategy* which stated that 'consultation needs to shift so that employees are consulted directly rather than *via* trade unions' and that 'the role of trade unions needs to be marginalised by greater focus on direct communication and consultation, but without an overt statement to this effect' so that 'employee support for the trade unions should therefore decrease over time' (Transport and General Workers Union). Faced with such challenges, the Transport and General Workers Union, for example, has prioritised education on Human Resources Management (HRM) and Total Quality Management (TQM), producing educational materials which clearly address HRM/TQM in terms of ideology, changes in industrial relations and changes in production (Transport and General Workers Union).

The point to emphasise here is that before working on practical strategies for bargaining, making positive responses to HRM/TQM, shop stewards have needed to develop a broad critical understanding, including a critical understanding of why management may be introducing HRM/TQM, in the first place; could it be that education in political economy is re-emerging?

Similar points can be made about trade union education and training in response to privatisation and compulsory competitive tendering/market testing. To address the specifics of bargaining, in response, trade unionists need a broad and critical understanding. This needs to include a critical understanding of the wider context for these strategies for restructuring. Such understanding is the prerequisite for developing alternative strategies, based upon quality public services as well as quality jobs and training for those who are employed to provide them (GMB/T & G, 1995). The more that bargaining is decentralised, the wider the need for this type of broader education amongst shop stewards.

Trade union education and training has increasingly needed to take account of the changing composition of the labour force, too, in order to reach those at the sharp end of these strategies for restructuring. These particularly vulnerable workers include casualised workers, part-time workers, often women, and other disadvantaged groups who move in and out of paid work. Reaching these groups has been identified as a priority task in a number of unions (eg, Transport and General Workers 'Link-Up'), and the educational implications have also been identified.

For example UNISON has emphasised education and training, including basic education, for these most disadvantaged groups, and developed strategies to reach them *via* the community as well as *via* the workplace. This concern has vital potential implications for the discussion of community-based approaches in the latter part of this chapter and subsequent chapters. In a recent evaluation of its Return to Learn Programme UNISON found that they had been reaching low-waged and part-time workers (traditionally the hardest to reach) and that taking part in the programme had contributed to participants' developing confidence and motivation for further study. Afterwards, 59 per cent had gone on to further study or training, 29 per cent had taken on additional responsibilities at work and 23 per cent had increased their involvement in the union (quoted in Tuckett and Burch, 1995: 6).

Meanwhile, employers have also had to address some contradictory pressures in the face of global restructuring. Market-led approaches have predominated, in education, and more typically training. In Britain, this has led to deregulation, relying on individual employers to provide training to meet skills shortages, within the national training framework of National Vocational Qualifications. But, conversely, as Forrester and Ward have pointed out, the reality is that there has been increasing concern that this deregulated framework is not meeting overall skills needs (Forrester and Ward, 1995; National Commission on Education, 1993; Keep and Mayhew, 1994). And, as a recent survey demonstrated, 49 per cent of employers had not even heard of National Vocational Qualifications and 72 per cent were not interested in them (Callender and Toye, 1994).

In response, some employers, both in Britain and beyond (including the US), have developed not only specific training schemes but also much broader educational initiatives, through Employee Development (ED) programmes, to provide a variety of general learning opportunities for their workforces. The objectives have been to develop better skilled and educationally equipped workforces, to enable companies to compete more effectively in the global economy. (Incidentally, ED schemes have also been linked to strategies to promote the 'new industrial relations' (Moore, 1994: 10), which relates back to the previous discussion of HRM/TQM; employers wanting to change attitudes and working practices, to increase 'flexibility' and enhance productivity (Payne, 1993).)

The best known of these ED schemes have included the Ford programmes (jointly negotiated with the trade unions in the US and then in Britain, because the trade unions have also seen increased educational opportunities as being to the advantage of their members), Rover, Baxi Heating, Peugeot Talbot and Lucas Aerospace (Forrester *et al*, 1993) These schemes have proved extremely popular, and both employers and trade unions have been surprised at the high level of take-up, and the increased self-confidence and the enthusiasm for learning which has been generated. How far then does this all go towards meeting employers' objectives? This relates back to the questions about lifelong learning as a potential instrument of domestication, or as a potential instrument of change.

So far, this summary of workplace-based education and training has focused upon experiences in Britain. There are parallels to be pointed to, as well as differences with experiences elsewhere. Some of these will be summarised, before moving on, in the final sections of this chapter, to focus upon education and training for those outside or on the margins of the workplace.

Some international comparisons and contrasts

Chapter Two provided illustrations of workers' education outside Britain, as well as within it. These included examples from Scandinavian Folk High Schools and Trade Union High Schools, which, in turn, influenced developments in North America, alongside the other influences on workers' education there. Although there is not the space to develop this here, trade unionists have also succeeded in bargaining for resources for broadly-based educational provision in a number of countries, including bargaining for Paid Educational Leave (PEL). The Italian experience has been particularly notable here. Some eight million workers were entitled to the 150 hours' study time which had been agreed for PEL in the seventies, in the aftermath of workers' struggles in the late sixties (Yarnit, 1980). Whilst some of the courses which were provided were criticised (for example for being too academic), others were clearly linked to workers' concerns, offering a critical understanding of experiences of life and of work. 'Best results', it was argued, 'have occurred where the programmes have taken account of what's going on in the workers' movement and the world of work and have developed teaching which always relates to this' (quoted in Yarnit, 1980: 218) – the legacy of Gramsci's work, building workers' education through the factory councils.

In terms of experiences in the South, the previous chapter included references to work-based education and training, as well as to community-based education and training, in Tanzania and Cuba, for example. Work-based education was to contribute to strategies for transformation, with all the strengths and with all the inherent limitations of these strategies. Lovett, for example, has criticised strategies for Participatory Action Research, which formed part of TANU's wider strategy for transformation, in Tanzania. This, he suggested, failed to grapple with the underlying structural problems and, instead, involved offering a fundamentally inadequate and somewhat populist approach to development based upon self-help (Lovett et al, 1983: 108-10).

Just as in Britain, workers' education has been promoted from alternative perspectives, too, for domestication as well as for transformation. Hopkins, for example, has illustrated both transformatory objectives and objectives to promote social harmony, both of which underpinned support for the Indian Central Board for Workers' Education, for instance. 'The essence of workers' education is that it should teach the workers to be dutiful and should inculcate in them a sense of duty and reverence. It is necessary for the working class to acquire the habit of cheerfully undertaking the tasks entrusted to them' (quoted in Hopkins, 1985: 29).

India provided the largest example of government-run workers' education in the non-Communist Third World in the post-war period, with co-operation from employers as well as from the trade unions, although the leadership were also distrustful, apparently 'suspecting that stability, conformity and "responsibility" were the major goals' (Hopkins, 1985: 117). Commenting more generally upon the impact of state funding on workers' education, Hopkins concluded that this varied from one context to another; but that the greater the strength of the labour movement, in general, the greater the chances of independent trade union education.

As an example of trade union education which was not only independent but very specifically geared towards transformation, the Congress of South African Trade Unions (COSATU)'s approach illustrated ways of developing economic and political understanding as the precursor to democratic government in post-Apartheid South Africa. Together with the Trade Union Research Project and the Economic Trends Group, COSATU produced an education handbook for shop stewards, on *Our Political Economy: Understanding the problems* (COSATU, 1992). This handbook effectively provided a crash course in political economy in very accessible format (complete with instructions on how to read graphs) specifically to set the framework for critical discussions about strategies for transformation in post-Apartheid South Africa. What was the starting point, in terms of the economy, and what were the prospects for growth, sector by sector? Most importantly, how could the economy be restructured in order to redress the yawning inequalities, in terms of race as well as class and gender, which had characterised South Africa under Apartheid? And how could the economy be reoriented to meet social needs, and to promote sustainable development, growth with redistribution?

Clearly these questions had no straightforward answers, in an economy where growth had been falling off in the eighties, and where black adult unemployment was 45 per cent; domestic problems which also had to be understood in the context of the wider international pressures and constraints on any one economy. The point which is being made here is not that the handbook provided ready-made solutions. But it represented an interesting example of independent education, to promote participation in developing strategies for transformation. In its own words, the handbook was to provide the point of departure for

COSATU to 'go forward to address solutions and plan a democratic economy for the future' (COSATU, p.73). As the general secretary of COSATU commented, subsequently, 'There have been good ideas, including at COSATU congress', ideas about councils in the community and councils in the workplace, to promote the Reconstruction and Development Plan for growth with redistribution, but what was needed was a 'coherent programme ... as a focus to activate and dynamise these structures'. And without 'mechanically transporting other experiences, we need to look at mass programmes which have been implemented in other revolutionary transitions, such as Nicaragua and Cuba', in order to draw lessons for mobilisation, not just around economic development, but also around 'literacy, inoculation, land reform and housing, which involve the masses of our people' (Shilowa, 1995). The South African experience provides subsequent examples of education and research, too, both in relation to the development of alternative economic strategies, and in relation to strategies for transformation, more generally.

Reaching those outside or on the margins of paid work

Before moving on to these, though, there remain questions to be addressed about education and training for those who are outside the world of paid work, or at least peripheral to it, the unemployed and the under-employed and marginally employed. As the references to Gelpi's analysis at the outset of this chapter suggested, the exclusion and marginalisation of the unemployed, the under-employed and the casually employed also needs to be understood within the wider framework of global restructuring, in the world of production. Here too, there have been competing approaches: at one end of the spectrum, education and especially training/retraining, geared towards fitting the excluded and the marginalised more closely to the changing requirements of the labour market; at the other end of the spectrum, critical education and training to promote collective consciousness and action-empowerment (Forrester and Ward, 1991: 247-9).

In practice, of course, this latter approach does not preclude the need for specific skills training, and support with preparing a *curriculum vitae*, handling job interviews and all the other ways in which the unemployed and the marginally employed can improve their employment prospects (inasfar as the jobs are there to be filled in the first place, of course). But schemes which are narrowly focused on economic goals and industrial needs are, it has been argued, of dubious value, particularly in areas of high unemployment. As McGivney and Sims have shown, this has become more clearly recognised at international level, as unemployment has risen. Quoting a Unesco statement in 1985, they illustrate how 'adult education must not be confined solely to activities of an occupational and economic nature. The development of individual autonomy and collective self-sufficiency calls for the

development of the critical faculties and a sense of civic responsibility'
(quoted in McGivney and Sims, 1986: 11).

Even within the context of government-supported programmes for
the unemployed which have been geared towards training/retraining to
meet the changing requirements of the labour market, there have been
examples of adult educators succeeding in widening the agenda. And
these examples have included both practical knowledge and skills
(including knowledge of welfare rights) and wider educational objectives. For example, community-based courses, which have been more
effective in reaching women, have included social/political issues, such
as the politics of health and welfare issues, as well as issues of sexism
and racism (Fraser and Ward, 1988).

And there have been examples of courses which have specifically
focused upon developing critical understanding of the political economy
of unemployment, and collective approaches to developing alternatives.
Northern College, for instance, has worked with the WEA to develop a
residential course on 'Understanding Unemployment' (as part of other
programmes run by local unemployment centres) together with a two-
week follow-on course. In addition, Northern College has reached many
others who have been outside or marginal to paid work, for example
through the college's 'Community Activists' Course'. Running through
these programmes has been a commitment to education, to enable
participants to develop both critical consciousness and the ability to
develop effective collective action strategies, within the community as
well as within the workplace (FEU/REPLAN Project Report, 1985).

Similarly, since 1992 Ruskin College has also organised a rolling
programme of courses for those outside or on the margins of paid
work, 'Changing Directions'. Once again, whilst the course does provide
participants with support in their job-seeking, the aim is far wider; to
support participants, individually and collectively, to gain the knowledge
to challenge their circumstances – knowledge for transformation and
change (Hughes and Schofield, 1994: 124-5). 'Changing Directions' also
includes a focus upon cultural activity. As one of the participants
explained: 'We were asked about Dylan Thomas (whose work featured
in the programme) when we applied to the TEC for funding; the chap
there thought we should be spending each week writing CVs and learning how to fill in application forms. Why? What's the point? There are
19 people chasing every single job in Oxford. We do realise that having
a good CV is important, but for our own self-respect and self-help we
need drama and discussion, poetry and literature to learn about
ourselves, about what we can offer society and about the best way
forward' (quoted in Hughes, 1995).

Set up in response to rising unemployment in Oxford, as the motor
industry laid workers off, the course set out to enable participants to
'make sense of what is going on in the economic and political sphere in
Britain and further afield that explains growing unemployment and
changing labour markets. This is in part to challenge a sense that many

bring with them that being unemployed is a personal failing. It is also to explore the implications of such changes in relation to wider definitions of citizenship' (Hughes, 1995). This brings the focus on to community-based analyses of the local economy within its wider context, and strategies for change, at the local level and beyond.

Community-based PAR to analyse the local economy

In Britain, as elsewhere, there is a history of community-based analyses of the local economy, Participatory Action Research, and education initiatives to set the scene for the development of alternative approaches. In recent decades, with the 'rediscovery' of poverty, the government's own Community Development Project (CDP) was a key influence in this field. The Home Office launched CDP, with 12 local projects, in 1969, to find new ways of meeting social needs in areas of high social deprivation, through promoting self-help amongst the deprived and through promoting improved co-ordination of services at central and local government levels.

The CDP projects, in operation, soon came to question these original assumptions, focusing, instead, upon the root causes of increasing poverty and deprivation. The key issue here was identified as industrial restructuring, as capital struggled to raise productivity and profitability in the face of international competition. These processes of restructuring, in turn, led to factory closures, relocations, speeded-up assembly lines, labour shake-outs, rising unemployment and low wages in Britain's older industrial areas (Gilding the Ghetto). As the CDP Report *The Costs of Industrial Change* (CDP, 1977) demonstrated, industrial restructuring took different forms in different towns and cities. But there was a common core of experiences, described in terms of 'the making and breaking of local economies' which were key to the causes of increasing poverty and social deprivation.

CDP's analysis of these local economies and the wider causes of their decline did not remain confined to academics, professionals or even politicians. Being action projects as well as research projects, the CDPs also included local programmes to share this developing analysis with local workforces and local communities. In Liverpool, for example, the local CDP supported the pioneering adult education work of Keith Jackson and colleagues at the Liverpool University Institute of Extension Studies. As Lovett *et al* have emphasised, 'the Institute team consciously sought opportunities to engage local people in hard social analysis which attempted to link local issues and problems within a wider social economic and political context' (1983: 34). Although a range of courses on different subjects were provided, the work was particularly distinguished by its provision of high quality education to enable working class activists to analyse their situation and develop more effective action strategies as a result.

As two of the educators, Ashcroft and Jackson, commented

themselves in 1974, adult education, like community development, was a relatively marginal activity, overall; when they left the area, it would no doubt be much as they had found it when the project started work, 'a massive monument to an exploitative society; a squalid and oppressive slum which nobody ought to tolerate . . . . The best we can hope for', they concluded, 'is that more people who live there will recognise this too, and that their frustration will lead to anger and an informed determination to change it' (Ashcroft and Jackson, 1974: 63). In fact, their work did support informed strategies for change, in the project area, in Liverpool more generally and beyond (Yarnit, 1980). And these Liverpool experiences, incidentally, were also part of the background to the development of Northern College, at the end of the seventies.

Meanwhile, other local CDP projects were also developing action research initiatives around the local economy and related social and political issues, working both with local workers' organisations and with community organisations. These initiatives included the Coventry Workshop, for example, and the Trade Union Studies Information Unit (which arose from the work of the Newcastle and the North Tyneside projects), together with other initiatives which were directly influenced by this work (for example, work in London's Docklands, and TUCRIC, in Leeds, which in turn led to a series of initiatives with unemployed workers and community organisations, from the base of the university department of adult continuing education) (Foster and Hodgson, 1979).

Subsequently, in the eighties, a range of initiatives by progressive local authorities, including Sheffield and the Greater London Council (GLC), also drew upon these experiences and analyses. For example, in working towards the GLC's Industrial Strategy (GLC, 1985) and Labour Plan (GLC, 1986), the GLC provided resources to local and London-wide trade union and community organisations. This was so that they could organise workshops and develop their own analyses of the underlying causes of the problems within the local economy, and put forward their own perspectives on alternative strategies and programmes for change. (Incidentally, these included projects in East London, which were able to draw upon previous work in Docklands.) In Sheffield, for example, the local authority also developed education programmes for its own workforce, targeting those with least formal education or qualifications, both to meet their individual educational needs and to enable them to participate more effectively in developing services to meet local needs in the community (the Take Ten programme). And subsequently, drawing in turn upon the experiences of Take Ten in Sheffield (and via Northern College), Ruskin, for example, developed similar programmes with Oxford City Council and Oxfordshire County Council (Hughes and Mayo, 1991). There was, then, a significant amount of cross-fertilisation and exchanges of ideas and experiences within and between these different initiatives.

The history of municipal socialist projects to promote adult education for change, and Participatory Action Research around the local economy has already been written up elsewhere (e.g. Boddy and Fudge, 1984; MacIntosh and Wainwright, 1987; Blunkett and Jackson, 1987). Just to provide one example for illustration here, the West London Report was produced, for the GLC, through research officers working directly with trade unionists and local community organisations, as well as with local political representatives. This collaboration included a three-day series of workshops, a form of public inquiry, in which trade union and community organisations, women's organisations and black and minority ethnic group organisations put forward their views and concerns. The West London Report became a key document, setting out both the analysis of the problems within the local economy (within its wider regional framework) and developing a strategy for addressing the problems. This strategy was about alternative approaches to local economic planning. And it also contained more immediate proposals and projects for meeting local employment, training and social needs. These became the basis for subsequent policy, too, at least within one of the local authorities in the West London area.

In the very different climate of the nineties, there are still, nevertheless, examples of action research to develop alternatives of these types. For example, the Greater London Association of Trades Councils, working together with professionals from research (including trade union research backgrounds) and adult education, recently produced such a programme, *Can the Capital Work?* This initiative was to support campaigning for alternative strategies to tackle unemployment in London, within the framework of alternative strategies nationally, taking account of European factors. And it was 'part of a campaign aimed at uniting the employed and the unemployed to impose on the politicians the policies which alone can make 'full employment' more than a virtuous slogan' (GLATCs, 1994: 1). As a campaigning tool, the booklet concluded with very practical suggestions for ways in which trades councils could involve the local unemployed, women's organisations, pensioners' groups and anti-racist groups, together with suggestions for how to take these questions up at the political level, and how to gain access to more information and research on economic issues.

This last point is important too; as Lovett, for example, has argued in relation to PAR more generally, involving people in becoming researchers in no way removes the need for theoretical rigour and professional expertise. Professionals should not abdicate from this, in some ill-thought-out attempt simply to identify with the people, expecting PAR to emerge spontaneously. 'To arrive on the scene empty-handed (ie, without theoretical insights and professional skills) is to mystify the whole process', Lovett argued, pointing to what he saw as some of the mistakes of the Tanzanian experiences, amongst others, to illustrate his point (Lovett *et al*, 1983: 110). Similar points about the importance of theory and rigour were emphasised in the Liverpool Institute of Extension Studies work, for example (Ashcroft and Jackson, 1974). This relates back to discussions about the relationship between theory and practice in Chapter One, and the role of theory, more generally, in the development of critical consciousness, in the work of both Gramsci and Freire.

Community-based initiatives

Meanwhile, the unemployed, the under-employed, the marginally employed and those who work with them as educators and researchers have, of course, emphasised the importance of immediate, concrete programmes and projects, as well as critical consciousness for developing longer-term strategies for change. There have been varieties of examples, some of which have already been mentioned in previous chapters. Internationally, for instance, the Antigonish Movement provided a model of adult education to promote co-operative economic development, a model which has been applied in the South, as well as in the North.

There have been examples of local community economic development emerging through adult education programmes. And there have been examples of adult education programmes which have been far more specifically aimed at promoting community economic development, working with the excluded and the marginalised in a variety of settings.

An example of the first type comes from the Welsh mining valleys, in the aftermath of the defeat of the miners' strike (1984-5). Demoralisation ensued, with pit closures and redundancies, and the loss of associated welfare, cultural and recreation provision. In this depressing scenario, Amman Valley, adult education classes brought accessible programmes to local communities. In particular, they reached the women who had been effectively unreached *via* traditional forms of provision.

Skills training was available (eg, in basic computing), but there was also broader educational provision, which developed people's understanding of the situation. This was an important ingredient in enabling groups to develop strategies for change. In particular, people worked together to develop community enterprises and community projects to meet local needs (including childcare, youth provision, collectively organised community care and credit unions) (Reynolds, 1995). 'There was a sense', Reynolds argued, in which 'this move into business activity was a logical progression within a developing holistic view of community revival. The new businesses and the education and development activities rapidly became mutually dependent' (*op cit*).

The point about the case of Amman Valley Enterprise is not, of course, that this is unique; on the contrary. But this type of approach precisely illustrates some of the inherent contradictions within market-led approaches to adult education and training. Local community economic development in the Amman Valley, South Wales, emerged through broad adult education in the community, rather than through very specific skills training, alone. Ironically, in some ways, this vital point has been accepted by some government ministers (although government policy, overall, continues to be deeply affected by market-led approaches, emphasising specific skills training for the changing labour market). For example, Tim Boswell, as minister responsible for adult education, agreed that 'it is quite unusual for adults who have not had the best experience with the formal education process to move straight into a qualification-bearing course. I entirely accept that adults may be drawn back into the world of learning by joining, for instance a non-vocational course which may instill the confidence needed to update their skills' (quoted in Tuckett and Burch, 1995: 6).

Meanwhile, an example of the second type of initiative is provided by the Community Development Studies Unit (CDSU) at Magee College, in Derry, on the border between north and south, in Ireland. This border context has been marked by state and para-military violence, with divided communities and very high levels of unemployment, poverty and deprivation, especially amongst the Catholic communities. Here, in Derry, the objective of the programme of critical education and specific training has been targeted, from the outset, at addressing the problems of endemic unemployment and marginalisation. The roots of this programme have been identified as coming from both the North and from the South (from the educator's previous experiences of community development in Zambia and South Africa) (Shanahan and Ward, 1995). And in terms of theoretical roots, Freire's work has been influential, in this context, drawing as Freire has upon insights from both Christian (including Catholic Christian) and socialist thought. The work of Korten and others, who have been concerned with transformation in terms of people-centred, sustainable development, has also been influential in this context (Shanahan, forthcoming).

From 1987, the work at Magee College has been supported by the European Union, and linked into community economic development through university-based adult education in Ireland, north and south. The Magee course is 'a mixture of critical education with basic vocational training, validated by the University of Ulster', a curriculum 'concoction' which has been advocated by the Council of Europe for adult education with the long-term unemployed (Shanahan and Ward, 1995). Social sciences are included, along with practical skills including IT, to encourage critical thinking, and then to support participants in developing specific plans to meet community needs. Forty unwaged people (unwaged community activists and volunteers) attend the course, for 40 weeks a year, spending three days a week in college and two days back in the community, working on a practical project, an exercise in Participatory Action Research.

In general, funders like to see concrete results, in terms of unemployed people getting back to work; or at least in terms of community businesses and co-operative developments established, for example. And academic institutions tend to have their own agendas, too, in terms of academic standards, student numbers, validation, etc. The staff at Magee have worked to balance these agendas with their own concerns to create curriculum space for the creative and critical involvement of the 'excluded', supporting collective approaches in the community. Community groups use the Magee course to gain access to knowledge and skills. Whilst this can and does lead to community economic development initiatives, groups can and do also use the Unit to address wider structural issues of class, gender, ethnicity and ecology.

The Magee Unit has been evaluated as a success, in terms of enabling unwaged participants 'to develop confidence in their ability to influence change and to organise community projects into stand-alone co-operatives' (Shanahan and Ward, 1995). However, the staff have also been very self-critical; the longevity of small businesses and co-operatives is often problematic, and jobs are all too often poorly-paid. But nevertheless, cultural capital, in the forms of knowledge, resources and skills, have been redistributed in a validated programme of study with high academic standards, they have argued. And third-level educational resources have been opened up to excluded groups in Magee and elsewhere. This evaluation emphasises, once again, the vital importance of the interconnections between critical analysis and practical projects, the importance of maintaining both rigorous standards and active community participation/PAR, valuing theory as well as practice.

So, the experiences which have been summarised in this chapter so far seem to point in the following direction – the key importance of adult education and participatory action research, both in the workplace and in the community. This is with the aim of developing a critical understanding of the local economy, within its wider context, as the prerequisite for developing strategies and programmes for change and transformation. What, then, would this imply in practice? What would be the implications for the curriculum and for PAR agendas? And how might this be negotiated with adult learners; respecting the importance of starting from where they are, but not coming empty-handed, and expecting alternative approaches simply to emerge, spontaneously?

Bearing in mind this last point in particular, setting out a model of 'how to do it' would be unlikely to be helpful, even if such a model could be devised, let alone devised in ways which would be equally applicable in very different circumstances. The following set of questions, somewhat more modestly, merely suggests some headings, which adult educators and community workers might find useful, as a checklist, to begin the process of compiling the local community economic profile.

Some of these questions may be answered on the basis of existing information, including official statistics, together with local reports. Additional information and reports may be available through the relevant trade unions, local universities and colleges, and through the media. The PAR process may also need to involve the collection of additional information, including the use of interviews and/or local surveys. (For further discussion of community profiling, see Hawtin *et al*, 1994.)

Some possible headings for a checklist for compiling a local community economic profile

1. What is the local economic base, and how has this changed, historically?

    What are the major industries/services, locally, both in terms of their economic strength/profitability and in terms of the employment which they each provide, locally and beyond (which are not, of course, necessarily the same)?

    What are the key trends in these industries/services, sector by sector? Are the different sectors growing or declining, in terms of profitability and/or in terms of employment, which, in turn, needs to be measured, both in terms of the numbers of jobs involved and in terms of the quality of these jobs/pay, security and conditions?

    Who owns/controls the key firms, and where do they fit, in the wider context? For example, are any firms part of a multinational corporation, and if so, where does this particular plant fit into the multinational's wider interests?

    Who owns/controls the land, and how does this affect what is produced, and how? (This last question applies in different ways, in urban areas, and in rural areas, including rural areas in the South.)

2. How is the local economy being affected by wider policies, at local, regional and national levels, and beyond?

    Local policies may be attempting to encourage inward investment, for example, and/or discouraging particular types of industries, through land use planning policies, for instance.

    National policies may be key to the overall level of investment, and/or national policies may be driving down wages and conditions, as part of market-led strategies to promote profitability, in the face of global competition.

    European-level policies may be key to the prospects for particular sectors, as well as having vital implications for the economy, more generally.

    And international factors, such as trade agreements, for example, may be key to the prospects for particular sectors, and to their competitors, internationally.

    More generally, social policies, at different levels, may be having major effects, such as reducing the number and/or quality of jobs in the public service sector, as a result of spending cuts and/or privatisation/market testing.

3. What is the composition of the local labour force?

Where do local people work, and what jobs do they do? Who works locally, and who works outside the area?

What qualifications and skills do local people have, and who has access to which types of education and training? And conversely who does not have effective access to education and training, for whatever reasons?

How is the local labour force divided in terms of gender, race and age, as well as in terms of social class? Are particular groups, such as women, migrant workers, rural workers, older workers, young people or people with disabilities suffering from particular disadvantages?

4. What about all the *unpaid* work which is being performed in the local community?

What about all the caring work which is being performed, looking after children, older people, and people with disabilities? And what about unpaid work, being active in community organisations, for example? This work has value, and takes time, even if this is not recognised in financial terms.

What about unpaid work, growing food, in rural areas? This may be vitally important, especially in some Southern contexts.

Some unpaid activities may become part of the waged economy; for example, when local groups/co-operatives set up community nurseries, or bid for community care contracts. But social needs are not necessarily most effectively met in this way, nor is sustainable people-led development necessarily advanced, through such forms of marketisation.

This type of checklist may seem extremely crude to policy makers, whilst still seeming relatively daunting to community activists and local trade unionists. Ken Livingstone, MP and former leader of the controversial GLC, commented that his book on the Programme for the Nineties did not have a chapter which was identifiably addressing economic issues because nobody would have read it (Livingstone, 1989). Such may be the popular reaction to anything labelled 'economic issues', at least in Britain. So could such a checklist actually be useful to local people? How would it apply, for example, to the analysis of the context for participants on the 'Changing Directions' course at Ruskin College in Oxford?

Without attempting to answer, in any detail, there are some broad indications of relevant aspects to be explored here. Despite being located within the most prosperous region of Britain, Oxford, as the participants on the 'Changing Directions' course are only too well aware, has been characterised by increasing poverty, and a widening gap between rich and poor, over the eighties and early nineties. The numbers living in low-income families increased by 30 per cent in Oxford over this period. Unemployment fell, in the late eighties, but rose again to around 16 per cent for men by early 1993 (Noble *et al*, 1994).

In trying to develop a critical understanding of their deteriorating situation in Oxford, how far would these types of questions point participants in a useful direction? The changing economic base has clearly been identified as a key factor, and particularly the loss of jobs in the car plants in Cowley, East Oxford, which shed half their jobs between 1988 and 1992 (although some production does remain, in Oxford). The effects of these changes on the local workforce in Oxford and the surrounding areas included both unemployment and lower pay, as former car workers found themselves forced to take alternative jobs which paid less; the only jobs then available to them (Noble and Schofield, 1993).

To understand the decline of employment in the motor industry in Oxford, however, in turn involves understanding the corporate strategies of rationalisation and disinvestment, 'driven' as the introduction to the story of the Cowley Workers in Oxford, explains, 'by the desperate search for profits under conditions of global competition' (Ward, 1993: 2). And in particular, the story of job losses at Cowley involved the policies of the Thatcher government in pushing through the privatisation of Rover, the last and what has been described as the most problematic relic of the state-owned British Leyland motor manufacturing conglomerate. In the event, the sale (to British Aerospace) was controversial, and 'sweeteners' to promote the sale had to repaid, on the orders of the European Commission. One of the other international dimensions to this story included collaboration with the Japanese manufacturer, Honda, which was also making major investments outside Oxford, in Swindon. (Typically this was intended to bypass the trade union activism which had characterised Cowley, in the past – although more recently, at Cowley too, a new deal was agreed, which has been described in terms of the new management techniques. This deal has been seen as being geared towards 'centralising and weakening the trade unions' base and powers, and developing the "team" concept' and full flexibility (A Cowley Worker, 1993: 205).

In addition to the impact of national and indeed international policies, local authority policies were also relevant in the Oxford context. In particular, the City Council carried out a public inquiry, in 1990, to explore what might be done to save jobs. In the event, the report recommended accepting the reality of the closures and co-operating with Rover and Arlington Securities to develop alternative employment on the land which would become vacant, as a result. This has been described by a critic in terms of the 'conversion of a major economic and social issue concerning the employment of a sizeable group of Oxford residents into a property development issue' (Thomas, 1993: 226). Whether or not former car workers would find suitable employment in the redeveloped industrial and commercial space was, of course, another question, which brings the discussion to the labour force itself. How likely were they to gain jobs in the newly-developed commercial space, for instance, or to compete for professional jobs, either in Oxford or outside? (This latter question has relevance because there are also Oxford residents who commute to London and elsewhere, daily, especially to fill professional and managerial jobs.)

Without going into further detail here, the impact of these redundancies also needs to be understood in the context of the labour force, and the qualifications and skills of the former workforce, in East Oxford. Most of the jobs were semi-skilled, requiring few, if any formal qualifications. This was a relevant factor, in understanding why it was so difficult for former car workers to take up well-paid jobs in the more buoyant service sector, including the university (the old Town and Gown divide, a divide which has more recently been described in terms of 'The Tale of Two Oxfords' (Schofield and Noble, 1993: 258). And meanwhile, manual jobs in other parts of the service sector, including the National Health Service (local hospitals being major sources of employment in Oxford), were themselves increasingly affected by pressures on public spending, including pressures directly resulting from compulsory competitive tendering.

Overall, the impact of the changes in Oxford has been borne particularly severely by the most disadvantaged sections of the population; working class people without formal qualifications and skills, and particularly older workers, and young people, unable to find jobs with a future. Black people, and especially black youth, are particularly disadvantaged. Black people make up only some 3 per cent of the population in Oxfordshire, but constitute some 10 per cent of the unwaged. Women have been particularly prone to part-time, low-paid, casual work, there being insufficient new full-time service jobs to replace the full-time jobs lost in manufacturing. And women have had to carry particular burdens, in picking up the pieces, both as second earners, trying to maintain the household income, and through their unpaid work in the family and in the community.

This last point about the importance of unpaid work has, at least, been recognised as an important issue for public policy, in terms of support for developing community initiatives and community education and training, through the regeneration strategies which have been planned, as part of Oxford's Single Regeneration Budget initiative. (This represents a joint initiative, supported by government, local authorities, the TEC, local employers and local voluntary and other organisations, to promote regeneration in the area which has been most seriously affected by the redundancies).

In summary, then, some of the questions from this checklist, would seem to have bearing on the analysis of the context in a city such as Oxford. In addition, in Oxford Participatory Action Research can start from the basis of a range of materials, including official statistics, local authority reports and specialist research into poverty and deprivation, completed in the university (Noble *et al*, 1994; Rowntree, 1994). And through the Oxford Motor Industry Research Group, academic researchers worked together with local trade unionists, the Oxford and District Trades Council and community activists, to tell the story of the Cowley Automobile Workers in Oxford, and to put the case for change, from an alternative perspective (Hayter and Harvey, 1993).

From this alternative perspective, Gelpi's emphasis on the key importance of changes in the world of production are central. Increasing social exclusion and increasing social needs in Oxford needed to be analysed in terms of their underlying causes, restructuring in the local economy, in response to increasing international competition. This needs to be analysed together with the impact of policy interventions, at local level, and national level and beyond. In fact, of course, this emphasis upon the centrality of the world of production is also shared by those who start from market-led perspectives, although resting on fundamentally different assumptions and very different policy conclusions, both in terms of economic solutions and in terms of social solutions. Which last point brings the discussion on to the theme of the next chapter.

References

Ashcroft, B. and Jackson, K. (1974) 'Adult education and social action', in D. Jones and M. Mayo (eds) *Community Work One*, Routledge and Kegan Paul.

Blunkett, D. and Jackson, K. (1987) *Democracy in Crisis*, Hogarth.

Boddy, M. and Fudge, C. (eds) 1984) *Local Socialism*, Macmillan.

Callender, C. and Toye, J. (1994) 'Employers' take-up and usage of NVQ/SVQs', *Employment Gazette*, November, pp. 417–22.

CDP (1977) *The Costs of Industrial Change*, CDP.

CDP (undated) *Gilding the Ghetto*, CDP.

COSATU (1992) *Our Political Economy; Understanding the problems. A handbook for COSATU shop stewards*, COSATU Education, Johannesburg, South Africa.

A Cowley Worker (1993) 'The unions and the closure', in T. Hayter and D. Harvey (eds) *The Factory and the City*, Mansell.

FEU/REPLAN Project Report (1985) *Adult Unemployment and the Curriculum: A manual for practitioners*, FEU.

Forrester, K. and Ward, K. (1991) 'Adult education and trade union centres against unemployment', in K. Forrester and K. Ward (eds) *Unemployment, Education and Training: Case studies from North America and Europe*, Caddo Gap Press, California.

Forrester, K. and Ward, K. (1995) 'Choosing to Learn? Employee Development Schemes Assessed', unpublished paper, Department of Adult Continuing Education, University of Leeds.

Forrester, K., Payne, J. and Ward, K. (1993) 'Adult Learners at Work; Final Research Report', University of Leeds.

Foster, J. and Hodgson, K. (1979) 'New directions – the need for local research resources in labour movement', in CDP/PEC, *The State and the Local Economy*, PEC.

Fraser, L. and Ward, K. (1988) *Education from Everyday Living*, NIACE, Leicester.

Gelpi, E. (1979) *A Future for Lifelong Education: Principles, policies and practice*, Manchester University, Department of Adult and Higher Education, Monograph 13.

Greater London Association of Trades Councils (1994) *Can the Capital Work?*, GLATCs.

GLC (1985) *The London Industrial Strategy*, GLC.

GLC (1986) *The London Labour Plan*, GLC.

GLC (undated) *The West London Report*, GLC.

GMB and T & G (1995) *New Model DSOs: Strategies for survival and success*, a joint TGWU/GMB Publication.

Griffin, C. (1987) 'Ettore Gelpi', in P. Jarvis (ed.) *Twentieth Century Thinkers in Adult Education*, Croom Helm, pp. 280–97.

Hawtin, M., Hughes, G. and Percy-Smith, J. (1994) *Community Profiling: Auditing social needs*, Open University Press, Buckingham.

Hayter, T. and Harvey, D. (eds) *The Factory and the City*, Mansell.

Hopkins, P. (1985) *Workers' Education: An international perspective*, Open University Press, Milton Keynes.

Hughes, K. (1995) 'Really useful knowledge: adult learning and the Ruskin Learning Project', in M. Mayo and J. Thompson (eds) *Adult Learning, Critical Intelligence and Social Change*, NIACE, Leicester.

Hughes, K. and Mayo, M. (1991) 'Opening up personal development: a workplace learning initiative', *Adults Learning*, 3, 4, pp. 99–100.

Hughes, K. and Schofield, A. (1994) 'What has Dylan Thomas got to do with getting people back to work?', *Adults Learning*, 5, 5, pp. 124–5.

Keep, E. and Mayhew, K. (1994) 'The changing structure of training provision', in T. Buxton, P. Chapman and P. Temple (eds) *Britain's Economic Performance*, Routledge, pp. 308–41.

Livingstone, K. (1989) *Livingstone's Labour: A programme for the nineties*, Unwin Hyman.

Lovett, T., Clarke, C. and Kilmurray, A. (1983) *Adult Education and Community Action*, Croom Helm.

MacIntosh, M. and Wainwright, H. (eds) (1987) *A Taste of Power: The politics of local economics*, Verso.

McGivney, V. and Sims, D. (1986) *Adult Education and the Challenge of Unemployment*, Open University Press, Milton Keynes.

McIlroy, J. (1992) 'The demise of the National Council of Labour Colleges' (pp. 173–207); 'The triumph of technical training?' (pp. 208–43) and 'Trade union education for a change' (pp. 244–75), in B. Simon (ed.) *The Search for Enlightenment*, NIACE, Leicester.

McIlroy (1995) 'The dying of the light', in M. Mayo and J. Thompson (eds) *Adult Learning, Critical Intelligence and Social Change*, NIACE, Leicester.

Moore, R. (1994) 'Ford EDAP: breaking through the barriers', in *Adults Learning*, 5, 9, pp. 225–26.

National Commission on Education (1993) *Learning to Succeed: A radical look at education today and a strategy for the future. Report of the Paul Hamlyn Foundation*, Heinemann.

Noble, M. and Schofield, A. (1993) 'After redundancy', in T. Hayter and D. Harvey (eds) *The Factory and City*, Mansell, pp. 231–55.

Noble, M., Smith, G., Avenell, D., Smith, T. and Sharland, E. (1994) 'Changing Patterns of Income and Wealth in Oxford and Oldham', Department of Applied Social Studies and Social Research, University of Oxford.

Payne, J. (1993) 'Too little of a good thing? Adult education and the workplace', *Adults Learning*, 4, 10, pp. 274–75.

Schofield, A. and Noble, M. (1993) 'Communities and corporations: rethinking the connections', in T. Hayter and D. Harvey, *op. cit.*, pp. 256–74.

Shanahan, P. and Ward, J. (1995) 'The university and empowerment', in G. Craig and M. Mayo (eds) *Community Empowerment: A reader in participation and development*, Zed Books.

Shilowa, S. (1995) 'Recapture the revolutionary imagination', *Morning Star*, 20 May, p. 6.

Reynolds, S. (1995) Amman Valley Enterprise: A case study of adult education and community revival', in M. Mayo and J. Thompson, *op. cit.*, pp. 242–52.

Thomas, M. (1993) 'Planning, property and profits', in T. Hayter and D. Harvey, *op. cit.*, pp. 209–27.

Transport and General Workers Union (undated) 'Cadbury Limited: Human Resource Manipulation?', leaflet written and produced by Transport and General Workers Union on behalf of Cadbury Conference shop stewards, including USDAW, AEEU and T and G.

Tuckett, A. and Burch, E. (1995) 'Learning for a lifetime' *Education Guardian*, May 16, p. 6.

Ward, S. (1993) 'Introduction', in T. Hayter and D. Harvey, *op. cit.*, pp. 1–7.

Yarnit, M. (1980) 'Second chance to learn', in J. Thompson (ed.) *Adult Education for a Change*, Hutchinson, pp. 174–91.

Yarnit, M. (1980) '150 Hours – Italy's experiment in mass working-class education', in J. Thompson, *op. cit.*, London pp. 192–218.

Chapter Five

Adult education and training: Responding to changing social needs

This chapter starts from the conclusions of the previous chapter – social needs and their relationship to changes in the world of production. How have different approaches to adult education and training supported communities in analysing and responding to changing and intensifying social needs, needs related to increasing poverty, ill-health, poor housing and environmental concerns? And how can adult educators support communities in developing holistic approaches to meeting these social needs, within wider strategies for development and regeneration, strategies for transformation, both in the South and in the North? The focus in this chapter will be upon community-based approaches to health, housing and planning located within the context of changing social policies and decreases in the resources which are being made available to meet these increasing needs.

The previous chapter argued for the importance of analysing social needs in relation to changes in the productive sphere – the world of work and the social relations which underpin the economy. The example of health needs illustrates this approach as follows. Starting from immediate issues, critical approaches to adult education move on to raise underlying questions about the root causes of ill-health. As a case in point, in the *Community Workers' Handbook* (which drew upon Freire's approach) Hope and Timmel illustrated a method – Werner's 'But Why Method' – which had been developed in Zimbabwe, to probe the root causes of community health problems. The community health worker/educator starts from the presenting problem:

'The child has a septic foot'
'But why?', asks the health worker/educator
'Because she stepped on a thorn' (without shoes)
'But why has she no shoes?'
'Because her father cannot afford to buy her any'
'But why can he not afford to buy her shoes?'
'Because he is paid very little as a farm labourer'
'But why is he paid so little?' (quoted in Hope and Timmel, 1984: p. 59).

Similar dialogues would result, for example, from questioning as to why a baby was so ill from diarrhoea, or why a poorly nourished young child was at risk of dying from measles. Such dialogues would raise issues of poverty and deprivation, including environmental deprivation and deprivation in relation to sanitation and clean drinking water, as well deprivation in relation to affordable medical care. This takes the discussion straight on into the economic causes, as well as the social and political causes of ill-health.

In the current context of global restructuring, together with reductions in governments' social spending, the rate of improvement in children's health has fallen off. The truth is that children's health and welfare has actually deteriorated in the poorest countries in the South, especially in Sub-Saharan Africa (Cornia et al, 1987). Lower incomes and higher food prices have resulted in poorer nutrition, whilst cuts in government health spending and increased charges for medical care put services beyond the reach of the very people who may be in greatest need of them.

In parallel, although, of course, from a very different starting point, growing inequality of income in Britain has been accompanied by growing inequalities in health. Poverty, the Social Justice Commission suggested, 'should carry a government health warning' (Commission for Social Justice, 1994: 44). 'The damage done by unemployment is also clear', the Report continued, both in terms of physical health and in terms of mental health, including increasing vulnerability to depression and suicide (the suicide rate having risen particularly sharply amongst young men). Whilst unemployment is especially damaging to psychological health, insecure employment has been shown to have very similar, although less extreme, effects (Burchell, 1993). Taken together, unemployment, casualisation and low pay are major factors in increasing health problems in Britain and beyond.

Meanwhile, health problems are exacerbated by the poor housing and deprived environmental conditions of the most disadvantaged groups in society. In Britain, the poorest children, as the Commission for Social Justice also pointed out, 'are twice as likely as those from social class 1 to die from a respiratory illness' (respiratory illnesses being linked to damp housing conditions). They are 'more than four times as likely to be killed in a traffic accident' (again this may be linked to environmental conditions, especially lack of safe play space). 'And the poorest children are more than six times as likely to die in a house fire' (which may be linked to cheap but unsafe heating, for example from paraffin stoves) (Commission for Social Justice, p.43).

The previous chapter focused upon *economic* factors, in the context of global economic restructuring and Structural Adjustment Programmes. This set the framework for analysing community- and workplace-based strategies for addressing poverty, low wages, casualisation and unemployment, at the local level and beyond. This chapter focuses upon *social* aspects; and this, in turn, relates to the restructuring of social policies, as well as economic policies. Whilst these underlying changes in social policies vary significantly from one national and regional context to another, there are some common threads and common pressures to be addressed.

Broadly, these common threads and common pressures in the restructuring of social policies can also be analysed in terms of the competing approaches which were summarised in Chapter One. On the one hand, market-led approaches to social policy, like market-led approaches to economic policy, also start from the key role of the free market, as the co-ordinator of the economy and the dynamic factor in economic development. Once the free market is operating effectively, its supporters argue, then the benefits of economic growth can 'trickle down' to benefit even the least advantaged groups in society. Economic growth can then provide the resources for social spending, on health and education, for example, and on housing and social services. But social spending must never be allowed to hamper the essential needs of the economy, or to divert resources away from productive investment.

On the contrary, in fact, the burden of public spending on social welfare can be reduced, according to this approach, and resources deployed more effectively, if market mechanisms are also promoted *within* the health and welfare services themselves. So, for example, privatisation, and competitive tendering, feature significantly in market-led approaches to health and welfare services, as part of overall strategies to reduce public spending (so that resources are concentrated on productive investment) and to achieve better 'value for money'. Public responsibilities are to be constrained, and private provision is to be promoted, according to this market-led perspective. And in parallel, there should be enhanced responsibilities for individuals and their families. In the words of the US free marketeer Charles Murray, the strategy which he advocates is 'to have central government stop trying to be clever (with interventionist social policies) and instead get out of the way . . . ' (Murray, 1990: 34).

Meanwhile, alongside this emphasis upon the role of individuals and families, market-led approaches to social policy have also emphasised the potential value of the contributions to be made by the voluntary and community sectors. Community participation and self-help, in particular, can reduce public spending, whilst ensuring that the services which *are* still provided with public resources meet local needs as effectively (including cost-effectively) as possible. Community education can be particularly relevant here, in terms of supporting self-help in the community.

This type of approach to the restructuring of health and welfare services has been very marked in policy debates amongst the New Right, in both Britain and the United States. The ripple effects of these debates can be traced far more widely elsewhere in Europe and beyond (Glennerster and Midgely, 1991; Mayo, 1994; Craig and Mayo, 1995). Community participation and self-help feature significantly, too, in responding to and attempting to offset the effects of market-led Structural Adjustment Programmes. Cuts in social spending as a result of Structural

Adjustment Programmes have particularly affected the poorest and most vulnerable groups in the poorest Third World countries in the South. So, for example, in response, community-based initiatives may help to offset the impact of reduced services and/or increased charges for services, by providing voluntary labour and/or through community-based financing to keep services going. This may help to pay for health workers and buy drugs for local clinics, for instance.

In particular, women, who generally carry the prime responsibility for families' health and nutrition, can play an enhanced role in these types of initiatives. Women may have the key role in developing self-help treatments, for instance. For example, if community health education programmes can enable women to treat babies for diarrhoea – the number-one infant killer – using home-based oral rehydration treatments, the need for more expensive treatments in health posts or hospitals can be reduced (Cornia, 1987).

Community education to promote self-help has been advocated then as part of strategies to cope with the effects of market-led economic and social policies. But, conversely, community education has also been advocated as part of *alternative* approaches, both to meet immediate social needs, and to work towards challenging the underlying, root causes of these immediate problems. Ultimately, according to this alternative approach, communities' health and welfare cannot be maximised without taking account of underlying economic as well as social factors. Brecht's poem *A Worker's Speech to a Doctor* has been quoted, in this context, to illustrate precisely these connections with the underlying economic and social causes of ill-health.

'Are you able to heal?' the worker asks the doctor, when
The pain in our shoulder comes
You say, from the damp; and this is also the reason
For the stain on the wall of our flat.
So tell us;
Where does the damp come from?
Too much work and too little food
Makes us feeble and thin.
Your prescription says:
Put on more weight.
You might as well tell a bulrush
Not to get wet . . . (quoted in Widgery, 1979).

According to this alternative approach, then, community education in relation to health has to be about more than meeting immediate needs, however important these immediate needs are. And community education has to be about more than technical training to meet these immediate needs most effectively. Community education, from this alternative perspective, needs to go on, to pose questions about the root causes (the 'but why' questions) and to raise the interconnections between the different factors, in holistic ways.

The importance of developing holistic approaches links back to the issue of community profiling, which was raised in the previous chapter. This involves analysing local needs 'for the purpose of developing an action plan or other means of improving the quality of life in the community however defined'. As Hawtin *et al* explain, 'Of course social researchers and those charged with meeting social needs and providing services know about the relationships between, for example, poor housing and ill health or unemployment and depression. However, practice has often been slow in reflecting this reality. So policies designed to combat poor housing, ill health, unemployment and mental health problems are still often formulated and implemented in isolation from each other. Community profiles which are comprehensive in their coverage will challenge that bureaucratic departmentalism as well as accurately reflecting the reality of people's lives' (Hawtin *et al*, 1994: 5). This type of holistic approach needs to involve communities actively at every stage of the process, they argue – participatory action research. And Hawtin *et al*'s approach also implies that meeting these needs requires improved and better resourced services, too, rather than relying on community self-help on its own (whether or not that was the objective of the policy-makers who initiated the community profiling in the first place).

In practice, of course, even the most convinced free-marketeer finds difficulty in proposing that public provision might be totally replaced by self-help, whether by individuals or by communities attempting to pull themselves up by their own bootstraps unaided. Nor have self-help groups, themselves, typically seen their role as *supplanting* rather than *complementing* the role of publicly-supported and professionally-provided services (see eg, Powell, 1987; Richardson, 1984; Wann, 1995). The market, by itself, is not sufficient, in the view of some of those who have been most enthusiastic supporters of self-help. Collective efforts are needed, too, 'to provide for each other what the market cannot provide' (Wann, 1995: 101). On the contrary, in fact, as Wann has argued, self-help is about 'sharing knowledge, skills and power – the antithesis of a marketplace where the fittest survive and the weakest go to the wall' (*ibid*). But self-help, according to this type of perspective, also requires public investment, including public investment in education and training for self-help groups.

In summary, then, self-help, and community participation more generally have gained very widespread support in recent years. In both Britain and the US, for example, there has been a wave of interest in the rediscovery of 'community' and the new 'communitarianism' which has been advocated by Etzioni and others. 'The term community is on many lips today', as Atkinson, for instance, has argued, including politicians of both left and right. (Atkinson, 1994: 1). The new 'communitarianism' challenges the overall dominance of market-led approaches, whilst still emphasising the potential for community-based approaches to encourage citizens 'to take a greater responsibility for their own lives and for the quality of the society in which they live' – attempting to square the circle? Similar enthusiasm for self-help, community participation and the role of the voluntary/NGO sectors can be identified, in relation to development issues, in the South. Over the past decade or so, it has been argued, the voluntary/NGO sector, has 'moved closer to centre stage' in policy terms, 'with greater diversity, credibility and creativity than ever before' and with greater capacity to influence key decision-makers (Clarke, 1991: 3-5). More generally, it has been argued that 'the hope for dealing with the global development crisis rests not with the development industry, but with the great social movements of contemporary society including the peace, environment, women's and human rights movements' (Korten, 1990: ix).

But beneath this apparently common, shared enthusiasm, there have been significant differences in underlying approach and perspective. These have ranged from the World Bank and international organisations committed to market-led approaches, on the one hand, through to a broad range of organisations committed to challenging the *status quo* and developing community participation for empowerment and transformation, for people-centred, sustainable development, at the other end of the spectrum (Craig and Mayo, 1995). And this diversity of approach and perspective is reflected in the diversity of the voluntary/community/NGO sector itself, from small self-help groups to large voluntary sector organisations with publicly-funded contracts to provide services, and from local advice and advocacy groups through to international agencies and people's movements (Brenton, 1985; Thomas, 1992). There is no necessary or neat correspondence between these different approaches and the variety of organisational types which implement them, in practice.

In terms of community education and training, there are key differences of approach, too. These range from education and more particularly training to promote the more circumscribed versions of self-help, through to community education and training and participatory action-research to explore the root causes of social problems and to promote strategies for transformation. As some of the examples which will be summarised in this chapter illustrate, there are inherent tensions here, too. Holistic approaches to community health education tend to raise questions about root causes, for example, whether or not that was the original intention of the sponsoring or funding agency. And conversely, transformatory community education initiatives also tend to focus upon some very practical and far more limited issues (such as technical issues of management and contracting in the mixed economy).

Community health education

So, to move into the discussion of examples; firstly community health education, which, as McGivney and Murray have demonstrated, has 'for many years been a central part of Primary Health Care,' as well as a 'specialised division of adult education' (McGivney and Murray, 1991: 17). Adult education and primary health care/health education share common underlying principles and analysis, they have argued, starting from people's immediate needs and their capacity to understand these critically, and then to develop action strategies and act upon them. McGivney and Murray have also pointed out that adult educators and health professionals have not necessarily recognised these common principles and methods in the past. Since the late seventies, though, there has been an increasing focus upon more holistic approaches to community health education and development. McGivney and Murray have provided examples of community health education involving both users and promoters of projects, in a continuous process of learning, using a diverse range of participatory methods. There is a whole literature in this area of development.

But, as has also been suggested, over recent years there has been an increasing focus upon community health education within the context of market-led strategies to contain health spending, whilst attempting to offset the social damage resulting from the implementation of Structural Adjustment Programmes. There are major tensions here, and competing pressures, pressures which, all too often, bear especially severely upon women, when they are called upon to find the additional time and the energy for self-help initiatives. (This can mean adding community labour to women's existing commitments, in productive labour and in reproductive labour, in the family; women's 'triple burden' in Moser's terms; see Moser, 1989). As studies such as Walt's have shown, these attempts to pass the costs of community health initiatives on to communities themselves, in the harsher financial climate of the eighties, have been problematic. Typically, poorer communities lack the resources to take on these responsibilities themselves, unaided. To be successful, in terms of preventative approaches to health care, community health initiatives need to be resourced as part of wider support for primary health care (Walt, 1990).

To point to these limits and tensions, however, is in no way to devalue the positive potential of community-based approaches to health education and to development, more generally. Walt and Wield, for example, have pointed to the positive achievements of community health education in Mozambique, drawing upon the experiences of self-reliance and prevention, in the liberated zones, during the struggle for independence from the Portuguese colonisers. After independence 'each Mozambican was to be involved in health education' (Walt and Wield, 1983: 29; Walt and Melamed, 1983). And this was to be directly linked to the new 'Frelimo' government's strategy for collective and democratic participation in socialist transformation.

But there were massive difficulties in implementation, especially given the lack of resources due to the impoverished legacy of the colonial past. These difficulties were subsequently compounded as a result of increasing violence and civil disorder as a result of the activities of the

RENAMO rebels, who were supported by the Apartheid regime in neighbouring South Africa.

There are some parallels here with experiences in Nicaragua, as Chapter Three explained in summary. Under the Sandinista government, health education had been a key element of the National Literacy Campaign. After close consultation with the local community organisations (the 'Defence Committees'), a follow-up manual, *Health Lessons for Literacy Workers*, was produced. The objective was to stimulate dialogue about themes such as the lack of clean water, inadequate sanitation and poor nutrition, so that, as people developed their knowledge and understanding, they would develop the confidence to tackle these problems. Some 30,000 health volunteers were trained in the first year of the new government to work on health education and change in their local communities. Mass vaccination campaigns followed, too, as part of this community-based approach to adult education and health.

As Chapter Three also pointed out, as the war with the Contras developed, resources were diverted to the war effort (although health resources were protected as far as possible). There were additional problems, as clinics and hospitals became the targets of Contra attacks. After the defeat of the Sandinista government, the situation deteriorated even further. Dramatic cuts in public services were required as part of the market-led restructuring, which was linked to the IMF loan. Health services were seriously affected as a result.

Volunteers in the Community Movement, however, determined to continue their grassroots health work, pressurising the government for services, under the slogan 'Together in the Defence of Life'. And in addition to working directly on health issues, the Community Movement has been active in campaigns to defend people's access to land in order to grow food, because, as Plunkett has pointed out, 'The deterioration in people's health will continue as long as they are unable to feed themselves. No amount of health education or care will remedy the vulnerability of malnourished adults or children' (Plunkett, 1995: 203). This point emphasises, once again, the links between community health education and the problems of economic and social development more generally.

So far, this discussion has focused upon Third World experiences, but there have been parallels, in Britain, and other First World contexts, and ideas and experiences have been exchanged between North and South. In Britain, the Community Health Movement together with the Women's Health Movement grew, from the late sixties and seventies, linking a positive view of health with collective approaches to the social causes of ill-health (CDF *et al*, 1988). Community health projects have focused upon better access to information and resources and increased self-confidence amongst people in local communities. The aim has been to promote improved working relationships between professionals and service users, and greater public influence over health policies and resources.

Some of these objectives can be achieved through community education targeted at individual users. But the broader goals of influencing health policies and campaigning against the social causes of ill health relate to more collective forms of community education. Participatory action research has been relevant here, too.

There has been a wide range of community health education initiatives of this more collective and participatory type. In addition, the Women's Health Movement has ensured that issues of gender have been raised as central to community health, as well as issues of class (in parallel with the concern about the gender implications of health in the South). This was not simply that women have tended to take responsibility for health within families, but because health also raises fundamental issues of power and control, in terms of gender as well as in terms of class.*

For example, Chapter Two referred to community education, as well as workplace education projects, through the WEA in the North-Western District, projects which included Health Education for Women (North-Western WEA, 1988). Through this pioneering project, 'substantial numbers of women who previously had had little to do with adult education became involved in courses being organised by the Workers' Educational Association' (ibid, p.1). Whilst women, in both community and workplace settings, wanted access to information through these courses, they also wanted far more than that. Women were also wanting to explore ways of developing their rights for choice and control, including control in childbirth, birth control and fertility. In addition, women were wanting to explore ways of changing underlying power relationships, between women and men, as well as between professionals and users, in the wider context of public resources or lack of resources for health care. And women were also wanting to raise issues about the underlying causes of ill-health (including accidents in the workplace).

In WEA tradition, the courses involved participatory methods, especially group discussions, as well as role plays, for example. And the courses were free, with childcare provided, to make them genuinely accessible to women, regardless of their incomes or family responsibilities. There was also a focus upon follow-up activities, such as the development of self-help groups (and a limited number of such groups were set up, although more might have been achieved, in this respect, if more resources had been available). There were, the evaluation report concluded, no magic formulas for increasing women's participation, in the community or in the workplace, but women's health courses had a valuable part to play in the process. This was especially so, since they were reaching women who had not previously been involved in adult education.

---

* (These issues include the most basic rights of women to have control over their own bodies, their own fertility and their own sexuality.)

Community health education has been particularly relevant for women. But it has been relevant, too, in a range of ways, to a wide variety of groups concerned to challenge their oppression and exploitation. Racism, in society in general, and racism in relation to health, more specifically, has compounded the particular forms of oppression which are experienced, for example, by those with disabilities or mental health problems. These are problems whose underlying causes, in turn, relate to wider structures of exploitation, oppression and discrimination in society. So, for instance, black people with mental health needs have been more likely to experience compulsory treatment, but less likely to be offered psychotherapy or counselling, which might have supported them and prevented the need for more serious forms of intervention. These problems have been compounded by the lack of transcultural therapy and counselling to meet their needs in appropriate ways (Webb-Johnson, 1991).

Community health education, broadly defined to include support for self-help groups and self-advocacy groups, can contribute to more positive outcomes here. Downer and Ferns, for instance, have emphasised the potential importance of self-advocacy by black people with learning difficulties, to challenge their oppression from racism, combined with disablism. 'Black people with learning difficulties', even more than white people with learning difficulties, 'are seen as child-like, pathetic and in need of "care"; or as threatening, aggressive and in need of "control" ', they argue (Downer and Ferns, 1993: 139). 'Care services', as they point out, 'and many of the professionals who work in them are not aware how often black disabled people have power taken away from them, often by services themselves' (ibid, p.139). Self-advocacy can help 'to reduce negative experiences and increase positive experiences for black people with learning difficulties', they argue (p.140), and groups which have been trained in self-advocacy can help people to know what they want and to be stronger in standing up for their rights, with greater self-confidence. There is a vital role here for support services, including education and training, provided, of course, that this education and training support is offered on the groups' own terms. (Although, as Downer and Ferns also point out, of course, even this will not break down the barriers faced by black people with disabilities if other people, including relevant professionals, 'do not really want to listen' (p.143).

There is, then, a widening range of opportunities for adult educators to support communities of interest, those who share and identify common interests and experiences of oppression, and who share a commitment to challenging these forms of oppression. In the British context, the implementation of Care in the Community, following the NHS and Community Care Act, has brought some of these issues to the fore, and especially so in view of the policy provisions for involving users and carers. Once again, this demonstrates some of the inherent tensions within market-led approaches to health and welfare. On the one hand, market-led approaches emphasise individual choices and the role of market-led service provision, reinforced by self-help, to contain public spending and ensure value for money. And on the other hand, this entails increasing pressures for more resources for improved, more appropriate and less discriminatory services, and for addressing the underlying causes of ill-health, once users are consulted and the Pandora's box of user and community participation is opened.

Issues of ageism are important here, too, as well as issues of sexism and racism. Summarising the range of initiatives which have been developed to involve older people in planning and evaluating community care, Thornton and Tozer have reflected that there has been a great growth, although much remains to be done. And this growth of initiatives has included educational work, in order to support and equip older people to participate. For example, this has been the case with training programmes to provide skills for participation *via* the Greater London Forum for the Elderly. 'A variety of initiatives have illustrated how older people can be encouraged to achieve self-development, both individually and collectively. It seems important', Thornton and Tozer add, 'that appropriate support is available, whether through access to information or the development of confidence and specific skills, if older people are to contribute to community care in effective ways' (Thornton and Tozer, 1994: 22). Similar points have been emphasised in the study by Martin and Gaster, for instance, demonstrating that a developmental approach to consultation 'implies support for processes of empowerment', including knowledge and understanding, through seminars and joint training (Martin and Gaster, 1993: 49).

Amongst the examples of collective approaches which Thornton and Tozer quoted in this context, is the case of the Oxford Pensioners Action Group (OXPAG) who participated in an action research project, to explore older people's views on the development of Community Care services and to feed this into the Community Care planning process. OXPAG had a history of lively activity in the area, both in representing their members' views, through regular consultation processes, and through direct campaigning, taking part in local, national and international (European level) campaigns on issues of direct concern. This particular project of Participatory Action Research was carried out in partnership with Ruskin College, with the active support of key professionals and with a grant from a charitable fund. This provided the basic resources to enable the interviews to be completed and the report compiled. So the project provided an example of PAR, supported with local adult education resources. And the project also raised a number of broader issues, as the following summary explains. This sets the project within the framework of more holistic approaches to health and community care, which, in turn links back to the holistic approach to community profiling which was outlined in the previous chapter and in the first part of this chapter.

OXPAG has been a strong and well-organised pensioners' group, building upon the organisational networks which have been built up over the years in the city. In particular, key members of pensioners' organisations in Oxford have included a number of former trade union activists. On retirement, they brought their previous organisational and political skills and contacts with them into the pensioners' movement. And unsurprisingly, given the traditional manufacturing base which was described in outline in the previous chapter, former Cowley car workers were well represented in these networks. OXPAG, itself, is a federation of different groups, including the Transport and General Workers Union's retired members' group.

OXPAG is represented on a number of organisations which are concerned with health and welfare issues in the area, including the Community Health Council, and these issues are regularly discussed at the lively and well-attended public meetings which OXPAG organises. In addition to a small grant to assist in the organisational work, at the time leading up to the PAR project a professional social worker with relevant responsibilities for Community Care used to attend OXPAG committee meetings, by invitation, to provide information and advice. This was a relevant factor, because this professional's information and advice was trusted and valued, and this trust set the context for the high levels of co-operation which subsequently characterised this project.

Whilst OXPAG had important background knowledge and experience in getting involved in Community Care planning issues, however, their overall focus was far wider, covering campaigning on pensions and benefits, as well as on a range of local issues. And OXPAG's view of health, itself, was a wide and inclusive one; members were involved in 'Agewell', which, as the title suggests, is concerned with promoting the active well-being of older people, *via* access to leisure, recreation and adult education, for example. This included access to adult education programmes at Ruskin, planned by and for older people themselves (Hughes, 1992).

The involvement of the pensioners in planning for Community Care for 1992-3 depended on both the commitment of the planning authority, and the key professionals concerned, and, of course the commitment and energy of the pensioners themselves. As part of this involvement, they decided that they needed far more systematic information about the views of pensioners, including the views of those pensioners who did not come to meetings (whether because they chose not to, or because attending meetings or clubs was difficult for them, in practice. This was, of course, a major problem, especially for the less mobile, and for those who were housebound altogether). In the event, OXPAG worked together, drawing upon the research support available to them, to plan the research, design the questionnaire, pilot it, and then analyse the findings and compile the report.

The findings, which were summarised and fed into the consultation process, included some very specific views about service planning. For example, there was widespread concern about the reorganisation of home care services, to concentrate resources on those in greatest need (pensioners generally thought that the resources for this service were inadequate and that the service was far too restricted). In general, in fact, pensioners' criticisms were about the insufficiency of services, rather than about the type of services which were provided. Pensioners wanted more of the same, rather than different services. The survey also demonstrated the disturbing probability that considerable numbers of older people were not receiving benefits to which they were entitled (an issue which was fed back to relevant professionals, for further and immediate action). There were also particular questions about whether older black people were receiving adequate services, and why they were so under-represented, for example, amongst the users of many of the clubs and day centres in the area. This raised issues about the accessibility and the appropriateness of services provided. OXPAG subsequently explored some of these issues further, working together with black older people's groups.

More generally, however, the survey confirmed the view that older people, in general, were very active and involved already in community care as providers of care. There was evidence of widespread mutual support; older people providing neighbourly services for each other (such as shopping for a neighbour if she or he was unwell). And older people were often carers themselves, caring, for example, for a partner with disabilities. (This finding is in line with findings from other studies.)

Whilst pensioners did have strong views on health and welfare issues related to community care, however, their views on well-being were much wider than that – a finding which was consistent with their wider campaigning interests. The inadequacy of pensions was a major concern; adequate incomes being considered essential to well-being. Community safety was a matter of concern too (they wanted more 'bobbies on the beat'). And transport also emerged as a major issue, both in relation to transport to health and welfare services, and in relation to transport to leisure and recreation services, more generally. Their priorities for well-being included access to clubs (such as lunch clubs) and to a range of hobbies and leisure interests, including community education provision. Their views on community care and well-being more generally fitted into a holistic approach – an approach which older people were actively interested in promoting and pursuing; although with the caveat that their interest in being consulted was dependent on seeing some tangible changes. Taken together, then, the results of this PAR project by older people in Oxford provides further inputs to the first outline sketch of the type of Community Profile which began to emerge in the previous chapter. This, in turn, brings the discussion back to the question of holistic approaches and alternative strategies, and to the case of Oxford, as an example of some of the dilemmas of developing such strategies in practice. But before moving on to this, there are issues to be summarised around housing, land use, planning and the environment, more generally.

Community education and housing, planning and environmental issues

At the outset of this chapter, it was suggested that there has been a long history of connections here: connections between health and well-being, on the one hand, and housing and environmental concerns, on the other. Housing, planning and environmental questions have been centrally important to community development, and to community education, in urban contexts especially, although the way in which these concerns have been addressed has, of course, varied. In particular, environmental issues have taken on new, and far more explicit, prominence as environmental movements have developed, globally, in recent years.

In the British context, tenant action has been a specific focus. There has been a long history of community action around housing issues, dating at least from the First World War, and even earlier. Tenants organised around immediate issues such as rent levels and housing conditions, and they also organised campaigns over housing policy, and tenants' rights more generally (Cowley, 1979; Smith, 1992). Community educators have supported these tenants' initiatives in a variety of ways, providing examples of technical support as well as examples of adult education in support of community action and wider political strategies for change.

For example, the adult educators who worked with the Liverpool Community Development Project provided educational sessions, on the implications of major changes in housing policy (*via* the Housing Finance Act, which was being debated in 1972). These educational inputs covered aspects of the political economy of housing, as well as more practical issues relating to the organisation of a rent strike. The tenants went on to political campaigning (putting up tenants' candidates in a local election). Further political education sessions ensued – a process which shaped subsequent thinking about approaches to working class education, including Second Chance to Learn, in Liverpool (a joint university and WEA initiative) and the establishment of Northern College in 1978 (Yarnit, 1980). Northern College continued this strand of working with tenants and tenants' organisations, both within the area and beyond (including educational work with tenants' federations more widely). This work with tenants has taken place alongside Northern College's continuing work with trade unions, credit unions, women's organisations, black groups and organisations of people with disabilities.

More recently, experiences of tenant education and training at Northern College have illustrated some of the tensions inherent in government social policies, together with some of the tensions inherent in different approaches to adult community education and training. The provision of affordable rented housing has been particularly seriously affected by reductions in public expenditure. Market-led approaches to publicly-rented housing, in the eighties, and beyond, have also promoted privatisation (through council house sales), together with a range of policies to increase the scope for market mechanisms, and to reduce the role of the traditional providers of publicly-rented housing – the local authorities.

In summary, Grayson has argued, the focus of government policy for tenant education and training is for training for participation in management co-operatives. These tenant management co-operatives are, in turn, key to government policies for managing marketisation in housing; breaking up the traditional predominance of public (ie, local authority) housing in the rented sector. Tenant management co-operatives were to promote tenant choice, and to encourage self-help and the most effective use of scarce resources for housing management, although the underlying decisions about the level and allocation of these resources would remain with central government. Grayson has drawn parallels here with market-led policies for the local management of schools and for trusts in the National Health Service. 'Managing the crisis of government funding in this way has become standard throughout the Welfare State', he has argued. 'The blame for service cuts is neatly deflected on to local, apparently democratic or responsive management rather than their political fundholders' (Grayson, 1995). The net effect on tenant activists, he has concluded, has been to pressurise them into a network of organisations and institutions, to socialise them into participation in terms of managing the problems, rather than campaigning or organising politically around housing issues and social change.

In parallel, tenant education has gained a higher profile, but through becoming more focused upon training, as part of more tightly defined and managed processes. The Department of the Environment, Grayson suggests, has been looking to promote tenant training in relation to rigorously identified competencies and training outputs. But despite these pressures, Grayson suggests, tenant organisations have not been fully incorporated. On the contrary, in fact, 'there is still a massive membership of tenants' organisations', and there is evidence of a revival of interest in self-financing mechanisms, amongst tenants, in order to maintain their independence (ibid).

And even within existing schemes, adult educators have developed training programmes which do include the wider (ie, political) issues, alongside the more technical aspects of tenant training for participation. Grayson refers to the experiences of this broader approach, at Northern College, as well as through Fircroft College in Birmingham (colleges which, it will be recalled, both drew upon the ideas of Freire in developing their distinctive approaches, as well as drawing upon the traditions of Highlander and the Folk High Schools).

In the case of tenant education and training, this distinctive approach involved both content and methods, including the political economy of housing, and doing so in ways which gave tenant organisations space to join in planning the curriculum in participative ways. 'Thus', Grayson concludes, 'spaces do still exist but radical practice can only occupy them if training for incorporation and mystification is challenged' (*ibid*). Quoting from Lovett's views, he points out that the choices are clear; on the one hand a more limited, instrumental approach to training, without encouraging dreams of a new society; and on the other hand, a wider approach to education for critical thinking: a process of action and reflection.

Education for critical thinking on housing, in addition, involves education for critical thinking on wider land use planning and environmental issues. In the context of this chapter, there is space only for the very briefest of summaries. But the point does need to be made that the housing crisis, so visibly demonstrated by the presence of so many homeless people in Britain's cities, is not the product of housing policies alone. Land use planning policies and property development processes have also been important factors within the wider context of underlying patterns of economic and social change. During the eighties, in particular, market-led approaches to planning in Britain emphasised the importance of deregulation. Public intervention was to be kept to a minimum, with some limited 'pump-priming' to encourage the private property market to promote the most profitable forms of regeneration. The benefits of these developments would then 'trickle down', in terms of housing, as well as in terms of economic and environmental regeneration.

London's Docklands was to be one of the show-pieces of this approach. But after a decade of market-led planning, critics have argued, this was a dream turned to nightmare. In practice, the market had not simply been left to its own devices, because substantial public funds were deployed to subsidise the land and infrastructure in order to encourage private property developers to invest. There were criticisms of the effectiveness of this approach from a range of viewpoints, including the Audit Commission. Docklands was a contradiction, in its own market-led terms. And far from the benefits trickling down, Docklands 'turned into a nightmare of deregulated planning and massive over-development' (Coupland, 1992: 161). In particular, land was developed for what were thought to be the most profitable uses, especially offices and some luxury housing, which had the effect of pricing out less profitable uses, such as affordable housing.

The end result was increased economic and social polarisation; which had been precisely what community planning initiatives in Docklands, and in London more generally, had been trying to avoid. In contrast, community planning initiatives had been working to involve local communities, together with planners, in developing alternative approaches to regeneration. Community planning started from social needs, rather than market-led definitions of what might be most profitable. And community planning initiatives have included co-operative and non-profit-making schemes for affordable housing and local amenities, as in the case of the Coin Street development on London's South Bank, for example (Nicholson, 1992).

Community planning requires both technical knowledge and a critical understanding of land use planning and property development processes – as well as a critical understanding of the underlying economic and social pressures which are affecting the area in question. And this, in turn, entails community education and training and access to research support. There are a range of examples to illustrate this point, including examples from the CDP and the GLC experiences which were raised in the context of the previous chapter. In London, a powerful example has been provided more recently, in the case of controversies over the redevelopment of King's Cross. This site of 40 ha of under-used land is just north of the King's Cross and St Pancras railway stations, on the edges of London's metropolitan centre. A local action group was established in 1987, when it was feared that redevelopment proposals would concentrate upon office developments, together with an international railway development (for the Channel Tunnel link.) In contrast, local people wanted redevelopment proposals which would address social needs (including the need for affordable social housing). In the event, there have been changes of policy anyway (with changes in the plans for the Channel Tunnel terminus, as well as changes in the perceived profitability of office developments with the downturn of the London office market since 1989). But at the time, the 'umbrella' campaigning group, the Railway Lands Group, understandably feared that they faced a major threat to the area, and they needed research support, urgently.

With grants from the local councils and from the Royal Institute of British Architects (RIBA) Community Architecture fund, they were able to find technical support from a team of planners from University College, London. With this support, they went on to develop their own alternative plan for the area, which sought a compromise between financial pressures for viability, on the one hand, and community needs, on the other (especially the need for affordable social housing). The work was consolidated at a 'planning weekend' in 1990.

This event, which has been described as being 'extremely stimulating', brought together professionals, local activists and residents in 'a five-day brainstorm'. Together, through this process, this group generated the alternative draft plan. As a result, local people gained increased confidence that 'alternatives are really possible, and that further moves could be made away from the office city towards meeting more social needs and goals and having a much greater diversity of activities' (Edwards, 1992: 180). This was a very particular example of community education and training, and participatory action research, in practice. The plans were subsequently given the second of two prizes for innovation awarded by the Royal Town Planning Institute and RIBA for the London region. The prize of redevelopment to meet social needs, in practice, has typically been more problematic, however.

More recently in Britain, there has again been increasing focus upon community participation in comprehensive approaches to regeneration.

(This renewed interest can be related back to the discussion of some of the inherent limitations of the more extreme versions of free-marketeering discussed earlier in this chapter). Government programmes such as 'City Challenge' and the 'Single Regeneration Budget' initiatives have specifically required community participation (Atkinson and Moon, 1994; Blackman, 1995). So what does this actually mean, in practice? In summary, initiatives such as City Challenge *have* provided some space for community participation. But there are inherent tensions within this type of framework, including tensions in relation to community education and training associated with it.

To come back to Oxford, some of these points may be traced in that city's successful bid, in 1994, for a 'Single Regeneration Budget' (SRB) bid to regenerate the Blackbird Leys/Cowley area. From the previous chapter, it will be recalled that this part of Oxford had been particularly seriously affected by the loss of jobs in the motor industry, as the Rover plant was restructured. The employment and social problems which resulted from these changes in the manufacturing base formed part of the case for arguing that the area needed additional government resources for a renewal programme when the bids for the SRB bids were prepared. In addition, and this was particularly crucial, in terms of the government's priorities, (which emphasised the importance of private sector participation), local employers were prepared to involve themselves. Rover led the way, here, with a key financial contribution to the new Training Centre (part of its social responsibility to the area, to assist in the re-adjustment process). The Training Centre's focus was upon providing specific skills to enable local people to take up jobs, together with training to support business start ups.

The 'partners' for this SRB bid were the local authorities, together with the Training and Enterprise Council and other private sector interests, and with educational and community organisations. These latter interests did include, for example training projects for women, and for black and minority ethnic groups, and there was some provision for supporting community projects, including credit unions. But the very tight timescale for putting the bid together, coupled with the uncertainty about what, if anything, might ultimately be funded, made it extremely difficult to involve a wider range of community organisations more fully (although efforts were made to consult local people).

At the time of writing, the SRB was still at a very early stage. The point to emphasise here, is not, of course, that there is no scope for community participation, or for positive programmes of community education as well as training. But the structure of the programme has inherent tensions – between the goals of comprehensive regeneration with community participation, on the one hand, and the constraints of government guidelines, coupled with market-led priorities, including market-led priorities for training, on the other hand. In the earlier discussions, there were, for example, proposals for community education outreach work, and for a very broad approach to this, drawing upon the experiences of training agencies, including the women's training centre, together with the churches, the WEA and Ruskin. The aim was to meet the educational interests of individuals as well as their immediate training needs, and to meet the needs of community organisations, concerned to explore the underlying economic, social, political and cultural aspects of their situation – as the prelude for developing strategies for change – adult community education for transformation.

In addition, there are inherent difficulties within any small area based programme for regeneration. Neighbouring housing estates were suffering from similar problems – high unemployment, underemployment, casualisation, low wages and poverty, together with the social problems which are associated with these. Yet, any benefits from the SRB were supposed to be concentrated in the target area, according to the ground rules. This poses major questions about how comprehensive such an approach could really be, citywide. And there are inherent difficulties, more generally, in local responses to problems which clearly involve wider interests, both wider private sector interests, and wider government interests and policies.

The scope for effective community participation in shaping regeneration programmes of this type is problematic, then. To analyse the space available, the room for creative manoeuvre, requires a critical understanding of the different interests involved, the powers as well as the policies of the key stakeholders. The land and property development interests are potentially important factors to analyse here as well as the interests of the major employers, and the (limited) powers and policies of local government, as well as the (more extensive) powers and policies of central government. This, in turn, raises other aspects of the community profile which needs to be compiled, through participatory action research; aspects which emerge in the following chapter.

References

Atkinson, D. (1994) *The Common Sense of Community*, Demos, London

Atkinson, R. and Moon, G. (1994) *Urban Policy in Britain: The city, the state, the market*, Macmillan.

Bingham, J., James, A. and Mayo, M. (1993) 'Including older people in community care planning', in P. Berseford and T. Harding (eds) *A Challenge to Change*, National Institute of Social Work, pp. 89–98.

Blackman, T. (1995) *Urban Policy in Practice*, Routledge.

Brenton, M. (1985) *The Voluntary Sector in British Social Services*, Longman.

Burchell, B. (1994) 'The effects of labour market position, job insecurity, and unemployment on psychological health', in D. Gallie *et al.*(eds) *Social Change and the Experience of Unemployment*, Oxford University Press, pp. 188–212.

Clarke, J. (1991) *Democratising Development: The role of voluntary organisations*, Earthscan.

Commission for Social Justice (1994) *Social Justice: Strategies for national renewal*, Vintage.

Community Development Foundation, Health Education Authority and Scottish Health Education Group (1988) *Action for Health*, CDF. Cornia, G. (1987) 'Economic decline and human welfare in the first half of the 1980s', in G. Cornia *et al.* (eds) *Adjustment with a Human Face*, Clarendon Press, Oxford, pp. 11–47.

Cornia, G. (1987) 'Social policy-making: restructuring, targeting efficiency', in G. Cornia et al. (eds) *ibid.*, pp. 165–182.

Coupland, A. (1992) 'Every job an office job', in A. Thornley (ed.) *The Crisis of London*, Routledge, pp. 25–36.

Cowley, J. (1979) Housing for People or Profit?, Stage One, London

Craig, G. and Mayo, M. (eds) (1995) Community Empowerment; a reader in participation and development, Zed, London

Downer, J. and Ferns, P. (1993) 'Self-Advocacy by Black People with learning difficulties' in P Beresford and T Harding, A Challenge to Change, National Institute of Social Work, London, pp. 138–146

Edwards, M. (1992) 'A Microcosm: Redevelopment Proposals at kings Cross' in Thornley, A. (ed) The Crisis of London, Routledge, London, pp. 163–184

Glennerster, H. and Midgely, J. (eds) (1991) The Radical Right and the Welfare State, Harvester Wheatsheaf, London

Grayson, J. (1995) 'Training the Community- The Case of Tenant Training' in Mayo, M. and Thompson, J. (eds) Adult Education and Critical Intelligence, NIACE, Leicester

Hawtin, M., Hughes, G. and Percy-Smith, J. (1994) *Community Profiling: Auditing social needs*, Open University Press, Buckingham.

Hope, A. and Timmel, S. (1984) Community Workers' Handbook, 1, Mambo Press, Gweru, Zimbabwe

Hughes, K. (1992) 'Opening Doors for Older Learners' in Adults Learning, Vol 4, No 4, 1992

Korten, D. (1990) Getting to the 21st Century; Voluntary Action and the Global Agenda, Kumarian Press, West Hartford, USA

McGivney, V. and Murray, F. (1991) *Adult Education in Development*, NIACE.

Martin, L. and Gaster, L. (1993) 'Community Care Planning in Wolverhampton' in R Smith et al., (eds) Working Together for Better Community Care, SAUS, Bristol

Mayo, M. (1994) Communities and Caring; the mixed economy of welfare, Macmillan, London

Moser, C. (1989) 'Community Participation in Urban Projects in the Third World' in Diamond, D. et al., Progress in Planning, vol 32, part 2, Pergamon, Oxford.

Murray, C. (1990) The Emerging British Underclass, IEA Health and Welfare Unit, London

Nicholson, G. (1992) 'The Rebirth of Community Planning' in A Thornley (ed) The Crisis of London, Routledge, London, pp. 119–133

Plunkett, H. (1995) 'The Nicaraguan Community Movement: In Defence of Life' in G Craig and M Mayo (eds) Community Empowerment; a reader in participation and development, Zed, London, pp. 194–205)

Powell, T. (1987) Self-Help Organisations and Professional Practice, Maryland NASW Press, Silver Springs, USA.

Richardson, A. (1984) Working with Self-Help Groups: a guide forlocal professionals, NCVO, London

Smith, J. (1992) Community Development and Tenant Action, Community Development Foundation, London

Thomas, A. (1992) 'Non Governmental Organisations and the Limits to Empowerment' in Mackintosh, M. and Wuyts, M. (eds) Development Policy and Public Action, Oxford University Press, Oxford

Walt, G. (1990) Community Health Workers in National Programmes, Open University Press,

Walt, G. and Wield, D. (1983) 'Post-independence: Constructing the new health services in Mozambique' in Open University Course U 204, Third World Studies, Open University Press.

Walt, G. and Melamed, A. (eds) (1983) Mozambique: Towards a People's Health Service, Zed, London

Wann, M. (1995) Building Social Capital; Self help in a twenty-first century welfare state, IPPR, London

WEA/North Western District (1988) Health Education for Women, WEA/North Western District, Manchester

Webb-Johnson, A. (1991) A Cry for Change- An Asian Perspective on developing Quality Mental Health Care, Confederation of indian Organisations, UK.

Widgery, D. (1979) Health in Danger, Macmillan, London

Yarnit, M. (1980) 'Second Chance to Learn, Liverpool: class and adult education' in Thompson, J. (ed) Adult Education for a Change, Hutchinson, London

Chapter Six

Analysing political power and building alliances for transformation

This chapter starts from the questions which were posed at the end of Chapter Five: questions about how to analyse local power structures, and key stakeholders' interests. How can we develop a critical understanding of the sources of power, and the limitations of power, at the local level, as the basis for developing strategies which are realistic and effective in the here and now, as well as having longer-term potential, in terms of the goals of transformation? What is the nature and extent of the interests which need to be challenged? And how do we identify the potential for building alliances between those with shared interests, where these interests converge?

There are key questions, here, for adult education for political participation, community participation and citizenship, questions which relate, in turn, to underlying differences of approach, within adult education and training. But before engaging with these debates about different approaches to adult political education, and education for citizenship, there are terms which need to be clarified. 'Power', itself, has been conceptualised in different ways, with divergent implications for the analysis of the structures and sources of power, whether locally, or more generally. And community power structures, in turn, have been subjected to varying types of analysis, depending upon the theoretical approach which has been adopted.

What is meant by the term 'power'? Weber's definition of power as 'the chance of a man (*sic*) or number of men to realize their own will in a communal action even against the resistance of others who are participating in the action' has been taken as a classic starting point in political sociology, emphasising that power consists in the ability to get your own way, even when others oppose your wishes. Ultimately, power rests upon the ability to coerce; but coercion does not need to be exercised when power is seen to be legitimate, and therefore to be obeyed. Typically, then, the modern state has the means of coercion – the police, the criminal justice system, the armed forces.

But most people accept the state's power as legitimate authority, at least for most of the time. And even if they break particular rules, themselves, most people accept the legitimacy of most of the rules – in general – or at least as far as others are concerned (their own rule-breaking behaviour being seen, perhaps, as a justifiable, or at least an excusable exception). This point about power and legitimacy is important in relation to subsequent discussions about political education and consciousness. The issue of legitimacy has already been raised in the context of the discussion of Gramsci's approach to this, in Chapter One, together with Gramsci's emphasis on the importance of challenging the dominance of ruling class ideology, questioning the legitimacy of the *status quo*.

So far, then, power has been conceptualised in terms of two aspects, coercion on the one hand, and legitimacy on the other. Lukes has taken this discussion further, distinguishing three dimensions of power (Lukes, 1974). The first dimension of power relates to 'decision-making': who has the power to affect which decisions? Lukes distinguishes this from the second dimension of power, power in relation to 'non-decision making'. This second dimension involves the power to reduce the options available, or to keep issues out of the decision-making process altogether. For example, a community might be consulted about which of two routes they would prefer for a proposed new road, but not about whether they want such a new road at all.

The third dimension of power, according to Lukes, is the underlying power to shape people's wishes and preferences; so that they do not even recognise the reality when power is used in ways which are detrimental to their interests (Lukes, 1974). For example, the oppressed may be socialised to accept their situation as inevitable, normal, even as legitimate. They may internalise the views and values of the oppressor. This corresponds to the situation which Freire identified when he pointed out that the oppressed can become the 'host' of the oppressor, inside themselves, 'having internalized the image of the oppressor and adopted his guidelines' (Freire, 1972: 23). This was the situation which, he argued, needed to be analysed critically, and challenged, through conscientisation.

This third dimension of power brings the discussion closer to Marxist approaches. Marxists have gone on to argue that power has to be understood, ultimately, in the context of the mode of production. And in capitalist society power has to be understood in terms of the relations between those who control the means of production and those who produce surplus value. This does not mean, of course, that capitalists, the ruling class, and the state, can simply be equated, the one with the other; the ruling class, in political terms, need not necessarily be the dominant economic class, in any particular case.

But it does mean that the framework within which political power is wielded is constrained by the requirements of capitalist production (which includes the reproduction of capitalist social relations). So political power is not free-floating, or randomly distributed, according to Marxists. Nor is the distribution of bias or the restriction of options – Lukes's second dimension of power – randomly distributed. On the contrary, in fact, according to Marxists, these biases operate to reinforce the legitimacy of capitalist relations of production; or in more common parlance, to reinforce the view that 'there is no alternative' to the predominance of the market economy; and that 'there is no alternative' to the common sense of market-led approaches to tackling economic, social, political and cultural issues (Therborn, 1982). This brings the discussion back again to Gramsci, and to his emphasis on the importance of understanding, through political education and political struggle, that there *are* alternatives.

How, then, have these different approaches to the conceptualisation of power related, in turn, to the analysis of power and community power structures, in practice? Classic American sociological debates on community power structures in the post-Second World War period focused upon whether power was concentrated in a 'power elite', typically dominated by local businessmen, as Hunter's study of Atlanta argued (Hunter, 1953). These elites could be identified through the powerful reputations of their members, locally.

Alternatively, through focusing upon the outcomes of particular decision-making processes, rather than upon the reputations of the supposedly powerful, Dahl argued that no such concentrations of power within a 'power elite' could be identified, locally. On the contrary, he argued that studying the outcomes of decision-making, over an issue such as urban renewal plans, demonstrated that there were different and competing interest groups involved in a bargaining process. So the trade unions, for instance, as well as business interests, competed alongside the local university, whilst the local authority acted as the arbitrator, negotiating to achieve an outcome which would be acceptable to all sides (Dahl, 1961). Everyone had power, at least potentially, and the local state was neutral.

In contrast, critics, including Marxist critics, have argued that focusing upon the outcomes of decision-making is insufficient. To understand the nature and sources of power also requires focusing upon 'non-decision-making': which are the issues which never reach the formal political agenda at all? Which issues are literally out of the question, and why? This was the approach which informed the Inter-Project Editorial Team of the Community Development Projects' analysis of state intervention, to tackle poverty and deprivation, within 12 localities in Britain.

Their report *Gilding the Ghetto* (CDP, 1977) argued that government had defined the problems of the older industrial areas as marginal problems, in need of minor policy adjustments – more co-ordination of services here, a little more community spirit and self-help there. What had not been placed on the public agenda were the underlying problems of capital restructuring, the dynamics of the making and breaking of the older industrial areas. Nor was the role of the state (in promoting restructuring strategies to enhance the profitability of private capital) put into question.

In practice, then, according to this type of approach, local community power structures cannot be fully understood by 'reputational' approaches, to identify who has the reputation for being powerful, as individuals or groups. Even community power studies which are based upon the analysis of the outcomes of decision-making processes are insufficient, by themselves. Power within local communities can only be fully analysed, according to this approach, by taking account of the underlying interests of capital, and state policies towards these interests, at both local and national levels. Typically, this also requires taking the analysis even further, because local plants may be owned by wider conglomerates, and even if they are not, they would still be crucially affected by wider market factors. As globalisation has proceeded apace, this last point has become even more relevant.

How, then, does this discussion of the analysis of community power structures relate to debates about adult political education and education for citizenship? There has been a history of concern with adult political education, as part of wider concerns with education for citizenship. In the pre-war period, the Association for Education for Citizenship was established to address the need for education for democracy, in response to the rise of totalitarian dictatorships. Bertrand Russell's lecture on Education for Democracy argued the case, in general, for an approach which would enable people to form their own views, and to be rather 'impervious to eloquence and propoganda' (Russell, 1937: 11). This related to a liberal approach, based upon the rights of individual citizens, an approach which stood in strong contrast with the devaluing of individual citizen's rights under totalitarianism.

Whilst emphasising individual rights, rather than collective rights, this liberal approach has some parallels, too, with more collective and more directly engaged political approaches. For example, Freire has reflected upon the importance of maintaining the distinction between political education and political propoganda, in ways which have some echoes of Russell's comments. So whilst arguing for the importance of politics in adult literacy work, and for the impossibility of neutrality, Freire has also emphasised that adult educators should not be in the business of giving people political 'lines': 'we do not have the right to say to the illiterate that the only good thing is to belong to the (Brazilian) Workers' Party', he pointed out, to illustrate this point. 'No. I do not have this right.' Freire has, however, argued that the adult educator has the duty to make political issues explicit, in critical ways. 'I have the duty to say that there are five, six, seven parties' he explained. 'I have the duty to discuss the ideology and the political choices of these different parties. I have also the duty of telling them which is my choice. I do not accept the neutrality which is to have a kind of hypocritical posture in the world.' 'What I cannot do', he concluded, however, was either to lie, 'or to impose my choice upon them' (Freire, 1995: 65).

In the British context, education for citizenship has been debated again in recent years, both in relation to children's education (education for citizenship being a required cross-curricular theme in the National Curriculum) and in relation to adults. Citizenship has been emphasised, and the rights of individual citizens enshrined in the Citizen's Charter, as 'one of the central themes of public life in the 1990s', in the Prime Minister John Major's words (Citizen's Charter, 1991: 2).

The Speaker's Commission on Citizenship added official recognition of some of the implications of citizenship, in terms of adult education. 'If adequate support is to be made available to enable men and women to organize themselves, and influence decision-making locally and nationally, adult education and community development are of paramount importance', the Report argued (*Report of the Speaker's Commission on Citizenship*, 1990: 39).

At this point, inherent tensions begin to emerge. On the one hand, the Conservative government's approach to citizenship was based upon emphasising individual rights and responsibilities. The Citizen's Charter was quite specifically not intended as a 'recipe for more state action: it is a testament of our belief in people's right to be informed and choose for themselves' (*Citizen's Charter*, 1991: 2). And this, in turn, fits into the market-led approach, with individuals making choices in the marketplace, with as little interference from the state as possible. Allen has summarised this approach in the following terms: 'the proper restricted role of the state is to enable free market forces to work unfettered by restrictive practices and to enable Active Citizens to accumulate wealth and to monopolize other scarce experiences' (Allen, 1992: 131).

Such an approach, based upon the Citizen's Charter, has been subjected to a number of criticisms, including the criticism that this represents a 'flimsy weapon' for the most deprived and excluded groups in society, 'people who have only one landlord to turn to, only one school to which they are entitled to send their children, only one doctor who serves their neighbourhood, and – at best – only one employer who might give them a job' (Donnison, 1994: 23). In addition, and more fundamentally, Donnison argued, in his contribution to the Commission on Social Justice, that this approach offers only the right to question the ways in which particular services are – or are not – delivered to them. 'Useful though those are, they are not the citizens' rights which enable people to question the way in which their society is evolving – to ask for a different kind of transport system, for more public housing or for housing allocated to different kinds of people, for example' (Donnison, 1994: 23). In Allen's terms, the space for critical reflection and dissent is lacking (Allen, 1992).

What are the implications, then, in relation to adult education for citizenship? Adult education for citizenship of the Citizen's Charter type would focus upon individual rights, together with some reference to the duties of patriotism and voluntary work, it has been suggested (Heater, 1992). As it had already been pointed out, in an earlier report by the Advisory Council for Adult and Continuing Education, adult political education needs to provide the information and skills 'which enable people to understand political processes and to participate in the determination and administration of public policy' (ACACE, 1983: 1).

But this is not simply a technical issue. If adults are to respond critically to all forms of indoctrination or propaganda (in the tradition set out by Bertrand Russell, and reinforced by Crick and others more recently) then they need critical education as well as technical training. One of the contributions to the ACACE report recognised precisely these tensions. Adults really needed to be educated to analyse power and the roots of power, Ridley suggested, if they were to participate effectively, whether as individuals or as members of organisations such as tenants' or parents' groups. Whether or not the state would decide to pay for such forms of political education, rather than confining the use of public funds to more limited forms of 'role education' (ie, education and training for the roles of tenant representatives or parent representatives) was seen as more problematic, however (Ridley, 1983). There are echoes, here, of some of the discussions about community education in the previous chapter, including the discussion of different approaches to tenants' education and training.

This relates to the type of more fundamental questioning which has been raised by Donnison and others. Education for citizenship, in this alternative framework, needs to promote 'a process of dialogue and commitment, rooted in a fundamental belief in the possibility of public life and the development of forms of solidarity that allow people to reflect and organize in order to criticize and constrain the power of the state and to overthrow relations which inhibit and prevent the realization of humanity' (Giroux, 1989, quoted in Smith, 1992: 106).

The implications of this latter type of approach for the analysis of community power structures are major. The 'Community Profiles' section, on local power structures, would need to go far beyond the 'reputational' approach to listing the individuals and the organisations which were perceived to hold power in the area, although that would be a relevant starting point. The analysis of 'outcomes' of decisionmaking processes would also be useful, to test out the ways in which power was being wielded locally by key actors and organisations. But that would need to be supplemented, in turn, by an analysis of the underlying interests, and the wider pressures on these, whether as a result of public policies, or whether as a result of external market forces. This is a potentially major undertaking, in terms of education and training, to enable the local community, including the local workforce, to tackle such a profile, through Participatory Action Research.

Analysing community power structures

Community power structure research of this type has been a feature of the Highlander Research and Education Center, for example. As Gaventa has commented, there are numerous examples (from Highlander's work and elsewhere) where people have 'learned to research their own power structures through gaining access to courthouse records about property transactions, tax rates, housing codes, land and mineral ownership, government records about company finance, military industries and so forth' (Gaventa, 1991: 123). In addition, workers and communities have learned how to research into the corporations which affect them, both locally, and in terms of their international connections and interests. And Gaventa has also drawn attention to the relevance of 'right to know' movements, involving workers, communities and professionals who share concerns about the environmental effects of toxic chemicals being used in their areas, for example.

Highlander provided numerous examples of this type of research support, to enable people to become researchers, to investigate for themselves, as well as drawing upon the research of professionals, and learning to use official statistics critically. Gaventa has located this approach within the 'European Gramscian tradition, which considers the capacity of every person to be an intellectual, and to develop a popular, organic knowledge that converts spontaneous common sense into "good sense"' (Gaventa, 1991: 127).

What does all this mean in practice? The following example provides an illustration. Drawing upon published materials on Highlander's work, adult educators from the William Temple Foundation in Manchester and Ruskin College ran an educational session with community groups, along these lines, at a residential weekend in the college, in 1992. This weekend, it should be emphasised, was part of a longer process of educational work with the groups in question, over a period of months, or longer, in some cases. So the work which was completed over the residential weekend was followed up, and developed, on an on-going basis. There was no way in which the issues involved in completing useful community economic profiles and community power profiles could have been disposed of within such a residential weekend, without such follow-up. Although this particular session was only one small part of a longer-term programme, the process of tackling some of the issues which were raised in the session may still provide some illustration of the approach, more generally.

The Highlander materials which were used as the basis for planning the session started with some reflections on power, from the written account of a woman activist who had worked with Highlander. She began by describing herself as a person who, initially, used to think that the American system was everything that she should believe in. But then the mines closed and people lost their jobs in her local community. This situation forced her to rethink her position. Her first reaction was to think that 'we had done something wrong'; that the mines closures were somehow the fault of the local workforce. It was only later that she learned that the company was still in the black; the mines could have been kept open and the workforce was in no way to blame. The company could simply make more money 'by leaving us stranded without jobs', because higher profits could be obtained by investing elsewhere.

Her deepened understanding of the situation came through working with Highlander. This process of analysis and critical reflection began
when she and her colleagues were asked about 'who was in charge' of
her area; who made the decisions; who owned what, which politicians
supported the miners or voted against them? Who had control?

From the analysis which followed this process of questioning, she
came to the conclusion that there was considerable overlap between the
people who had power in business circles, and the politicians with
formal political power, and that powerful professionals, including
lawyers and insurance people, worked alongside them. She learned
about some of the international connections involved. And she also
explored some of the connections between power and gender; being a
woman opened a lot of doors, she reflected, but it had been a problem
too, and not least amongst some of the older men in the community
who still thought that women's place was to be seen and not heard. She
concluded that her involvement in the research had been a wonderful
education, which had given her confidence and the ability to question:
'one day you wake up like me, a 38-year-old woman and you realize
that you have done all those things like you are supposed to. You paid
your taxes, you sent your children to school, you just accept. Then you
wake up one morning and you realize, it was the right way for the
multi-rich people, for these rich people in these wonderful houses, they
aren't hungry and aren't cold. But it's not the right way for you. Some
people just go back and accept it again. But I am not going to accept it.
I am going to bring about some changes.'

The community economic profile which the Highlander materials
outlined covered the ownership and uses of natural resources (including land) and the human resources in the area, education and skills
levels, incomes and poverty and where people worked in both formal
and informal economies. There was also information about health and
welfare, housing and other public services, and jobs in these, as well as
other key aspects of the local economy itself (sources of capital, banking, local and non-local businesses and enterprises, the informal and
domestic economy). So far, there are parallels with the discussion of
community economic profiles in Chapter Four. But the Highlander
approach did more than this, and took the process of developing the
community economic profile significantly further, by moving on to link
this to the question of power.

One approach to beginning to analyse the sources of power in the
community, which Highlander had developed, was to encourage
participants to brainstorm in small groups. What do we mean when we
talk about power? Who do we think has power to make economic
decisions and political decisions? Is there overlap between these two?
Where are decisions about issues such as jobs, education, community
safety, taxes, and public services actually made?

In subsequent discussions about the nature and location of power,
follow-up questions were suggested, to trigger further critical reflection

and analysis. For example, 'who would you see, if you wanted to get a public sector job?' was a question which could trigger further discussion about who controls these resources, and how important public sector jobs are in the local economy, as well as being important in terms of analysing the provision of local services. And this could lead to further questions about how decisions on different issues are taken – in public or behind closed doors? Which issues never emerge on the public agenda, in any case, and why is it that these issues are not subjected to public political debate? And who benefits from decisions which are taken or not taken, both directly and indirectly? What are the relationships between the people who take decisions and the people who benefit from these decisions? And how many people are involved in accepting the decisions which are taken by others (a trigger question which can bring out the fact that many decisions affect large numbers of people in the community, although these decisions may be taken by a relatively small number of people who have power concentrated in their hands – the power which the few can wield over the many)?

Through these discussions, power maps can be drawn up, and people can identify themselves in relation to these. This can then provide the basis for analysing where the power to take particular decisons lies, and how to develop strategies to affect these decisions. But it is not simply about assisting people to develop their understanding of the power that others wield, in their communities. The Highlander materials suggested that participants also needed to understand their *own* power in their communities, and as people, with power within themselves. This power can be used negatively, for example when men abuse their power over women in male-dominated societies, and white people abuse their power over black people. But conversely, people's power can be used positively and collectively, for change.

This approach raises the issue of empowerment, in terms of enabling people, individually, and collectively, to realise such power as they do have, and to use this power to the maximum effect. Even relatively powerless people have the potential for taking some power collectively, whether through their trade unions and political organisations or through women's groups, minority ethnic groups and community organisations. 'Empowerment', in this sense, is absolutely not based upon the view that power can simply be taken by anybody, in a society without underlying structures of bias. There *are* key structural constraints.

Rather, 'empowerment', in this sense, is based upon the view that even the exploited and the oppressed do still have *some* power. At the very least, they have the power to say 'no'. This power can be used, collectively, to challenge the powerful, and to work towards the longer-term goal of the transformation of existing power relationships. The objective here, though, is not to replace one set of powerful individuals and groups by another set – for the exploited and oppressed to become the exploiters and oppressors. In Freire's words 'the authentic solution of the oppressor-oppressed contradiction does not lie in a mere reversal of position, in moving from one pole to the other' (Freire, 1972: 33) but in transforming the very basis of power relationships, altogether.

A modified version of the Highlander community power exercise was worked through over the residential weekend in question. Participants tackled the questions in small groups, and their conclusions were brought back for joint discussions. Clearly, in the time available, it was not possible to explore the profiles in detail, although more detailed work could be taken forward, subsequently, through the continuing work with William Temple Foundation educators. Weekend exercises obviously do not substitute for the longer-term tasks of compiling official statistics, researching local companies, including their wider connections, listing local services and the range of local organisations, and surveying the views of local people and trade union and community groups. But even in the limited time which was available, this approach did lead to some critical explorations of the nature of power, and the sources of power, within the local communities in question.

The sources of economic power, in the context of restructuring, emerged relatively clearly, together with some of the connections between economic power and political power, and some of the constraints on local politicians as a result. So did some of the constraints which were due to central government policies, and central government controls on local government spending.

Some of the more contentious aspects related to the position of professionals in local communities. For example, social workers were amongst those who were identified as being powerful, with interests which conflicted with those of local people. In particular, they were seen as being powerful because they could take children away from the home, into the care of the local authority. Clearly, from the viewpoint of parents struggling to bring up their children, often in difficult circumstances, this *is* seen as a potential threat – even if social workers would be far less likely to see themselves, overall, as being particularly powerful. This provoked some discussion about the role of professionals and 'street-level bureaucrats' more generally, and the potential for building alliances between them and their clients, as well as the potential for conflicts of interest. Participants also reflected upon the question of their own power, both negative and positive, and considered strategies for working together, across the workplace/community divide, in empowering ways.

The discussion was realistic; people were only too well aware of the underlying constraints as well as the difficulties of building alliances to work for change. This fitted into the approach which had emerged from the Highlander materials. Underlying interests were to be identified, but possibilities for change were to be explored too. And potential allies were to be identified, in relation to particular issues, as well as potential opponents.

This final point about the identification of allies, as well as opponents, is one which will re-emerge, subsequently. How to distinguish between different types and levels of divisions and conflicts of interest; divisions *within* working-class communities, and divisions between different exploited and oppressed groups? The next chapter focuses specifically upon the role of adult education in addressing divisions in terms of race and gender, together with divisions between generations, young and older people, challenging discrimination and oppression, and respecting difference and valuing diversity, whilst developing joint strategies to tackle common problems.

But before moving on to these issues, the question of how to address divisions and conflicts of interest between different exploited and oppressed groups, within the framework of community power profiles, can be illustrated through an example of yet another type of conflict. The conflict, in this case, is based upon the religious divide cutting across working-class communities in Northern Ireland.

The context for this example is the Ulster People's College in Belfast, Northern Ireland, which was established in the 1982. The Ulster People's College has aimed to complement work in the field, 'to extend the process of action and learning in local communities; to reflect on their common problem; to learn from their different experiences and to discuss their cultural and political differences' (Lovett, 1995). The initiative was influenced by the radical independent tradition in adult education (including the work of Highlander, as well as the WEA, NCLC and Ruskin), a tradition which was to be applied to the particular circumstances of Northern Ireland, where social and economic problems were compounded by violence and sectarianism. The college was to provide an 'accessible secular, neutral venue where working-class people from both communities (ie, Catholic and Protestant) could come together to explore common problems and perceived differences' (Lovett, 1995).

Lovett has set out the background to this initiative. 'Working-class Protestants and Catholics were engaged in fighting the same problems of poverty, unemployment, redevelopment and the resulting alienation from those in authority' (Lovett, 1995). The problems were similar to those faced by working-class people elsewhere; but in Northern Ireland they were compounded by violence and sectarianism. Whilst there were a number of useful community education initiatives, in the seventies, Lovett argued, a more conscious and determined effort was required to grasp the nettle of community divisions and conflicts, and to work for peace and reconstruction.

The Ulster People's College has two major concerns: to assist people in both communities in searching for solutions to their many common problems (such as housing, unemployment, vandalism, lack of social and recreational facilities) and to 'help the two communities in Northern Ireland to communicate with each other, to appreciate and understand their respective traditions' (Lovett, *ibid*). This latter objective involved both developing understanding and respect for diversity, *and* developing a shared understanding of their common history and interests. The approach is not just non-sectarian, but anti-sectarian, exploring the root causes of sectarianism, in order to combat sectarianism.

The college provides short informal courses targeted at young people, women, community activists, trade unionists and peace and reconciliation groups. The starting point is where people are coming from, in terms of a critical understanding of their own culture and economic and social concerns. This then provides the basis for a critical understanding of current community divisions. Members of the different communities work together on these issues (with some separate discussions, too, where this helps to air issues more completely). There are residential weekends, seminars and conferences and some longer courses have also been developed in the college, including accredited courses in community development.

The aim is to promote social change, based upon anti-sectarianism, respect for people's identities, and the identification of common interests, across their diversities in Northern Ireland. This is political education in the broadest sense – political economy and the political situation in Northern Ireland, together with the political role of the churches, the role of the labour movement, and the cultures and identities of the two communities. Summarising the College's overall objectives, Lovett has referred to Freire's *Cultural Action for Freedom*; aiming to examine and explore people's communities 'in all their complexity in order to encourage the embracing of options which improve people's sense of identity, integrity, security and dignity. An emphasis on these manifestations of popular culture and politics from the base of society gives the People's College a specifically important function' (Lovett, *ibid*).

A community power profile in practice

Before moving on to other aspects of identity and diversity in the next chapter, this chapter concludes by summarising the discussion of community power structures so far. What would this type of analysis look like, in outline? In Chapter Four, the changing economic basis of Oxford was sketched out, as an example to illustrate a community economic profile. Oxford appeared again in the context of the discussion of regeneration strategies in Chapter Five. So how would an analysis of power in the city relate to the analysis of the local economy, which has already been summarised, and how would this, in turn, relate to debates about regenerating the local economy in Oxford?

In 1989, in response to proposals to close part of the Cowley car plant (the second of the three works), having already announced the loss of 2,500 of the 10,000 or so jobs, the City Council commissioned an independent inquiry into 'The Future of Cowley'. This inquiry gives a convenient starting point for the analysis of power, in the city and beyond; who were the key actors, and what were their different interests? How did these interests converge or diverge, and what, realistically, was the scope for alternative strategies, in response to the proposed closures?

The inquiry was headed by Lord McCarthy, an academic with relevant expertise. Together with his colleagues on the Panel, in 1990 he held some 23 public and seven closed sessions of the inquiry, receiving more than 80 submissions, over 200 letters and logging more than 400 telephone calls. This evidence, in total, provides a snapshot of the different interests involved. The report's conclusions also provide some relevant clues to the range of options which were seen as realistic by the different actors and interests concerned.

The Inquiry wanted to take evidence from the following: the Rover Company and Arlington Securities plc (the British Aerospace property development subsidiary), Cowley plant and other local trade unions, Rover group suppliers, Honda UK Manufacturing Ltd (Rover having links with Honda), employers and business organisations, the TUC locally (ie, the trades council) and nationally, Oxford City and County MPs and the region's MEP, the local authorities (the City Council, which was Labour-controlled, and the County Council, which was a 'hung' council), the European Commission, central government departments, House of Commons select committees, community groups, business advice agencies, specialist research organisations and others (including individuals with specialist knowledge, for example, of the motor industry). Most of these different types of interest did provide evidence, in the end. Broadly, this covered private sector business interests, including both manufacturing and property development interests, trade union interests, national government and local government (both politicians and professionals and administrators), as well as European Union interests, a range of community organisations, churches and voluntary organisations, professional researchers and other experts, and educational and training interests.

The management of Rover was conspicuous by its absence. They did not wish to give evidence directly (making the public hearings something of a performance of *Hamlet* without the prince?), although they did respond to the inquiry's requests for information, and provided details of their published plans.

In some ways, then, the most powerful interests were not fully visible at all. It was not just that the management of Rover were less than fully publicly accountable, either. The power of wider market forces emerged very forcefully, through the inquiry. In terms of the future of motor manufacturing in Oxford, the options were limited by the international framework; Japanese manufacturers, in particular, were achieving far greater productivity, with proportionately half the human effort required in European-owned plants; and European integration was expected to increase competitive pressures in the motor manufacturing industry. These market forces, reinforced as they were by EC policies, set the overall framework for the options available. Goverment policies for privatisation had also been a key factor in the fate of British Leyland/Rover.

In addition, property market considerations were also a key factor; the inquiry estimated that the site was worth between 40 and 50 million pounds. This could vary significantly, depending upon the way in which the site was redeveloped, for manufacturing or commercial uses, as a science park, a business park, or for retail uses, or some combination of these. There were clearly interests in promoting the most profitable commercial uses, including a university-based interest in a profitable science park. The site was seen as a prime site for development, because of the good transport links and the proximity of the university, in a city with an attractive environment in the relatively prosperous south-east region of Britain.

The local authorities' planning powers were limited here (and there were differences of perspective, anyway, between the city and the county). In summary, particular developments might be stopped, through the planning process, but such a decision could be overruled subsequently, anyway, by government, if the developers took the matter to an inquiry. Overall, then, it seemed as if the employers, together with the property developers, had very considerable power indeed; although even their powers were constrained by the wider pressures of market forces, including Japanese competition and increased competition as a result of European integration. As the report commented, in view of Rover's agreement with Honda, major changes at Cowley would involve persuading Honda to shift its entire investment strategy, and in addition the European Commission would have to be persuaded, against the tide of current EC competition policy. So Rover, too, was constrained by these wider pressures. What powers, then, if any, could be mobilised against all these pressures, for alternative strategies?

The inquiry concluded that the closures could not be prevented, and that the best deal on offer, realistically, would be to negotiate with Rover and Arlington Securities for balanced redevelopment on the site, to ensure that there would be some jobs which would meet the needs of the local workforce. In addition, the negotiated agreement should include some provision for training/retraining and career counselling, and a contingency fund, with contributions from Rover, to contribute to the local costs which resulted from restructuring. (This was the context for the subsequent plans around training and other regeneration projects, within the Single Regeneration Budget bid, which was discussed in the previous chapter.) But was this actually the best deal which could have been struck, given the balance of powers involved?

The critics argued that it was not. The report compiled by Schofield, *Cowley Works: Community Issues* (Ruskin Community Education Research and Training, 1990) set out the views which were discussed at a workshop which was held at Ruskin, that year, to explore the issues critically, from the perspectives of the local community and local trade unionists. The workshop set out to 'bring into focus the person who, as a worker, would be displaced by the plans of the Rover Group' and to 'discuss the development of community strategies which would reach the key community issues of the company's plans without either blaming or victimising those who would be most harmed by them or by leaving remedial action to the professionals' (*ibid*, p. 1). The workshop was a community education event, bringing together activists from Oxford with those who had been involved in anti-closure campaigns, and their aftermath, from elsewhere in Britain. Through these discussions, it was clear that a number of participants believed that more could have been achieved.

As a number of contributions to the inquiry had reflected, the process of restructuring had been very undermining for the trade union movement and for local communities, more generally. There was some sense of resignation as well as alienation. The trades council commented, at the Ruskin workshop, that half the basis of the trades council would be lost if the closures went ahead.

The trades council had organised a public meeting, with key speakers from the Transport and General Workers' Union, immediately the announcements about closure were made, but the local trades unions within the plant preferred to go for a low-key approach. Some of the critics argued that these local trades unions had accepted too much, too soon; infected with the 'new realism', it was argued, they had not made the most effective use of the (admittedly limited) bargaining power which they *did* still have.

The other major criticisms were levelled at the politicians. It was argued that it was not simply that local Labour politicians were limited by their restricted powers under a Conservative government committed to pursuing a market-led agenda (although clearly they were seriously restricted, in these respects). Even if the Labour Party had been in power, it was suggested, a Labour government would have had no commitment to more interventionist approaches to the economy; as one critic argued, 'there's no pretence that the Labour Party is going to be intervening or attempting to plan industry in anything like the sense that was spoken about in the 70s and early 80s' (*ibid*, p. 54). This point about the likely policies of a future Labour government was not in question, although the local Labour MP was personally strongly committed to do everything possible to save jobs at Cowley, within the given framework.

The final point to make here is that the workshop itself was part of a process of community and trade union education. As the local MP pointed out, campaigning against the proposed closures was potentially valuable, in addressing people's sense of powerlessness. And 'the value of the process of standing up and understanding why it has happened cannot be overstated' (*ibid*, p. 62). As another participant commented, the public inquiry had also been useful, in raising the issues and developing popular understanding and support on a wide basis, including churches and academics, as well as trade unionists and local community activists. (There were experts and professionals who worked alongside trade union and community organisations, sharing their knowledge, skills and research expertise, both as individuals and through the Oxford Motor Industry Research Project Group).

Concluding on the implications of the Cowley case, two of these academics commented on the limits which general and global conditions of capital accumulation put upon local action. 'We are dealing here not only with the particular behaviour of a particular company in a particular locality (however serious that may be), but also with the fundamental irrationalities of capitalism's 'creative destruction', in this case backed by a major and quite unnecessary run-down of British industry (seen as a stronghold of union power) by the Thatcher government after 1979' (Harvey and Swyngedouw, 1993: 13). But Harvey and Swyngedouw went on to argue that 'none of this implies that local action, such as anti-closure campaigns, is redundant or irrelevant to progressive social change. Only on the basis of such local action can clear limits be put upon the more violent aspects of creative destruction, while the linking together of community-based struggles is one vital thread in attempts to construct socialist alternatives to the irrationalities of free-market capitalism' (*ibid*, p.13-14).

The campaign, itself was potentially educative, then, as well as the more overtly educational events which were associated with it, according to this perspective – although the campaign was admittedly relatively low-key. In Harvey and Swyngedouw's view, the campaign 'never rose much above the level of mild exhortation and was powerfully influenced by the political shift on the left towards an attitude of public-private partnership, even in the absence of any evidence that the private side had any interest in such an arrangement' (*ibid*, p.23). The implications of these comments point towards the conclusion that, as some of those at the Workshop had argued, more could have been achieved if a more coherent sense of alternatives had been shared by a determined coalition of local trade union and community interests and local politicians.

This, of course, is not the same as arguing that local political interests and local business interests were identical, or even, necessarily, that there were substantial areas of overlap between them. The Labour council in the city took a public stand against the closures when they were first announced, and the local Labour MP was also clearly identified with this position (Hayter, 1993). The position was more complex, and the nature of the underlying structures of power involved needed more unravelling.

The inquiry did provide some illustrations of the structures of power in Oxford, and the key local actors and organisations involved. And studying the outcomes of the decision-making process does provide some relevant insights into local power structures and the links with the local economy. But that still leaves questions about the underlying structures of power, and the interests which were not fully visible, the underlying pressures from market forces, as well as from public policies at EC and national government level. And it leaves questions about alternative sources of power, within the trade unions and the local community, and within the political process. How fully were these sources of power utilised in an effective alliance, campaigning for common alternatives, or how far was this alliance limited by differences and divisions from within? And finally, how far did the 'new realism' limit the scope of demands for alternatives?

These final questions take the discussion back to the chapter's starting points about the nature of power, the different dimensions of power, and alternative perspectives on power and adult political education for empowerment. Without this, those with the least power, the most exploited and the most disadvantaged, may tend to be the least politically active; conscious of the extent of their powerlessness, they may lack confidence in the very possibility of an alternative (Percy-Smith and Sanderson, 1992). And this acceptance of the 'new realism' may, in turn, effectively reinforce their relative powerlessness, in practice.

References

Advisory Council for Adult and Continuing Education (1983) *Political Education for Adults*, ACACE.

Allen, G. (1992) 'Active Citizenship: A Rationale for the Education of Citizens?', in G. Allen and I. Martin (eds) *Education and Community*, Cassell, pp. 130–144.

CDP (1977) *The Costs of Industrial Change*, CDP Publications.

CDP (1977) *Gilding the Ghetto*, CDP Publications.

Dahl, R. (1961) *Who Governs*? Yale University Press.

Donnison, D. (1994) *Act Local: Social Justice from the Bottom Up*, IPPR.

Freire, P. (1972) *Pedagogy of the Oppressed*, Penguin Books.

Freire, P. (1995) *Paulo Freire at the Institute*, Institute of Education, University of London.

Gaventa, J. (1991) 'Towards a Knowledge Democracy: Viewpoints on Participatory Research in North America', in O. Fals-Borda and M. Rahman (eds) *Action and Knowledge*, Intermediate Technology Publications, pp. 121–131.

Harvey, D. and Swyngedouw, E. (1993) 'Industrial Restructuring, Community Disempowerment and Grass-roots Resistance' in T. Hayter and D. Harvey (eds) *The Factory and the City*, Mansell, pp. 11–25.

Hayter, T. (1993) 'Local Politics', in T. Hayter and D. Harvey (eds) *The Factory and the City*, Mansell, pp. 161–185.

Heater, D. (1992) 'Tensions: the Citizenship Ideal', in E. Baglin Jones and N. Jones (eds) *Education for Citizenship*, Kogan Page, pp. 19–34.

HMSO (1991) *The Citizen's Charter*, Cm 1599, HMSO.

Hunter, F. (1953) *Community Power Structure*, University of North Carolina Press.

Lovett, T. (1995) 'Popular Education in Northern Ireland: The Ulster People's College', in M. Mayo and J. Thompson (eds) *Adult Learning, Critical Intelligence and Social Change*, NIACE.

Lukes, S. (1974) *Power*, Macmillan.

Percy-Smith, J. and Sanderson, I. (1992) *Understanding Local Needs*, IPPR.

Report of the Independent Inquiry into the Rover Cowley Works Closure Proposals (1990) 'The Future of Cowley', Oxford City Council.

Ridley, F. (1983) 'What Adults? What Politics?' in *Political Education for Adults*, ACACE

Ruskin Community Education Research and Training (1990) 'Cowley Works: Comunity Issues', Ruskin College, Oxford.

Russell, B. (1937) *Education for Democracy*, Association for Education for Citizenship, London.

Speaker of the House of Commons (1990) *Encouraging Citizenship*. Report of the Commission on Citizenship, HMSO.

Smith, M. (1992) 'The Possibilities of Public Life: Educating in the Community', in G. Allen and I. Martin (eds) *Education and Community*, Cassell, pp. 105–117.

Therborn, G. (1982) 'What Does the Ruling Class Do when it Rules?', in A. Giddens and D. Held (eds) *Classes, Power, and Conflict*, University of California Press, pp. 224–248.

Chapter Seven

Adult and community education: Combatting discrimination and oppression

Like the previous chapter, this chapter is concerned with adult and community education and politics; but the focus shifts to the politics of oppression. Feminism has been key to this redefinition of politics. As Rowbotham has argued, 'one of the most remarkable characteristics of modern feminism has been its capacity for continual political innovation' (Rowbotham, 1992: 272). The take-off point was not simply the circumstances of women but a critique of the inadequacies of existing 'politics . . . for losing sight of the individual and of personal daily life' (Rowbotham, 1992: 272).

In contrast, the Women's Liberation Movement set out to widen the definition of the political, and in doing so to change daily life in the here and now, 'to live the ideal future relations in the present' as well as prefiguring an alternative future (Rowbotham, 1992: 273). Whilst focusing upon women's shared experiences of oppression, however, feminists have also focused upon the experiences which divide women and the ways in which gender intersects with class, race and sexuality in the global economy. In the Third World, Jawardena and Kelkar have argued, 'workers' and peasants' movements for social change, human rights issues, peace, ecology, struggles against communal violence, and antifundamentalist agitation are all important areas for feminist action' (quoted in Rowbotham, 1992: 291). Whilst the nature of these inter-relationships has been problematic and sharply contested, in the First World, too, black women and women of colour have also addressed the ways in which race, class and gender intersect.

This chapter focuses upon power relationships, and the interconnections between different aspects of exploitation and oppression, as the subject of adult education for transformation. In addressing these issues, adult educators have been concerned with issues of access. Why have particularly disadvantaged groups benefited proportionately less rather than more from adult education provision, and what can be done to improve their access to appropriate provision? Whilst these are important questions, which do need to be tackled, this chapter starts from the position that access is only part of the problem; and only part of the solution. There are also questions around content – access to what types of educational experiences? In Freire's terminology, are these experiences domesticating or liberating?

Are educationally disadvantaged groups being encouraged to participate within existing frameworks of social and personal relations, or – to put this in less polarised terms – are they also being enabled to explore the sources of their exploitation and oppression? Are women being offered opportunities to explore the sources of sexism? Are black and minority ethnic communities gaining opportunities to analyse the roots of racism? Are young people and older people having the space to unravel the causes of ageism? And are there opportunities to develop a critical understanding of the interconnections between different aspects of exploitation and oppression, which underpin the experiences of black youth or working class women, for instance? Without such understanding, the politics of the personal, organising around your own oppression, can degenerate, as Echols has pointed out, into the narrower position of 'organise around your own interests' (Echols, 1989: 10), potentially pitching white against black, straight against lesbian.

So these types of question about interconnections are key to the politics of 'everyday life', as outlined by Rowbotham and others; as enriching rather than substituting for existing definitions of 'politics' and the 'political'. As this chapter will also argue, these types of question are key in developing strategic alliances for transformation, based upon respect for diversity. There are parallels here with the anti-sectarian approaches to adult education in the Ulster People's College, which were outlined in the previous chapter.

The issue of access, then, is only part, albeit an important part, of the discussion about combatting the educational disadvantages of the exploited and the oppressed as part of strategies for transformation. But current patterns of participation in adult education clearly *do* reflect wider structures of disadvantage and social exclusion. These are illustrated in the findings of the NIACE study, completed in 1990 (McGivney, 1990).

This study confirmed that participants in adult education in Britain were disproportionately likely to be better-educated, already; the more education people started with, the more likely they were to pursue additional educational opportunities. Social class was a key factor, with levels of education relating to occupation. Research studies have consistently confirmed that mature students do not represent a cross-section of the adult population; 'adult education is largely the preserve of the middle classes' (Woodley *et al*, 1987: 85). And these class differences were key to understanding the pattern of women's participation. Middle class women were participating, when they were not constrained by problems of childcare, and/or by resistance from partners, whereas working class women were far less likely to participate (class inequalities compounding gender inequalities).

The groups least likely to participate, unsurprisingly, included women with dependent children, together with working class men as well as working class women in unskilled/semi-skilled jobs, unemployed people, minority ethnic groups and older adults. Non-participant adults can and do belong to more than one of these categories, making it potentially even less likely that they will participate. At this point, however, a note of caution is required. Whilst different forms of exploitation and oppression interact, and can reinforce each other, it is far too simple to conclude that different forms of oppression are necessarily cumulative, in such a straightforward fashion. As Rattansi, for example, has argued, class, gender and racism intersect in complex and contradictory ways. 'The notion of cumulatively disadvantaging oppressions, leading to inevitable failure, is belied by the educational responses of British Afro-Caribbean girls' who have actually been outstripping both Afro-Caribbean boys and white girls (Rattansi, 1992: 61–62).

NIACE identified different types of reasons for non-participation. Broadly these reasons can be considered in terms of the following categories; 'situational' barriers – a category which includes such factors as costs of courses, or lack of time to study; 'institutional' barriers – when institutions are geared towards young, white, middle class sections of the population, and are experienced as alienating by other groups; and 'dispositional' barriers – when people have had negative experiences of education in the past and/or perceive educational opportunities to be inappropriate or irrelevant to their needs. These different types of reasons have important implications for strategies for change. So whilst providing more effective information and outreach work, offering courses free of charge and ensuring that on-site childcare is provided are all vital steps in widening access for working class women with domestic responsibilities, even this will be insufficient if the institutions and courses in question remain unaffected.

The alienation which 'non-traditional' adult students can experience when they do move into 'mainstream' further and higher education institutions has been analysed by O'Rourke, in a chapter entitled 'All Equal Now?' (O'Rourke, 1995). Widening access, through adult education of the second chance variety, has been a major success story, in some ways, she argues. Adult education opportunities have been opened up for those who have been educationally deprived, deprivation which has often been compounded by other sources of deprivation, through gender, race, class and disability, and so forth. But these opportunities, such as New Opportunities for Women and informal pre-access courses, have themselves become more vulnerable in the current climate.

As Thompson has also pointed out, whilst Access has been a success story in many ways, these courses have also been seriously affected by the market pressures which have been exacerbated by New Right policies. 'In the process', she argues, 'something of the politics and passion has been lost. What counts as the culture and the curriculum of

Access, what informs the logic of accreditation . . . for example, owes less to the arguments about cultural politics and critical intelligence, feminism and empowerment, than to the need to generate 'customers' in line with the ideological and political consequences of applying performance indicators and free market economics to the practices of education' (Thompson, 1995).

And in the educational mainstream, there is increasing pressure to focus upon difference as a purely personal or individual concern, a matter for individual preference. The educational mainstream remains effectively untouched by the arrival of participants with far more varied backgrounds, interests and aspirations.

The 'equality' which results, O'Rourke argues, is a spurious form. Adults do not return to education on a 'level playing field'. Indeed, 'some of us don't even get onto the playing field. We're in the clubhouse making tea and sandwiches or even on the other side of the boundary wall, unaware there is a game to be played at all, or even we're trying to join in with only a partial grasp of the rules' (O'Rourke, *ibid*). This contrasts with the recognition of difference and the valuing of diversity which she considers to have been essential to the most successful experiences of adult education for equality in recent years. Institutions and their educational practices have to change. And so does the educational content. Existing biases in the selection and theorisation of knowledge have to be challenged, whether these are biases resulting from Eurocentrism, patriarchy, heterosexism, class biases, or some combination of these.

Looking at successful interventions in adult education in the recent past in Britain, Fryer has pointed to the particular richness of feminist initiatives. The publications which have resulted from feminist challenges has helped to popularise ideas and to open up topics of study 'that even two decades ago were largely hidden from view' (Fryer, 1992: 289). The expansion of women's studies has been crucial in opening up adult education for women. The range of courses for and about women has developed to include a very diverse spread of issues and concerns covering the workplace, the media, culture (including creative writing) community-based issues (including women's health) the family and gender relations, sexuality and violence against women. Educational methods have been affected too, Fryer has argued, in response to women's emphasis upon the value of relatively unstructured, less hierarchical approaches to learning; all positive aspects of adult education practice, in any case.

Thompson has similarly pointed to the achievements of the Women's Liberation Movement in challenging traditional educational methods, as well as in terms of deconstructing traditional forms of knowledge. At the same time she has also pointed to ways in which Women's Studies have faced potential co-option and neutralisation within the mainstream of academic institutions, in the current context (Thompson, 1995).

In parallel, Fryer has also pointed to the changes which have occurred through black studies and through adult education to challenge racism. This has included 'the recovery and celebration of history' as perceived by black women and men themselves and 'the examination of the consequences of imperialism and colonisation for the black experience' (*ibid* p.299). Whilst vitally important for black people, Fryer has argued that these challenges to working-class adult education are also vital for white students. The implications of this essential point are far-reaching, as the concluding section of this chapter will suggest.

So what have these developments actually meant, in terms of experiences of alternative forms of adult education? In the British context, the experiences of the Women's Education Centre in Southampton, which grew from the university's Adult Education Department's community education programme in the late seventies, provide illustrations. The Women's Education Centre was used predominantly by working class women, and was run on the basis of control by the members. Through the eighties, the Women's Education Centre weathered increasing attempts to supervise and control its work, withdraw funding from the creche, require women on benefits to pay course fees, and change its collective decision-making structures.

The experiences of women involved in the Second Chance for Women course at the Women's Education Centre have been written up collectively (Taking Liberties Collective, 1989). *Learning the Hard Way* provides a record of the struggles and achievements of a group of working class women, almost none of whom had any previous experience of writing. Despite the difficulties of their circumstances ('most of us were hard-up, two were in the process of getting divorced and two were in the middle of court cases', *ibid*, p.viii) the collective was determined to produce the book, as a book for women, rather than a book about women.

The book provides a powerful account of the obstacles which working class women face if they decide to return to education to improve their situations. 'In reality', they argue, 'the odds are stacked against working class or black women re-entering formal education and surmounting all the obstacles' (*ibid*, p.65). But when faced with situations such as the end of a marriage, a number of women do try to do precisely that, with the objective of gaining a better paid and more satisfying job. For others, the decision to return to study was born from 'sheer despair at the self-denial required of women in a world where we are often seen only in the context of our relationship to others' (*ibid*, p.66). Education was also seen as a way of taking more control over their lives, and as a means for enabling them to play a more active part in shaping their worlds.

But whatever the motivation, returning to study was by no means easy. In addition to overcoming the problems of self-confidence which affect so many mature students, these women faced the additional problem that 'back at the home base, it's likely to be business as usual' (*ibid*, p.68). Domestic labour and childcare is still their responsibility;

studying is not considered 'real work'. In addition to facing all these problems, and the financial problems which accompany returning to study, some women faced what amounted to sabotage from their partners, threatened by their potentially increasing self-confidence and independence. 'It seems to be a common phenomenon', they reflected, quoting a tutor on some of the tactics which were adopted by partners and former partners, especially at particularly crucial times like just before exams, behaviour ranging from stopping the maintenance payments to threatening to go for custody of children. 'Oh, it's classic. They always play up before the exams, throw a wobbler before the finals, we get it every year', this tutor commented (*ibid*, p.71). Sadly, the author's personal experience as a tutor of mature women students bears out the view that such occurrences are by no means rare – sabotage of this type does indeed take place.

The collective also provided a range of examples of institutional sexism and overt sexist behaviour towards women returners, both from staff and from male students. There were examples of class prejudice, too, which made women feel very strongly that 'they were the wrong sex and the wrong class in the wrong place' (*ibid*, p.79). There were also experiences of racism, and more general failures to tackle the issues of racism, poverty and powerlessness, adequately. Lesbian women encountered prejudice and discrimination as well, and all too often a deafening silence in relation to lesbian and gay issues. And these types of experiences occurred both on Access courses and in further and higher education. There were also examples of sexual harassment of women attending trade union courses. Across the board, from adult education to higher education, there were issues, too, about the content of the curriculum, whether these issues were about stereotyped assumptions about women's interests or about the invisibility of women and women's concerns.

Having set out these experiences of situational, institutional and dispositional barriers for women, the collective went on to discuss positive alternatives. At the Women's Education Centre in Southampton, women's education was based upon a number of principles, including the following; 'women-only classes, a curriculum which is based on women-centred knowledge; teaching-learning approaches which break down hierarchies between "experts" and "others"; an atmosphere which discourages the divisiveness of class privilege, racism and lesbophobia; the validation of personal experience; knowledge which is politically useful in the battle against patriarchy; good childcare; flexible timing; minimal fees and freedom from male interference and control' (*ibid*, pp.140-141).

The starting point was, as they pointed out, obvious: courses arranged at times which fitted in with domestic commitments, and an excellent creche. Fees were kept to a minimum, and could be easily waived, where necessary. As they explained 'For women with little money to call our own, arbitrary demands for cash as evidence of our commitment to learning is grossly insulting' (*ibid*, p.142), a point of continuing relevance in the context of increasing market pressures in adult education and further and higher education.

The curriculum was key, too. Although many women did seek to increase their chances of becoming more economically independent through courses specifically geared towards improving their employment prospects, there was also concern to learn together 'effective ways in which we can challenge patriarchy in our everyday lives for the benefit of ourselves and for women generally. Women's education, as we define it, is political education linked to women's liberation' (*ibid*, p.143) a definition which clearly relates to Rowbotham's definition of the political as including the politics of personal daily life, in the here and now, as well as prefiguring an alternative future.

The focus upon challenging gender relations related to the concerns with issues of race and class, with explicit commitment to black and working class women. As the collective explained, these issues had to be confronted; 'A commitment to feminism doesn't automatically eradicate racism, as many black feminists have discovered to their cost' (*ibid*, p.151) and similar points applied to heterosexism. Reflecting on discussions with some Latin American women, one woman commented that this had made her feel increasingly impatient with the complacency and liberalism of some British feminists and the failure to face up to the implications of 'gross inequalities of wealth and power and resources, the reluctance to hear what working class and black women are saying about class and racism, and the attempt to keep lesbian women quiet in case we give the Movement a bad name. The Latin American women were quite unequivocal. Social change for women needs to be both a political and economic revolution as well as a cultural revolution' (pp.160-161).

Combatting racism

The parallels with tackling issues of racism in adult education have already been suggested. Once again, there are vitally important issues around access to educational opportunities, situational as well as institutional barriers to be overcome. And once again, these issues also relate to underlying questions about the content, the nature of the curriculum, as well as about the delivery of adult education.

In a comprehensive guide, Dadzie has set out a practical set of proposals for improving adult education practice, as it affects black adult learners, based upon experiences of good practice (Dadzie, 1993). The urgency of the task of addressing these questions has been highlighted by the levels of unemployment which are experienced by black people. Consistently, black people have suffered from higher rates of unemployment than their white counterparts, and this has included black people with a high level of qualifications. Unemployment amongst black youth has been and continues to be a particularly serious problem.

In these circumstances, access to education and training opportunities has been seen as offering possible ways forward – despite the fact that even those black people who do have high levels of qualifications still suffer disproportionately from unemployment.

Dadzie sets out proposals for good practice in ways which address the key situational and institutional barriers. She starts with the importance of effective consultation with black and minority ethnic communities, to be followed up with outreach work. There are examples of precisely this type of partnership with black communities, as in the case of the Sheffield Black Literacy Campaign, for instance (Gurnah, 1993).

Institutions need to have comprehensive anti-racist policies, covering both students and staff. And courses need to be publicised in accessible ways, to reach potential students, and to reassure them, by presenting the information in accessible, user-friendly language, with positive images of black students and clear indications of the institution's commitment to equal opportunities and anti-racism. Guidance and student selection procedures need to be examined too, and students need to be provided with personal support, from tutors and possibly mentors, once they are enrolled (with mentors providing positive role models, from the student's own communities, to support and encourage them). And all these measures need to be monitored, as part of a continuing dialogue with black communities.

Whilst these measures all have value, as part of anti-racist strategies, however, the central core of anti-racist strategies involves the ethos of the institutions in question, and the curriculum itself. An appropriate ethos, as Dadzie describes this, is one 'which reflects an active commitment to anti-racism, cultural pluralism and access' (Dadzie, 1993: 79). And an anti-racist curriculum 'is one which incorporates the history, contributions and perspectives of black peoples into every aspect of its content amd delivery. Black issues and viewpoints are seen as integral rather than as a topic to be bolted on to an essentially Eurocentric syllabus' (*ibid*, p.99). This is not about emphasising cultural differences in ways which portray black people or cultures as 'curious' or 'exotic', as some forms of multi-cultural education have tended to do. Ultimately, anti-racist education, in contrast with multi-cultural education, emphasises the achievements and struggles of black people, within the framework of a critical understanding of the sources of racism.

In an essay on *Constructing the Other: Minorities, the state and adult education in Europe* Westwood has illustrated precisely these problems of Eurocentrism, and the connections between this and the historical roots of contemporary racist assumptions in Britain. She quotes from a speech made by the then minister of education, Kenneth Baker, to a Conservative Party conference, on the subject of traditional values, and the importance of children learning the main events of British history. 'Well, I'm not ashamed of our history', Baker is quoted as commenting. 'That's been our civilising mission', going on to emphasise 'the spread of Britain's influence for good throughout the Empire in the 18th and 19th centuries'.

As Westwood comments, 'The resonances with colonial discourses are very clear, the civilising mission, Empire and Britain as benign and more so, as epochs to be celebrated' (Westwood, 1991: 168).

The viewpoint of the colonised, of course, has been somewhat different; as Gandhi reflected when he commented, in response to a question about his views on this reputed British civilisation, that it would be 'a good thing'. This so-called civilising mission of the British had been justified, as Fryer has explained, to promote 'the moral and educational progress of the child-like natives they ruled over. Since black people were inferior', it was argued, 'the British who ruled them owed them a special obligation, not unlike the obligation that decent Englishmen owed to women, children and animals ... In its popular version, transmitted through schools, cheap newspapers, juvenile literature and the music-hall, racism told the British working-class that black people were savages whom British rule was rescuing from heathenism and internecine strife' (Fryer, 1988: 67). If anti-racist strategies are to be successfully developed, in adult education, or indeed in any other form of education, both Eurocentrism and the roots of racism itself have to be addressed as key problems in the curriculum.

Debates around multi-culturalism and anti-racism have featured in educational debates more generally, in recent years. Multi-culturalism has been criticised for neglecting the power relationships which underpin racism, focusing instead upon different cultures, as though these were all equally valued. The problem with this focus upon saris and samosas is that it may leave what Carby has described as a 'curious silence about, avoidance of, or inadequacy in addressing racism'. The following dialogue illustrates this point.

Schools: We're all equal here.

Black students: We *know* we are second-class citizens, in housing employment and education.

Schools: Oh dear. Negative self-image. We must order books with Blacks in them.

Black students: Can't we talk about immigration laws or the National Front?

Schools: No, that's politics. We'll arrange some Asian/West Indian cultural evenings (quoted in Brandt, 1986: 115).

In contrast, anti-racist education has been characterised as being concerned to develop understanding in order to combat racism, recognising that black people, far from being 'mere objects of racist practice', 'have been and are active in combating racism in society and education' (*ibid*, p.121).

In both theory and practice, however, there have been continuing debates about anti-racist education within the context of equal opportunities more generally. Anthias and Yuval-Davis, for instance, have decoded

some of the assumptions about 'good race relations', including the ideology of 'community' which has underpinned, in different ways, both
multi-culturalist and anti-racist schools of thought in the fields of education and service provision (Anthias and Yuval-Davis, 1993). They reflect
upon the criticisms of anti-racist approaches in practice, as set out in the
Macdonald Report, following the murder of a black school student in
Manchester, a report which characterised the brand of anti-racism in
question as being moralistic and simplistic, and excluding Whites from
the definition of the community. And they summarise Rattansi's
systematic critique of both multi-culturalism and anti-racism in education. Despite their apparently diametrical differences, Rattansi argued,
both approaches shared common weaknesses, failing to display sufficient awareness of contradictions, inconsistencies and ambivalences.

As Anthias and Yuval-Davis go on to point out, however, subsequent
approaches have addressed some of these weaknesses. The approach
which has been developed by Cohen, for example, has not only focused
on power relations within schools, but has also attempted to prevent
racist cultures from becoming part of the 'culture of resistance' of working class children. Racist 'common-sense' notions which children hold
about themselves and others have been tackled, in ways which have
been sensitive to what they describe as the 'shifting boundaries of
allegiances and groupings among children, in which complex notions
and articulations of race, sex, ethnicity, age and other constructions play
their part' (Anthias and Yuval-Davis, 1993: 161).

Although these arguments have been developed in relation to education within schools, there are parallels with some of the arguments
about multi-culturalist and anti-racist approaches in education more
generally, including adult education and social education with young
people, approaches which pose major challenges for white students, as
well as for black (Fryer, 1992). The type of approach which has been
developed in relation to schools, by Cohen and others, has also been
applied to the development of anti-racist strategies in youth work and
social education. Buck, for example, has explored the implications in
tackling racist behaviour, such as racist 'name-calling'. The use of racist
insults was often ambiguous and contradictory; young whites would
use terms such as 'paki', in 'wind-up exchanges' and then deny their
significance afterwards when confronted by the youth worker. 'I'm sorry
I said that. I didn't mean anything by it. I've known John all my life, for
years ... it didn't make no difference. I don't know why I said that
(Buck, 1990: 26).

Of course racist name-calling *was* significant, particularly given that
this study was carried out in an area where there was a background of
serious racial violence. The question was not whether racist name-
calling was significant, which it was, or acceptable, which of course it
was not, but how most effectively to confront it, as part of anti-racist
youth work strategies. The young whites used racist terms, but their
racial consciousness was 'highly fractured and ambiguous' (*ibid*, p.27).

They also exhibited a de-racialised 'common sense' which was a potential starting point to build on, in developing challenges to racist conscious- ness, building on 'those aspects of white common sense which contradict racist explanations' (p.30).

In commenting on effective anti-racist strategies in the aftermath of the Burnage school murder, the report included an example of good practice through a theatre group. This group involved young people in writing and producing a play about a Manchester boxer and political activist, the child of an African father and an Irish mother. The report commented that this type of cultural studies enabled the young people to learn about their lives and culture, about their relationships with each other at home and at school, about their attitudes to women and to race and class. Through the play, they unpacked the contents of sexist and racist culture. Anti-racist youth work of this type could be both educational and fun, offering young people alternative discourses on race.

As Buck recognised, however, this still left the vital question of how to tackle racist incidents, in the here and now. Whilst young people who used racist terms could be banned from using the youth club, as the youth workers' ultimate sanction, 'being banned' could also confer 'a degree of oppositional status on the young person involved (Buck, 1990: 29). One possible way forward, in tackling this, was to involve the young people themselves in taking responsibility for dealing with unac- ceptable behaviour, including confronting racist name-calling.

Such examples illustrate a far less simplistic approach to develop- ing anti-racist strategies, in education and in youth work, than some of the strategies which were criticised by Anthias and Yuval-Davis. Whilst critical of simplistic strategies to combat racism in education, however, Anthias and Yuval-Davis have also been critical of the fragmentation and divisiveness of particular approaches to 'identity politics.' One particularly problematic form of 'identity' politics relates to fundamental- ism, they suggest, with fundamentalist leaders defining themselves as the keepers of the 'true' way of life, the most authentic 'Others'. But, at the same time, 'fundamentalists are also perceived as a threat, and their "difference" as a basis for racist discourse' (Anthias and Yuval-Davis, 1993: 193).

Anthias and Yuval-Davis conclude by contrasting two very differ- ent approaches to 'identity politics'. Brant, on the one hand, sees identity as being at 'the heart of any transformatory project'. She rejects the logic of broad democratic alliances and rainbow coalitions, because, she argues, political action should be based on 'unity in diversity' (quoted in Anthias and Yuval-Davis, 1993: 196). In contrast, Bourne has argued that identity politics have come to replace political struggles which aim at 'social change' and the 'transformation of society'. Identity politics have become 'separatist, individualistic and inward looking. The organic relationship we tried to forge between the personal and the political has been so degraded that now the only area of politics deemed to be legitimate is the personal' (Bourne, 1987: 2, quoted in Anthias and Yuval-Davis, 1993: 195). They conclude by recognising the central importance of political struggles which do address the wider issues of class politics and the state, as well as addressing issues of race, ethnicity and gender, within society at large, and within their 'communities'.

Working with young people

This brings the argument back to some of the questions which were raised at the beginning of this chapter, questions about the politics of the personal as widening the definition of the political, rather than as narrowing the definition of the political to 'organising around your own interest'. The debate around 'identity politics' and 'cultures of resistance' and 'counter-cultures' relates to the discussions in the next chapter. But before moving on to this, there are questions to be addressed about age, youth and ageism, questions which also overlap with questions of class, race and gender.

Policy pronouncements on youth work, in Britain, as Jeffs and Smith have pointed out, illustrate public concern with the ways in which young people gain their identities as adults, and especially so in relation to young working class men, overlaid more recently with 'panics regarding the perceived behaviour of black young men' (Jeffs and Smith, 1990: 219). As Smith has also pointed out, 'every society is faced with the problem of how to ensure that successive generations are socialized into ways of thinking and behaviour which serves the community or the needs of particular groups within it' (Smith, 1988: 94). In capitalist society, young working class men have been seen as in need of specific attention, and young black working class men have been seen as even more problematic.

In periods of major restructuring involving high levels of unemployment, especially amongst young working class men, and most particularly amongst young black men, this concern turns to moral panic. Previous socialisation patterns and previous rewards for 'good behaviour' break down, as regular employment and a home of one's own become unattainable for so many adolescents. Although there has been increasing emphasis upon social control strategies – different versions of 'short, sharp shocks' to manage deviant youth – there has continued to be some concern with more preventative strategies, too. Social education, and informal education, through youth work, has been seen as one such means of contributing to this process of socialisation; the internalisation of the hegemonic culture, to use Gramsci's terminology.

Historically, social education has been an explicit objective of youth work since at least the earlier part of this century. Smith quotes the view that social agencies should not only 'amuse a young man but should also impart "polish", including teaching him to take off his hat upon entering the Department; to say "please" and "thank you", and to be civil; not to be impertinent; to mind his own business and refrain from personal comment. Opportunities will be found for showing him that chivalrous respect is due to womanhood. Cleanliness of person and apparel, and in a hundred other details can be encouraged in an unobtrusive way' (Baker, 1919: 13, quoted in Smith, 1988: 89). Youth work has been concerned not only with inculcating manners in the past, as this quotation indicates, but with underlying key values within capitalist society, and the reproduction of these.

Youth work, like welfare provision more generally, Jeffs and Smith argue, has been dominated by these bourgeois frames of value, even whilst providing services which have been needed. They refer to the 'frankly imperialistic and nationalistic' aims and direction of programmes such as some elements of scouting or the Duke of Edinburgh's Award Scheme (Jeffs and Smith, 1990: 219) and to the use of private sector sponsorships and promotions (reinforcing private market values) to illustrate this point.

Whether or not the young people who use the provision in question actually imbibe these values uncritically is, of course, another question, as Jeffs and Smith also recognise. Many young people, they suggest, 'will have little identity with the aims and values of the organisation, but are happy to use its services for as long as there is some benefit to them. They take opportunities and facilities and reinterpret them to their own ends.'

But as they go on to argue, 'we should not fall into the trap of thinking that the assumption of an instrumental orientation leaves them untouched by their experience of youth provision. Their encounter with middle-class attitudes and forms can simultaneously confirm them in their separateness and sustain a belief in their political and economic inferiority' (Jeffs and Smith, 1990: 211). They suggest that a sure test of the political and social direction of provision is to ask to what extent workers address questions of class, race and gender. 'Do they, for example, seek to encourage working-class young people to reflect critically on their experiences in the labour market? (or lack of experiences in the labour market) Or do they simply seek to ameliorate the situation?' (Jeffs and Smith, 1990: 221).

Reflecting on recent experiences, Jeffs and Smith come to the view that whilst there has correctly been some focus and good practice in work to combat sexism and racism, and some work on disability and sexuality, there has been less focus upon class. By approaching each specific aspect of disadvantage discretely, they argue, key connections between them have been missed; 'the basic structural and material circumstances which underpin and sustain inequality and injustice' (*ibid*, p.225), although they also point to the survival and development of radical traditions and alternatives. They quote Giroux on the value of approaches which allow people to challenge, engage and question the form of the learning process, and which offer young people the opportunity to 'speak with their own voices, to authenticate their own experiences' (quoted in *ibid*, p.226). In the view of Fisher and Day, this would be to work towards young people (in this case, young black people) developing their own sense of identity, purpose and direction (Fisher and Day, 1983).

In the development of alternative and 'liberating' approaches, Jeffs and Smith argue that one of the most important problems, perhaps the central problem, is how to address the ideological process by which one type of oppression is played off against another rather than understanding how one form of oppression links with another – there are parallels here with the points which were made in relation to gender and other forms of oppression. Yet, they argue, this process is not inevitable. It can be combated. Even within current constraints, youth workers can develop informal education with young people, based upon processes of critical dialogues, which do engage with the links between different forms of oppression.

In a subsequent publication, Smith has developed these ideas in relation to local education, in the widest sense, building on concepts of 'community', 'conversation' (drawing upon, but not uncritically transplanting, Freire's work on dialogue) and 'praxis'; action based upon reflection, which is also committed to human well-being and the search for truth and respect for others (Smith, 1994). Whilst this approach is absolutely relevant to working with young people, it is, of course, of far wider relevance in education for transformation.

The concepts of 'youth' and 'adolescence', like the concept of 'old age', are, in any case, socially constructed. Different societies, at different periods, define and mark transitions into adult status in different ways, just as they define and mark transitions out of the productive phase of adult status in different ways. As Smith has pointed out, 'Age is only one factor in determining experiences. Class, geographical location, gender, ethnicity and physical and mental 'ability' all can have a major bearing' (Smith, 1988: 94). Full adult status has been marked in different ways, with major variations in terms of class and gender, both in the past and present, depending on such factors as entry into productive work and marriage.

As it has already been suggested, periods of restructuring, such as the present, pose particular dilemmas for young people, and especially for young working class men, and for young black men, who are disproportionately at risk of being excluded from full entry into adult status, through regular employment and setting up their own household. This raises major problems about identity, problems which have their roots in social rather than individual causes. Social education which fails to address these root causes, or to link different experiences of oppression to these, would seem by definition inherently unlikely to succeed in enabling young people to gain identities as adults.

Challenging ageism

In parallel, as Phillipson and others have argued, the concept of 'old age' is also socially constructed, with important variations, in terms of class and gender. (Judges and members of the House of Lords, in Britain, may still be playing powerful roles in public affairs at a biological age when, typically, manual workers have long since been regarded as 'on the scrap-heap'.) More specifically, in capitalist society, in periods of boom, old age may be defined more flexibly than in periods of recession, when older workers may be encouraged/squeezed out of the labour market (Phillipson, 1982; Laczko and Phillipson, 1991). 'Early retirement' is a term which covers a range of outcomes, both voluntary and effectively involuntary (as some of the older workers in the motor industry in Oxford discovered: pressures could be applied which would encourage older workers to opt out, including simply keeping older workers on production lines where they struggled to keep up, rather than moving them to jobs where the pace was more realistic). (See earlier, Chapters Four and Five.) Without developing these arguments in any detail here, the point to emphasise is simply that one's identity, as an older person, like one's identity as a young person, is not exclusively an individual issue. This has key implications for adult education with older people.

As the proportion of the population over retirement (however defined) and the proportion of those categorised as very elderly has increased, there has been increasing focus, too, upon adult education for older people. As Midwinter and others have pointed out, education can be a positive experience; older people (contrary to negative stereotypes about declining capacities for learning), can and do enjoy learning, and this can make significant contributions to their health, well-being and morale (Midwinter, 1982). This has been clearly recognised, both in the community setting and within institutional care (Johnston and Phillipson, 1983), although current pressures on the funding of adult education in Britain pose potential problems in terms of access.

These developments have covered a range of initiatives, from pre-retirement programmes to assist people in adjusting from one status to another, to the spread of programmes offered in adult education more generally. In addition, there are examples of adult education initiatives with older people which have specifically addressed political issues from older people's perspectives. In Denmark, for example, older people have a national grass-roots association (Danage) which organises a range of leisure, education and cultural activities including travel, together with counselling and advice. Danage also organises political support on policy issues of concern to older people, political work which is reinforced through the educational programmes in question (including courses in public speaking, drawing up press releases and organising meetings, for example) (Pillay, 1990).

In Glasgow, when they established themselves in the early eighties, the Pensioners' Action Group East similarly began campaigning actively on issues of concern to older people, issues such as fuel poverty, health, transport and Post Office closures (local post offices being the places where pensioners drew their benefits) (Pillay, 1990). Educational needs were identified and met, needs which included organisational skills, as well as specific knowledge on benefits. The process of organising and campaigning has, itself, proved educational too, developing participants' confidence and belief in themselves. Similar points have been made about other older peoples' initiatives (Pillay, 1990). Through tackling issues of concern, collectively, older people have gained confidence and built upon their sense of their own identity. The processes have been educational, in the broadest sense, over and above the specific inputs which have been provided through adult education services.

There are connections here, too, with Smith's approach to local education, in terms of community, conversation and praxis. And there are connections with Gelpi's approach to Lifelong Education. As he has argued, 'the older person can learn, the psychologists tell us; but this scientific statement is not sufficient unless it is accompanied by a policy for the third age. It is not simply a matter of providing a course for retired people in a university, or of developing cultural activities in a community centre. What is necessary is to have a policy for community life, for housing, for the organisation of work, for culture, medical assistance, leisure, etc' (quoted in Griffin, 1983: 195). This, in effect, raises broader questions about knowledge content and about 'really useful knowledge', and not only for older people.

This also relates to the experiences of older people's organisations in Oxford, which were summarised in Chapter Five, experiences which drew upon adult education support, and developed Participatory Action Research in partnership. Through these experiences, it emerged so clearly that older people perceived their needs in holistic ways, relating to their needs for social change. Well-being, as defined by 'Agewell', meant health in the broadest sense, including access to leisure, recreation and adult education, as well as adequate transport and affordable housing, underpinned by a decent income.

Older people themselves, when consulted about what type of educational and recreational provision they would prefer, in an experimental project in Oxford, commented that they were 'fed up with Bingo'. Working with the Agewell Ruskin Group, this group of older working class people in East Oxford developed a proposal for alternative and more stimulating and relevant forms of educational provision. With local authority and voluntary sector support, they developed a model of participative education for people aged 50-plus, actively involving people in shaping their own learning (Hughes, 1992). The themes which emerged from this process included Early School Days (reminiscing), Health and Welfare and Myths about Ageing, and other activities, including play-reading, poetry and short stories, and working with numbers and statistics. Older people wanted to learn about a range of issues, to address their immediate concerns for action and change around welfare rights, for example, as well as to explore new horizons, including creative writing.

The outcome of this particular initiative was extremely positive, leading to a pack which was developed for use with other groups, and for work with housebound older people. The project demonstrated the extent of active interest amongst older people, even when they have had previously very limited and often negative experiences of education in the past. But their active participation did not simply happen spontaneously. As Hughes commented, initially 'there was a tendency for the Group to be fairly passive. Being entertained is what most participants had been used to. This made it more difficult to engage people in collective activities, as few had previously had their ideas sought out.' Feedback was positive. 'They stressed that this was a new experience for them, a different way of working with others, which took some getting used to. Participants clearly valued the opportunity to express themselves, and to have their experience valued' (Hughes, 1992: 100).

Whilst, more generally, older people certainly had specific perspectives and concerns, however, they also shared concerns with other groups and interests in their local communities. For example their concern with affordable public transport and with community safety. And conversely, older people, like younger people, had different identities too, differences in terms of class, race, gender and sexuality, as well as differences of locality (between urban and rural areas).

This final point about the differences between older people, as well as between younger people, takes the discussion back to some of the dilemmas which have already been posed about identity politics. How to be conscious of one's oppression and to organise around this, without letting this degenerate into the narrower position of organising 'around your own interests'? How to address the processes by which one type of oppression is played off against another, so that people 'are led to focus on their own specific form of oppression rather than understanding how one form links with another to constitute a structure of oppression' (Allman, 1988: 93, quoted in Jeffs and Smith, 1990: 226). How to avoid organising around specific oppressions coming, in Bourne's words, 'to replace political struggles which aim at social change and the transformation of society'? How to connect the politics of the individual and personal daily life, with wider political struggles, to widen rather than to fragment and dilute the definition of the political?

References

Anthias, F. and Yuval-Davis, N., in association with H Cain (1993) *Racialized Boundaries*, Routledge.

Brandt, G. (1986) *The Realization of Anti-Racist Teaching*, Falmer Press.

Buck, L. (1990) *Racist Name Calling and Developing Anti-Racist Initiatives in Youth Work*, Centre for Research in Ethnic Relations, University of Warwick.

Dadzie, S. (1993) *Working with Black Adult Learners*, NIACE.

154   Imagining tomorrow

Echols, A. (1989) *Daring to be Bad: Radical Feminism in America, 1967–1975*, University of Minnesota Press, Minneapolis.
Fisher, G. and Day, M. (1983) *Towards a Black Perspective*, Commission for Racial Equality.
Fryer, B. (1992) 'The challenge to working-class education', in B. Simon (ed.) *The Search for Enlightenment: The working class and education in the twentieth century*, NIACE, pp. 276–319.
Fryer, P. (1988) *Black People in the British Empire*, Pluto.
Griffin, C. (1983) *Curriculum Theory in Adult and Lifelong Education*, Croom Helm.
Gurnah, A. (1993) 'Mobilising communities for learning: the Sheffield Black Literacy Campaign', in L. Brook (ed.) *Serving Communities*, Further and Higher Education Staff College, pp. 75–81.
Hughes, K. (1992) 'Opening doors for older learners' *Adults Learning*, Vol. 4, No. 4, pp. 99–100.
Jeffs, T. and Smith, M. (1990) 'Young people, class inequality and youth work', in T. Jeffs and M. Smith (eds) *Young People, Inequality and Youth Work*, Macmillan, pp. 179–226.
Johnston, S. and Phillipson, C. (eds) (1983) *The Challenge to Adult Education*, Bedford Square Press.
Laczko, F. and Phillipson, C. (1991) *Changing Work and Retirement: Social policy and the older worker*, Open University Press.
McGivney, V. (1990) *Education's for Other People: Access to education for non-participant adults*, NIACE.
Midwinter, E. (1982) *Age is Opportunity: Education and older people*, Centre for Policy on Ageing.
O'Rourke, R. (1995) 'All equal now?' in M. Mayo and J. Thompson (eds) *Adult Learning, Critical Intelligence and Social Change*, NIACE.
Phillipson, C. (1982) *Capitalism and the Construction of Old Age*, Macmillan.
Pillay, C. (1990) *Adult Education, Community Development and Older People: Releasing the resource*, Cassell.
Rattansi, A. (1992) 'Changing the subject? Racism, culture and education', in A. Rattansi and D. Reeder (eds) *Rethinking Radical Education*, Lawrence and Wishart.
Rowbotham, S. (1992) *Women in Movement*, Routledge.
Smith, M. (1988) *Developing Youth Work*, Open University Press.
Smith, M. (1994) *Local Education: Community, conversation, praxis*, Open University Press.
Taking Liberties Collective (1989) *Learning the Hard Way*, Macmillan.
Thompson, J. (1995) 'Feminism and women's education', in M. Mayo and J. Thompson (eds) *Adult Learning, Critical Intelligence and Social Change*, NIACE.
Westwood, S. (1991) 'Constructing the other: minorities, the state and adult education in Europe', in S. Westwood and J. Thomas (eds) *The Politics of Adult Education*, NIACE.
Woodley, A. *et al.* (1987) *Choosing to Learn: Adults in education*, Open University Press.

Chapter Eight

Cultures of resistance, counter-cultures and counter-hegemony: Adult education for transformation

In this final chapter, the focus returns to some of the issues which were raised in the Introduction. In the increasingly globalised context of both production and consumption in the late twentieth century 'global village', traditional patterns of human relationships have been disintegrating. This has been characterised as a period in which economic and political crises have been accompanied by a crisis in the very beliefs and assumptions on which modern society has been founded. In Hobsbawm's words, this has not been 'a crisis of one form of organising societies, but of all forms', affecting both East and West, North and South (Hobsbawm, 1994: 11) – a crisis of beliefs and culture, in the broadest sense of the term.

In this increasingly homogenised, yet paradoxically increasingly fragmented and diverse 'global village', what might be the potential contribution of culture and cultural struggles? How might questions of culture and identity relate to wider debates about human consciousness and social change? And how might these debates, in turn, relate to adult education for transformation? As it was suggested in the Introduction, adult education for transformation has been theorised by Freire and others in terms of adult education for critical consciousness, conscientisation and praxis. And in these debates about changing identities and consciousness, it was suggested, culture has been characterised as both a key weapon of the powerful and as a weapon of the weak, who can and do use culture as a means of resistance (Wallerstein, 1991).

This chapter starts by summarising different definitions of culture, focusing upon two approaches, both of which have relevance in terms of these underlying questions. Both types of definition have featured centrally, too, within debates about the role of adult education and adult education's potential contribution to wider strategies for social change. This, in turn, takes the discussion back to questions of identity, language and consciousness, to cultures of resistance and counter-cultures. The role of theatre, amongst other forms of the arts, provides specific examples to illustrate some of these debates, both in Third World contexts in the South, and in First World contexts, such as Britain. The chapter concludes by revisiting some of the more theoretical issues which were summarised in the Introduction and in Chapter One, questions posed by Gramsci and others about the nature of the inter-relationships between the world of ideas and the material world, and questions about the importance of the battle of ideas and the potential contribution of lifelong education for transformation.

So what has been meant by the term 'culture' both in general and in relation to debates about adult education, more specifically? Culture can be and has been used in very different ways, ranging from definitions of 'culture' as the arts and media in society (which can then be sub-divided in various ways, to differentiate, for example, between aesthetics/high-brow, middle-brow and low-brow/popular culture) through to a much broader definition of 'culture' as a way of life, values and beliefs, in a particular society (the anthropological approach) (Wolff, 1991). Raymond Williams, whose writings and teaching in adult education, as well as higher education, have made such a contribution to left culture in Britain, reflected that the 'idea of Culture, in contemporary English thinking, is of considerable complexity. It is widely current in history, in criticism, and in sociology, yet often without definition, and obviously with a marked range of meanings' (Williams, 1993: 57). Culture, as he went on to point out, is a term which has developed in meaning over time, from a relatively clear definition, in terms of a process of training and refinement – the culture or cultivation of the mind – in pre-industrial society, through to a more complex notion in the nineteenth century – an idea of culture involving responses to change and the consequences of change.

In addition to the notion of culture as the intellectual side of civilisation, the general body of the arts, Williams identified a broader usage, of culture as a whole way of life. In the words of Dewey, which he quoted to illustrate this point, 'The state of culture is a state of inter-action of many factors, the chief of which are law and politics, industry and commerce, science and technology, the arts of expression and communication and of morals, or the values men prize and the ways in which they evaluate them; and finally, though indirectly, the system of general ideas used by men to justify and to criticize the fundamental conditions under which they live, their social philosophy' (quoted in Williams, 1993: 57).

Such a usage clearly involves different approaches to society and to social change; on the one hand, culture represents a way of life and the justifications for this; the ways in which the processes of legitimation take place; the hegemonic culture, in Gramsci's terminology, which relates to a particular set of relations of production. In terms of the competing perspectives which were outlined in Chapter One, in the current context this would relate to societies based upon market-led perspectives and ideologies. And conversely, culture also comprises criticisms and alternative perspectives, the development of counter-hegemony, in Gramsci's terminology, geared towards transformation.

In Williams's view then, culture was certainly not confined to the general body of the arts and highbrow aesthetics. Culture, he argued, was ordinary. 'Every human society has its own shape, its purposes, its own meanings' (Williams, 1993: 90). And, as he went on to argue, cultures are constantly being made and remade, in individual minds, in response to processes of change. 'A culture has two aspects; the known meanings and directions, which its members are trained to; the new observations and meanings which are offered and tested.' Cultures involve both traditions and creative responses to change, according to this view, and culture, itself, involves both the arts and learning, and a whole way of life. Whilst critical of many aspects of Marxism, in theory and in practice, Williams also took the view that Marxists were correct in analysing the connections between culture, thus broadly defined, and the underlying system of production, and the class divisions which relate to it. Whilst recognising the impact of economic change, and the biases inherent in bourgeois culture, then, Williams went on to argue for the importance of working class culture, with its emphases on neighbourhood, mutual obligation and common betterment. Whilst drawing upon Marxist insights, however, Williams was also critical of particular sectarian approaches to Marxism. And he specifically rejected his experiences of dogmatic practices, when Marxists had been prescribing particular approaches and cultural forms as the only progressive way forward. 'To try to jump the future', he argued, 'to pretend that in some way you *are* the future, is strictly insane' (Williams, 1993: 94). This was, of course, precisely Freire's criticism of left sectarians, suffering from an absence of doubt, those for whom 'tomorrow' is decreed beforehand, inexorably pre-ordained (Freire, 1972: 18).

Introducing *Border Country*, McIlroy and Westwood reflected upon the limitations of the social democratic approach which Williams espoused, as well as its strengths. He underemphasised some of the structural barriers and conflicts of interest in capitalist societies, they suggested, and took 'far from adequate stock of the fractures of working class community, of the barriers to a common culture and the difficulties inherent in its creation, of Edward Thompson's counterposing to Williams's "culture as a whole way of life" "culture as a whole way of struggle" '(McIlroy and Westwood, 1993: 17) – issues which re-emerge in the final section of this chapter. Others have pointed to different tensions and limitations within working class communities, to the changes which have occurred over time, and across different localities, and to the divisions within them, including the fundamental divisions arising from the sexual division of labour (Clarke, 1979). But this is absolutely not to undervalue Williams's legacy. And in particular, within this legacy, McIlroy and Westwood celebrated Williams's contribution to and belief in adult education and his continuing commitment to the working class.

These connections between culture, as broadly defined, and adult education, which Williams so valued, have a long and contested history.

And this was particularly the case in relation to the narrower, more specific definitions and approaches to culture in the past. In the pre-war period, culture (in terms of its narrower definition as literature and the arts) was especially disputed – seen by some traditionalists in adult education as 'soft', 'women's subjects', not to be taken as seriously as the 'hard' subjects such as political economy – although this was also fiercely contested. More recently, in the post-war period, it has been argued, the focus of these debates in working class adult education shifted; it was the 'cultural struggle' which attracted many radicals into working in adult education. 'Many felt', Steele has argued, that 'a decisive shift from the politics of the point of production to the politics of representation, ideology and hegemony was strategically necessary if a new political "common-sense" was to be constructed. If art and literature were to serve the people, the argument ran, a critical popular consciousness had to be developed' (Steele, 1995).

This was key to the development of what came to be called Cultural Studies, he argued. The teaching of cultural subjects in adult education was linked to the development of the New Left, and to attempts to create an alternative sense of national identity in place of that associated with imperialism and oppression. There were attempts to encourage 'worker-writers' as part of building this alternative, and there were attempts to interpret the cultural heritage of the past, in the light of Marxism. Steele quotes Thompson's view that the goal was to win people for life and not wait for a new kind of person to appear until after Socialism has been won. 'We must change people now for that is the essence of all our cultural work', which seems to imply a view of culture as a way of life and struggle, as well as in terms of the educational role of the arts, more specifically.*

In the post-war period, Steele argued, however, Cultural Studies moved into the academic mainstream, and contemporary Cultural Studies became separated from the political economy of culture. Excessively anxious to avoid economic reductionism, in its more extreme manifestations, Cultural Studies tended to become distanced and increasingly ironic and even nihilistic in the case of some post-modernist approaches. But Steele has also pointed to alternative approaches, including the work of Harvey, for instance, which have succeeded in avoiding both crude reductionism and distanced nihilism, approaches which have important potential, in relation to adult education and Cultural Studies as a project of popular education. Questions of culture, identity and consciousness have been key to debates about adult education and change, then, as these debates have developed over time, in different

---

* These different aspects emerge in the current context too, as previous chapters have illustrated, with community-based adult education initiatives to encourage creative writing, and initiatives to promote the critical study of the cultural heritage of the past, as well as initiatives based upon a broader definition of culture, identity and consciousness.

contexts. In the present context, these questions have a particular focus, because of the changes associated with globalisation, changes which have themselves been contradictory and contested, both in general, and in relation to issues of culture, identity and consciousness, more specifically. As Hall, amongst others, has argued, globalisation cannot simply be interpreted as the triumph of the West, spreading across the world, incorporating differences, whether this triumph is viewed in terms of the productive process, or in terms of cultures and identities. Whilst it has indeed become increasingly possible to jet across continents, eating comparable meals, reading the same books, listening to the same music, watching the same films and television programmes, even collecting comparable artefacts as 'souvenirs', this is not the entire story. At the same time, indeed partly in direct response to increasing homogenisation, there has been increasing emphasis, too, upon difference, and the distinctiveness of different cultural identities. As Hall has pointed out, this return to the local can be a form of resistance, a defensive response to globalisation, the struggles of the margins to reclaim some form of representation for themselves (Hall, 1991).

As Hall has also pointed out, these are processes of change. Cultures and identities are never completed, 'they are always, as subjectivity itself is, in process' (Hall, 1991: 47). Indeed, the earlier origins of the term 'identity' imply both sameness and continuity, 'permanence amid change and unity amid diversity'; in more modern usages, the 'struggle to define the self' linked to the 'way in which a community constructs conceptions of people and life' in a changing world (Plummer, 1993: 271). The quest for personal identity in the late twentieth century can thus be seen as part of the quest for cultural identity, which has acquired such importance precisely because of the extent and the degree of global change, changes which have both positive as well as negative features. In Hall's view, for instance, it is from these processes of change, and mixing, that some of the most exciting cultural forms have emerged. 'Creolisation' has been creative. Musical traditions (which have developed and changed as they have moved across continents, from Africa, *via* North America and Latin America, back and forth, including Britain) provide just one set of examples.

But conversely, there are negative aspects too. Wallerstein, for example, has pointed to the ways in which cultures and identities can be subjected to commodification – turning cultural artefacts, even national heritages, into 'exotic' consumer items. And an increasing emphasis upon identities and differences can, as the previous chapter suggested, be part of processes of exclusion towards the 'Other'; Englishness, for example, as constituted in terms of a colonial past and a racist present.

These issues relate to key and continuing themes in adult education. As Chapter One outlined, Freire's approach to the pedagogy of the oppressed emphasised the importance of confronting the consciousness of the oppressor, internalised within the innermost being of the oppressed. 'Only as they discover themselves to be "hosts" of the oppressor can they contribute to the midwifery of their liberating pedagogy' (Freire, 1972: 25). Adult education for transformation works for the development of critical consciousness and praxis, processes which, in turn, involve questions of identity and culture – ejecting the oppressor from within one's own head, to combat dehumanising negative self-images, and to struggle towards liberation. This approach to liberation, according to Freire, specifically entails the transformation of social relations, rather than liberating oneself at the expense of others (organising around one's own interests, even if this involves organising against the interests of other groups of the oppressed) or simply replacing 'the former oppressors with new ones' (Freire, 1972: 33).

Culture, language and identity

Shenahan, for example, draws upon transformatory notions, when he quotes the poet Yeats in relation to Irish experiences of the loss of culture and identity, through colonial exploitation and oppression. Yeats had referred to this in terms of the colonisers digging up the cultural rose-garden of the colonised, replacing this rose-garden with a cabbage-patch instead (Shenahan, forthcoming). Or alternatively, Shenahan has also quoted Synge, referring to these processes as 'The Devil's Own Mirror' of colonial and neo-colonial experiences, a mirror which would cast a squint across an angel's brow. These processes, it is argued, devalue the cultures of the oppressed, whether these are defined in terms of the arts, or defined, more broadly, in terms of a way of life, leaving the oppressed with a devalued sense of themselves and their potential for working creatively for liberation and for social transformation.

Challenging these negative definitions and self-definitions becomes key to the development of critical consciousness. An example of a particularly striking image, here, was provided by the Australian Aboriginal picture of an Aboriginal, with the face of a dog, wearing a dog collar with the tag 'Australian Citizen'. The caption underneath read 'In 1944 Aborigines were allowed to become "Australian Citizens." Aboriginal people called their citizenship papers "Dog Tags". We had to be licensed to be called Australian.' * Aboriginal culture was both an integral part of a way of life, which had been rural and, far from representing a nostalgic response to change, Aboriginal art was actively challenging contemporary forms of oppression, both rural and urban.

Adult education has been centrally involved in these types of struggles over cultural identity. Contemporary examples include classes in national languages, histories, and literatures, for instance. Irish language classes have already been mentioned, as a case in point, in Chapter Six.

---

* This image was displayed on the cover of the guide to an exhibition of Aboriginal Art, 'Aratjara: Art of the First Australians', at the Hayward Gallery, London, 1993.

In the context of sectarian divisions in Northern Ireland, an interest in the Irish language was itself perceived in terms of links with Irish nationalism, the Catholic community and opposition to the Unionist state. Irish language classes and classes in aspects of Irish history and literature have been problematic within adult education provision. There has been considerable interest, especially amongst Catholic communities, and classes have taken off, in some areas, and within particular projects.

Official support has been ambivalent, and there have been instances where such provision has been perceived as linked to nationalist politics, in ways which have been unacceptable to the state (public funding for particular voluntary and community initiatives being subject to vetting, to ensure that there would be no risk of funded projects supporting paramilitary organisations, either directly or indirectly). Yet despite what the critics have considered to be at best the indifference, and dearth of funding, and at worst the active hostility of the state, in the past, Irish language education and cultural activities have survived and developed within community initiatives (McKee, 1995). And more recently, as the situation has developed, there has also been increasing evidence of interest amongst Protestant working class communities. As Lovett explained, in his account of the Ulster People's College (discussed in Chapter Six) this was a vitally important aspect of their approach to anti-sectarianism, involving both communities, Protestant as well as Catholic working class people, in learning about their identities, cultures and histories, to develop a critical understanding of the current context, and a shared understanding of their common interests and the shared problems which they needed to confront.

Language classes and the rediscovery of cultural identity has, of course, been a feature of adult education initiatives in a wide range of contexts. The Gaelic language has featured in adult education in Scotland, too, despite a previous history of having been suppressed and eroded by the state, as in the case of Ireland. The suppression and distortion of local languages and cultures has been a common feature experienced by so many peoples who have been subjected to colonisation, whether by the British, or indeed by other colonial powers.

There are, of course, parallels, too, in relation to debates on uses of language and issues of identity and culture, and the oppression of women, and the oppression and exploitation of working class people. For working class women in Liverpool, for example, exploring their history as working class women was key to gaining self-confidence and pride. The report *I'm a New Woman Now* includes a poem written by a participant at a Women's History Group study weekend at Northern College, expressing her feelings on learning about the hidden history of working women's struggles in the past, and her pride, in realising that her view of herself had changed, in the process:

'this woman was a person all of her own,
Who'd fought for a place in history and now the truth is being
shown' (Cousins, undated: 51).

Cultural studies, in this case, included both an exploration of working
class women's history and way of life, and support in becoming a
worker-writer, expressing her own feelings through poetry. Similarly,
the Ruskin Learning Project, referred to in Chapters Five and Six, also
included these two elements: the development of creative writing, as
well as the critical exploration of the cultural heritage of the past. As
Hughes has commented, '"culture" is also an important dimension of
our work. It is "ordinary" in both the sense of being about where we
come from, who we are, what we want to be. It is also about a direct
involvement in shaping and changing meanings which in the process
challenges, demystifies and also shapes a critical appreciation of various
forms of cultural production' (Hughes, 1995). The Ruskin Learning
Project has included both sessions on political economy and sessions on
culture in the more specific sense of the study of the arts, literature,
drama and poetry, both practical sessions on tackling the daily problems
faced by the unemployed and the marginally employed, and sessions
on creative writing.

The questions about who shapes meanings, and how identities and
cultures are defined, are, of course, ultimately political questions. They
raise issues about power and democracy. There are connections, as
Kirkwood, for example, has set out, between what he has described as
'the key themes of our time' to do with 'the search for identity, the
meaning of authority, the nature of democracy, and the exercise of power'
(Kirkwood, 1990: 11). Definitions can be reinforced, through the interventions of the state, whether directly, or indirectly; or alternatively, they
can be reinforced through far subtler processes, the reproduction of
cultural hegemony, in Gramsci's terminology, just as definitions can be
resisted, and replaced, in a variety of ways, both positive and negative.

Examples from film

Examples of each of these can be found in the history of film; indeed,
film has been seen as particularly important, as the cinema became a
widespread form of entertainment. This has been partly because of the
mass potential of the audiences (some 40 per cent of the population
went to the 'pictures' at least once a week in the period just before the
Second World War in Britain; Stead, 1982). And it has been partly due
to the potential potency of the moving image itself. Film has been seen
as both potentially negative, a source of passive entertainment for the
masses, or even worse, an especially powerful propaganda weapon.
And conversely, film has been seen as an important tool for adult education, through appropriate documentaries, for example.

The documentary film movement in Britain and Canada, for
instance, set out to provide positive forms of adult education for social

reform; education from above. In the words of John Grierson, a key figure in the documentary film movement, putting this argument in extreme form 'you can also be "totalitarian" for good' purposes, as well as for evil purposes (Aitkin, 1990: 189). And film was also seen as a weapon of ideological struggle, both in Britain (for example through workers' film societies, showing documentary films on the Hunger Marches, or Spanish Civil War) and beyond. Whilst film making itself, as opposed to viewing films, has been relatively restricted within the context of adult education because of the costs involved in even the most modest productions, changing technologies, including video, have opened the field up in potentially new and challenging ways.

The use of film for direct agitation and propaganda has been discussed in the context of the early days of the Soviet Union, with the classic examples of the films of Eisenstein, including *October* (about the 1917 revolution), and *Battleship Potemkin*, which was banned from public showing in Britain. Lenin had remarked, in a much-quoted phrase, that 'of all the arts, for us, the cinema is the most important' (quoted in Taylor, 1979: 29). And in contrast, the use of film for propaganda has been discussed in the context of Nazi Germany, including the notorious *The Wandering Jew*, a piece of anti-semitic propaganda which was shown in Germany and in occupied Holland, for example (Taylor, 1979). This is an extreme case, however. Even Goebbels, who was responsible for propaganda in Nazi Germany, expressed the view that propaganda becomes ineffective the moment we become aware of it (Taylor, 1979).

There are also examples of far subtler versions of propaganda through the use of film, involving images which were to be shown, and images which were not to be shown. In Britain, in the inter-war period, the British Board of Film Censors had guidelines which covered not only matters of sexual morality and indecency, but also the following: 'references to controversial politics, relations of capital and labour, scenes tending to disparage public characters and institutions, realistic horrors of warfare, scenes and incidents calculated to afford information to the enemy, incidents tending to disparage our Allies, scenes holding up the King's uniform to contempt or ridicule, subjects dealing with India, in which British officers are seen in an odious light, and otherwise to suggest the disloyalty of the Native states or bringing into disrepute British prestige in the Empire' (quoted in Pronay, 1982: 103). There were also controls on showing 'liaisons between coloured men and white women'. The British imperialist way of life was not to be challenged in these ways, on public screens. As a result, Lord Tyrell is quoted as reflecting, in 1937, that 'we may take pride in observing that there is not a single film showing in London today which deals with any of the burning questions of the day' (quoted in *ibid*, p.122).

Whilst this may all seem slightly ludicrous, rather than anything more sinister, as a piece of history, there are, of course, more recent examples of uncomfortably topical films receiving relatively restricted showings. For instance, the French film *The Sorrow and the Pity*, (which tackled the myth that virtually the entire French population was actively involved in the Resistance, and illustrated the actual extent of anti-semitism in war-time occupied France), was considered to be problematic, in terms of being shown on French television, even though this was decades after the events in question (Macbean, 1975). And more recently, in Britain, there were delays in television showings of Ken Loach's film *Hidden Agenda*, about the conflict in Northern Ireland and the role of the British state. The point, of course, is not that there has been totalitarian censorship, but that the range of views, norms and values which are reinforced, or alternatively marginalised, can be affected in far subtler, although still vitally important ways.

More generally, this raises questions which are directly relevant to Gramsci's concept of cultural hegemony; the reinforcement of particular concepts of norms and values, in society, through the powerful medium of the moving image. The term the 'Third Cinema' was coined by Third World film-makers in the sixties, precisely in opposition to this type of cultural hegemony *via* the Hollywood movie which had become so prevalent on a global scale. Hollywood productions were seen as dominating their competitors, both in the West and in the Third World (with major and significant exceptions particularly that of India, which both produces and exports films on a major scale).

In contrast, the Third Cinema was to contribute to the development of alternative forms of culture and consciousness in the Third World (see eg, Pines and Willeman, 1989). The aim has been summarised by Solanas and Getino, for example, in terms of building not 'a cinema made for the old kind of human being' but 'a cinema fit for a new kind of human being, for what each of us has the possibility of becoming' (quoted in Ames, 1987: 100).

Whilst the intention was didactic, however, the process was to involve dialogue. This approach was particularly developed by Sanjines, for example, working in Bolivia and developing ways of involving local people directly in making films. As Sanjines explained, 'we realized that the people knew much more about misery than any film maker who might aspire to show it to them.' They did not want or need to be told about their situation, which they already knew only too well. 'The people are more interested in knowing *how* and *why* misery is produced; they want to know *who* causes it and *how* they can oppose them.' For example, he referred to the high level of political consciousness which characterised the Bolivian miners. In these circumstances, Sanjines argued, it was possible for local people to participate directly in shaping the film, spontaneously relaying their experiences. 'By eliminating the hierarchical structure of *a priori* film making, where everything is planned by the film-makers in advance, we took steps towards permitting genuine popular participation in the creative process of a film dealing with the history and destiny of the miners with whom we were working' (Sanjines, 1986: 42). (The film was *Courage of the People*.) Sanjines argued that this process was key, believing that 'a new language – liberated and liberating – cannot be born except through the exploration of and integration with the people's culture, which is living and dynamic. A revolutionary process does not exist, nor is it ever realized, *except* through the mobilization and dynamic participation of the people' (*ibid*, p.47).

Examples from theatre

Whilst film, television and video, along with radio, have been linked to adult education and community development, live theatre has also been seen as a potentially powerful tool. There have been strong traditions of alternative theatre in Britain, and even more so in Germany and the Soviet Union. Theatre has linked with strong cultural traditions in Third World contexts too, including a number of African countries. Popular theatre has been used in powerful ways within community development programmes. Theatre has been used for propaganda and for communicating information about development issues in didactic ways. And the use of theatre has been advocated as part of cultures of resistance against exploitation and oppression, 'as an integral part of any development strategy that is genuinely concerned with the need to better the lives of the majority' (Mlama, 1991: 18).

Exploring the history of workers' theatre movements in Britain and America, Samuel has drawn attention to the links between politics and theatre more generally. In Shakespeare's time, as the players' scene in Hamlet illustrates, theatre played an active role in the rivalries and intrigues of the court. And more recently, parliamentary commentators have reflected and continue to reflect upon the theatre of high politics. A political demonstration is necessarily, Samuel has argued, 'an act of street theatre, albeit one with a multitudinous cast, and a rhythm and tempo of its own' (Samuel *et al*, 1985: xv).

The idea of theatre as propaganda had long historical roots. In the late nineteenth and early twentieth century, the socialist movement was more concerned with bringing 'high culture' to the masses, but by the 1920s and 1930s, the focus had shifted towards a more iconoclastic, modernist approach, strongly influenced by experiments in Germany and the Soviet Union. Agitprop was street theatre of a directly committed kind, emphasising *Proletkult*, the culture of the working class and revolutionary social change. This was a theatre of ideas, rather than a theatre of 'illusion', divided from the audience and reality by curtains. Audiences were to be actively involved in this new theatre of ideas, and through 'dialectical realism' underlying social relations were to be unmasked (Samuel *et al*, 1985). The Workers Theatre Movement had links with the Plebs League and the National Council of Labour Colleges, which were discussed in terms of their role in the development of workers' education in Chapter Two. Street theatre of this type was used to attract crowds to street political meetings, and to collect funds and support for strikes. And street theatre was also used in support of international solidarity, such as the 'Meerut' sketch, in support of jailed trade unionists in India (Samuel *et al*, 1985). The aim was to organise, to educate and to agitate.

This approach to theatre was largely superseded in the latter part of the thirties, as left politics became more engaged with the politics of the Popular Front (which was based upon alliances against fascism, rather than such overtly working class politics) and as socialist realism replaced experiments with modernism in the international communist movement. The Unity Theatre, which became a focal point of alternative theatre, maintained both forms, however, and this survived into the sixties and the revival of radical theatre.

Alternative theatre groups, in this latter period, drew upon some of the radical ideas from the twenties to reach new audiences through street theatre, based upon simplicity, speed and topicality (Davies, 1987). Groups such as the Agitprop Street Players (later Red Ladder), the Brighton Combination and 7:84 performed plays about such subjects as industrial disputes, rent strikes and community planning and development issues. And projects such as the Albany, an independent community centre in South London, combined multi-media approaches to work with the local community as part of a community strategy 'to enable people to have more control over situations around them, to bring about changes where needed, to offer support services to families, individuals and community groups, and to work towards enriching the quality of life' (Collins *et al*, 1974: 171).

Community arts have played a vital role, then, in community education and community work and development more generally, despite increasing difficulties in the more problematic climate from the late seventies, and new areas have been opened up, in women's theatre, black theatre and gay theatre (Davies, 1987). There is not the space here for more than this passing acknowledgement of the wide significance of community arts work in Britain.

Popular theatre has had particular significance, too, in a number of Third World contexts, in the South. Theatre has been used to promote specific development messages, as well as to carry subtler cultural messages. And theatre has contributed to the development of cultures of resistance.

Both the British and the French, as colonial powers, tended to support cultural initiatives which encouraged European theatre in their colonies, it has been argued (Mlama, 1991). Whilst this could be seen as a form of cultural imperialism (culture being defined in the colonisers' terms) in practice, European theatre could raise potentially uncomfortable questions, too, and can still do so (Shakespeare's *Julius Caesar* has provided an example with particular resonance, in the context of countries which have experienced coups and counter-coups, and *Othello* provided another such example, in the context of Apartheid South Africa). But this focus upon European theatre, it has been argued, was to the detriment of support for local forms of theatre. It was only somewhat later, in the struggles for independence and following independence in many cases, that local theatrical forms and traditions came to gain fuller recognition (Mlama, 1991; Zakes, 1993). The potential contribution which popular cultural forms could make to development was recognised, at an international level, more recently still (with UNESCO becoming concerned to develop this potential, from the 1980s).

But the tradition of popular theatre in a variety of different contexts, in the South, has actually had a long history. In Ghana, for example, traditionally forms of theatre were used, with music and dance, as part of the ways in which young people were instructed into their way of life – culture, here, meaning both the arts of story telling, dance, music and drama *and* culture, in the anthropological sense, as a whole way of life. This type of traditional theatre was also strongly developed in a number of other African countries, including Kenya and Zimbabwe. Theatre was often very clearly didactic; there were vital messages to be conveyed. And this was a powerful medium (Mlama, 1991).

Popular theatre was also used as a tool of resistance, in a number of contexts, as part of struggles for liberation from colonial rule and from neo-colonial regimes. Examples here range from the use of theatre to organise support for Mau Mau in Kenya, for Frelimo in Mozambique, for ZANU in Zimbabwe (then Southern Rhodesia) and to build support for the Sandinistas in Nicaragua. Since then, theatre has been used, too, as a tool for development, in a wide variety of contexts, both development in general, and more specific aspects such as health education and development (McGivney and Murray, 1991).

Often, it has been suggested, this has been approached in overtly didactic ways, mirroring some of the approaches which had been applied in traditional forms. Mlama, for instance, has drawn parallels between some of the approaches which have been applied to using theatre, for development purposes, and Freire's criticisms of the banking approach to education. In both cases, the audience/adult learners may be seen as essentially passive, empty vessels to be filled with information, even if this information is 'for their own good' (health education messages, for example). And some of the forms which have enjoyed popularity, such as the use of puppets, for instance, have become less widely used, because they have been seen as too 'childish'; treating the audience in too simplistic a way (Zakes, 1993).

In contrast, Mlama has also provided examples of more interactive approaches, approaches which would seem to relate more closely to Freire's approach to education for conscientisation and transformation. For example, there were examples of theatre workshops in Zimbabwe where the villagers had actively engaged with the process of producing the play, shaping the content to reflect their own concerns and priorities for development. This type of approach was shared at a workshop on Theatre for Development, in Zimbabwe in 1983. Since then, however, Mlama has pointed to a more restricted climate, due to political shifts in Zimbabwe (Mlama, 1991).

One well-known example of theatre for development which raised very particular political problems was the case of the Kamiriithu Popular Theatre, in Kenya. In 1977, a number of university lecturers decided to put energies into reviving the Kamiriithu Community Education and Cultural Centre, at Limuru, to promote adult education for development and community development of a liberating nature. Literacy classes were part of an approach which aimed at conscientisation. Theatre was chosen as the medium for taking this process forward, to explore the causes of people's poverty and oppression, reflecting the strength of traditions of popular theatre.

Local people met and discussed the content of the play which they would produce, before requesting the novelist and playwright Ngugi Wa Thiong'O and the adult education and community worker Ngugi Wa Miri to produce a draft, using the local language. The play (in English, *I Will Marry When I Want*) subsequently emerged, following further discussion with local participants. Its success with local people has been attributed to the ways in which traditional cultural forms, including dances and songs of struggle, were incorporated in a play which centrally addressed the key issues of people's lives, 'their struggles, concerns and hope' (Mlama, 1991: 92). The play ends with the workers and peasants calling for the mobilisation and unity of the poor to end land-grabbing, poor working conditions and all-round exploitation and oppression.

Local people had worked together to construct the theatre for their play to be performed in. This theatre was razed, in 1982, in a government clamp-down on popular theatre. Ngugi Wa Thiong'O had already been detained in prison, and eventually he left the country, together with several of the animateurs, including Ngugi Wa Miri. Popular theatre had produced too much of a challenge.

The play certainly put across an unambiguous perspective on the sources of local people's poverty, exploitation and oppression. As one of the characters comments,

'I wouldn't mind, son of Gathoni,
If after selling away our labour
Our village had benefited.
But look at this village!
If all the wealth we create with our hands
Remained in the country,
What would we not have in our village?
Good public schools,
Good houses for the workers,
Good houses for the peasants,
And several other industries
In which the unemployed could be absorbed'.
... but
'The power of our hands goes to feed three people:

Imperialists from Europe,
Imperialists from America,
Imperialists from Japan,
And of course their local watchmen' (Ngugi and Ngugi, 1982: 36–37).

The play concludes with a call for unity.

'Development will come from our unity.
Unity is our strength and wealth.'

The final song calls to waken the workers, the peasants and the poor, who have tired of being robbed and exploited, 'tired of charity and abuses', calling them to unite and to organise, to work for a different form of development to meet local needs (Ngugi and Ngugi, 1982: 116).

Theatre has been and continues to be such a powerful medium, with the potential to pose questions about people's present realities, whilst raising questions, too, about alternative futures. Similar points were made, in paying tribute to Barney Simon, the co-founder of the Market Theatre in Johannesburg, South Africa, who died in 1995. The Market Theatre has been a unique project, both in theatrical terms and in terms of the challenging role it played under Apartheid. The Market Theatre, Mary Benson commented, 'was what all effective theatres aspire to be. It was of its time and place, but it dreamed of a different world that could be – while holding up a mirror of what was' (Benson, 1995).

Towards alternatives?

This brings the discussion back to some of the questions which were raised at the beginning of this chapter. How to move beyond the limitations of specific cultures of resistance, to explore the interconnections between them? How to develop a more coherent and critical understanding of the particular, within the context of the global? How to strengthen people's confidence that alternative futures could be possible, without claiming to be that future?

Cultures as defined in terms of whole ways of life, as well as in terms of the arts, are not, it has been suggested, free-floating sets of ideas, norms and values. On the contrary, cultures vary and change as they interact with changes in the material world, just as identities develop in process. The political economy of culture, itself, is key to a critical understanding of cultures, then, whether these are the cultures of the powerful, or the cultures of resistance. Both develop and change, as they interact with processes of change in the productive sphere, and both, in turn, affect these processes of change. Gramsci's approach to the role of ideas more generally emphasised both their great importance and their interconnectedness with the forces and relations of production. As processes of change gather speed in the late twentieth century this can be expected to affect the realms of identity and culture, as well as the realm of production, at an increasing pace of change.

If hegemonic cultures can be expected to be changing more rapidly than ever, rather than being static, then, so can alternative approaches to developing counter-hegemonic cultures. Williams's characterisation of working class culture emphasised the importance of neighbourhood, mutual obligation and common betterment, a whole way of life with norms and values which presented an alternative to the individualist competitiveness of bourgeois culture, the norms and values of the market-led approach. There are aspects of continuing relevance – but the details of Williams's picture of working class life seem extremely dated now. Such major processes of economic and social change have so affected the traditional working class communities which Williams characterised. And so have the alternative perspectives which have been developed, through other forms of challenge and change.

Some of these changes can be highlighted by comparing British working class culture, in the post-war period, to a more recent cultural challenge, originating in the United States. The term 'counterculture' has been used to describe a very different approach to developing an alternative set of norms and values, in the sixties. This 'counterculture' included both challenges to the predominant 'hegemonic' cultures of the capitalist West, as exemplified in New Left student political movements, and in attempts to create alternative ways of living, described by Roszak in terms of the mind-blown bohemianism of the beats and hippies (Roszak, 1969). This predominantly youthful 'counterculture' opposed the materialism, the elitism and the authoritarianism of American establishment culture, with its racism and its emphasis upon individualistic competition. Making love was counterposed with the predominant emphasis on making war (in the specific context of opposition to the Vietnam War). Music played a particular part in the development of this 'counterculture', with the greatest event being the Woodstock Festival of Life, in 1968, attended by some half a million participants. Whilst there are elements in common with the working class cultures as characterised by Williams, elements such as the emphasis upon collectivism and co-operation, rather than individualistic competition, the differences are also striking.

A contemporary version of a counterculture, a counterhegemonic project which set out to pose a fundamental set of challenges to the hegemonic culture, would need to include these critiques of individualism and excessive competitiveness in the market-led approach, counterposing these with the values of collectivism and co-operation. But a contemporary version of a counterculture would also need to take more account of a range of other challenges, including the challenges to previous definitions of the political, which have been posed by feminism, as Chapter Seven suggested. The politics of disability would have their place, along with the politics of sexuality and age.

In addition, the question of the environment and the case for sustainability has become centrally important to the development agenda, and this would also need to be fully addressed. As the Red-Green

Study Group has pointed out so clearly, without radical change towards the environment 'life on earth will be hell' (Red-Green Study Group, 1995). Environmental politics involve challenging an entire way of organising social life, requiring what has been described as a 'qualitatively new vision of how humans should live together with each other and with the planet' (*ibid*, p.4). The dialogue between traditional 'red' politics and environmental 'green' politics necessitates addressing real differences and tensions, as well as points in common. And environmental politics involves addressing global issues as well as local issues, taking account of and respecting the differences of interest between North and South, between those who have had access to more of the earth's resources and those who have had to make do with less.

But arguing for the importance of these various ingredients of a contemporary counterculture is very different from attempting to sketch its outlines. Such a task is beyond the scope or purpose of this book. The point to emphasise here is simply this. Like the hegemonic cultures which are to be questioned and challenged, counterhegemonic projects are constantly affected by processes of change. Consciousness changes, just as changing consciousness can itself promote change.

The author's own experiences, working in adult education, in different contexts, confirm the view that participants are generally only too well aware of their particular problems, the specific forms of their own exploitation and oppression. What they may be seeking may be ways of setting these experiences within a wider context, exploring the connections between their individual and collective experiences, and those of other groups, analysing the underlying structural sources of their problems, in order to develop more comprehensive and effective ways of addressing these. Adult education can play a key role here, providing potential ways of developing strategies for change which move beyond organising around one's own interests; enabling participants to gain the confidence to organise for transformation.

Commenting on the connections between culture, adult education, and political change, Freire has pointed to some of the influences on his thinking, including the influence of Gramsci. 'I only read Gramsci when I was in exile. I read Gramsci and I discovered that I had been greatly influenced by Gramsci long before I read him.'

Reflecting upon these influences, Freire went on to describe ways in which he had introduced discussions of culture to his literacy lessons in Brazil. 'I was full of happiness when I started to perceive the results of that discussion', he commented, 'when the illiterate workers realised that to make culture was also to transform a world which had not been made by them ... that we can transform a reality which we did not make, and we can transform the reality which we make. History, culture politics – all these things are made by us ... Thus they got much confidence in themselves through the simple discussion of culture', the confidence which they needed even to begin to contemplate transformation (Freire, 1995: 63-63).

References

Aitkin, I. (1990) *Film and Reform*, Routledge.

Benson, M. (1995) 'For freedom of the heart and mind', obituary of Barney Simon, *The Guardian*, Monday 3 July, p. 12.

Clarke, J. (1979) 'Capital and culture: the post-war working class revisited', in J. Clarke, C. Crichter and R. Johnson (eds) *From Working Class Culture*, Hutchinson, pp. 238–253.

Collins, S., Curno, P., Harris, J. and Turner, J. (1974) 'Community arts', in D. Jones and M. Mayo (eds) *Community Work One*, Routledge and Kegan Paul.

Cousins, L. (undated) 'I'm a New Woman Now'; Education for Women in Liverpool, Priority; c/o Educational Technology Centre, Liverpool.

Davies, A. (1987) *Other Theatres*, Macmillan.

Freire, P. (1972) *Pedagogy of the Oppressed*, Penguin Books.

Freire, P. (1995) *Paulo Freire at the Institute*, Institute of Education, University of London.

Hall, S. (1991) 'The local and the global: globalization and ethnicity' and 'Old and new identities, old and new ethnicities', in A. King (ed.) *Culture, Globalization and the World-System*, Macmillan, pp. 19–39 and pp. 41–68.

Hobsbawm, E. (1994) *Age of Extremes: The Short Twentieth Century*, Michael Joseph.

Hughes, K. (1995) 'Really useful knowledge: adult learning and the Ruskin Learning Project', in M. Mayo and J. Thompson (eds) *Adult Learning, Critical Intelligence and Social Change*, NIACE.

Kirkwood, C. (1990) *Vulgar Eloquence: From Labour to Liberation*, Polygon.

MacBean, J. (1975) *Film and Revolution*, Indiana University Press.

McIlroy, J. and Westwood, S. (eds) (1993) *Border Country: Raymond Williams in Adult Education*, NIACE.

McGivney, V. and Murray, F. (1991) *Adult Education in Development*, NIACE.

Mlama, P. (1991) *Culture and Development*, The Scandinavian Institute of African Studies, Uppsala, Sweden.

Ngugi and Ngugi (1982) *I Will Marry When I Want*, Heinemann.

Pines, J. and Willeman, P. (eds) (1989) *Questions of Third Cinema*, British Film Institute.

Plummer, K. (1993) 'Identity', in W. Outhwaite *et al.* (eds) *Twentieth Century Social Thought*, Blackwell.

Pronay, N. (1982) 'The political censorship of films', in N. Pronay and D. Spring (eds) *Propaganda, Politics and Film*, Macmillan, pp. 173–208.

Red-Green Study Group (1995) *What on Earth Is To Be Done? A Red-Green Dialogue*, Red-Green Study Group, Manchester.

Roszak, T. (1969) *The Making of a Counterculture*, Anchor, New York.

Samuel, R. *et al.* (eds) (1985) *Theatres of the Left 1880–1935: Workers' Theatre Movements in Britain and America*, Routledge and Kegan Paul.

Sanjines, J. (1986) 'Revolutionary cinema: the Bolivian experience', in J. Burton (ed.) *Cinema and Change in Latin America*, University of Texas Press, Austin, Texas, USA, pp. 35–48.

Shenahan, P. (forthcoming)

Stead, P. (1982) 'The people and the pictures: the British working class and film in the 1930s' in N. Pronay and D. Spring (eds) *Propaganda, Politics and Film*, Macmillan, pp. 77–97.

Steele, T. (1995) 'Unpopular culture and critical renewal', in M. Mayo and J. Thompson (eds) *Adult Learning, Critical Intelligence and Social Change*, NIACE.

Taylor, R. (1979) *Film Propaganda: Soviet Russia and Nazi Germany*, Croom Helm.

Wallerstein, I. (1991) *Geopolitics and Geoculture: Essays on the Changing World-System*, Cambridge University Press.

Wolff, J. (1991) 'The global and the specific: reconciling conflicting theories of culture', in A. King (ed.) *Culture, Globalization and the World-System*, Macmillan, pp. 161–173.

Zakes, M. (1993) *When People Play People*, Zed Books.

Globalization, adult education and training: Impacts and issues
Shirley Walters (ed)
ISBN 1 86201 026 9 (pbk); 1 85649 511 6 (hbk)
1997, 256pp, £14.95 (pbk); £39.95 (hbk)

Globalization has become a key shorthand for the times we live in, summing up some of the important changes affecting life in all parts of the world. And adult educators are having to come to terms with the processes involved and the implications for their own work. This book looks at the impact of globalization on adult education and training generally and on women in particular, and draws the lessons for adult education trainers. It explores adult education and training strategies towards women, workplace training and participatory approaches in diverse contexts and countries. The contributors focus on the notion of lifelong learning, its meaning and how to go about implementing it.

This book is the first in a series co-published by NIACE and ZED BOOKS on global perspectives in adult education and training. It includes well-documented material on the effects of globalization from both North and South. Launched at the UNESCO World Conference on Adult Education in Hamburg in July 1997.

SPECIAL OFFER to NIACE readers only. NIACE has arranged a privilege price of £35.95 (normally £39.95) for the hardback version – a saving of 10 per cent. Order direct from NIACE to take advantage of this excellent offer.

The learning divide: A study of participation in adult learning in the United Kingdom
Naomi Sargant
with John Field, Hywel Francis, Tom Schuller and Alan Tuckett
ISBN 1 86201 016 1
1997, 144pp, £20.00

This publication reports on a survey carried out by the Gallup Organisation in 1996. It highlights the full scale of the challenge which the UK faces in involving all its people in the learning society, and shows that the learning divide between the learning-rich and the learning-poor is growing. It shows that 60% of adults have not taken part in adult learning in the last three years; more men than women are currently learning or have been recent learners; age is a barrier; social class is still the key discriminator; and length of initial education is still the best single predictor of participation in adult learning.

The report includes the first full study of participation in Northern Ireland, and, with studies from Scotland and Wales, gives the most comprehensive coverage of the United Kingdom. With over 60 tables of statistical information, this report will provide an invaluable resource for researchers, academics, media and information officers.

Words in edgeways: Radical learning for social change
Jane Thompson
ISBN 1 86201 013 7
1997, 160pp, £14.95

Jane Thompson's books and essays have inspired and validated the work of radical practitioners in adult and community education not only in Britain, but also overseas – particularly in Ireland, Australia, New Zealand, Canada and the United States.

This is a collection of extracts, essays and conference presentations, written over a 20-year period, on working class and women's education. This volume covers the application of Marxist, sociological and feminist analysis to adult education; connections between the women's movement and adult education, and a collection of writings by women learners whose lives were restricted by poverty and family violence.

This book will be useful to students on adult and continuing education courses at Diploma and Masters level. It will also be of relevance to staff development activity, conferences and workshops in which matters of curriculum, political education, participatory learning, citizenship and social change are being discussed. Practitioners in adult learning and community education who are concerned about disadvantage and issues of inclusion and exclusion will also find the book valuable.

Electronic pathways: Adult learning and the new communication technologies
Edited by Jane Field
ISBN 1 86201 008 0
1997, 176pp, £14.95

What does the information society really mean for adult learning? A rapidly-growing range of communications technologies is being developed to support the adult learner. Telematics applications can have an impact on education, leisure and work, but adult educators and others involved in working with adult learners need practical help if they are to make the most of the opportunities.

This is the first book to place the new information and communications technologies firmly in the context of adult learning. It is written by adult educators who have used the new technologies to widen access to learning and promote independent learning. They have seen that it is possible to offer different ways to communicate and support learning, whether in college, the home, the workplace or other settings.

Case studies provide examples of the pitfalls involved, good practice identified and the opportunities available. The book is an accessible, informative and practical resource for all who are professionally concerned with developing adult learning.

Ethics and education for adults in a late modern society
Peter Jarvis
ISBN 1 86201 014 5 (hbk)
ISBN 1 86201 015 3 (pbk)
1997, 200pp, £35.00 (hbk), £17.95 (pbk)

Peter Jarvis analyses recent developments in the education of adults from an ethical perspective. Based upon the argument that there is only one universal good, and that all other moral goods are cultural and relative, he develops the position that education for adults is a site within which human morality is worked out. Examining both traditional topics, such as teaching and learning, and more recent ones, such as the education market, distance education and the learning society, Jarvis argues that educators need to be critically aware of the ethical implications of these developments. This is a topical book which should be of interest to everybody involved in education at every level and every age group.

Peter Jarvis is currently Professor of Continuing Education at the University of Surrey and Adjunct Professor of Adult Education at the University of Georgia, USA. He was previously Head of Department of Educational Studies at the University of Surrey. He is the author and editor of more than twenty books. He is also the editor of *The International Journal of Lifelong Education.*

Adults count too: Mathematics for empowerment
Roseanne Benn
ISBN 1 86201 007 2
1997, 224pp, £14.95

More and more adults are learning mathematics, either for work-related purposes, or as a qualification leading to a desired course of study. *Adults count too* examines the low level of numeracy in our society, the reasons why this is critical and the forces acting on adults which contribute to this state of affairs. Written to encourage the development of a curriculum which is tailored to the priorities and lives of individuals, Benn argues that mathematics is not a value-free construct, but is imbued with elitist notions which exclude and mystify. The book seeks alternative approaches to teaching mathematics which recognise the sophisticated mathematical techniques and ideas used in everyday work, domestic and leisure.

This book will be of interest to adult educators who teach mathematics or to mathematics educators who teach adults.

Adults learning
ISSN 0955 2308
Subscription rates: £30 (institutions); extra copies @ £15 each
£17.50 (individuals)
£15 (concessions for part-time tutors and adult learners)

The need for a professional journal for those concerned with adult learning has never been greater than now. The majority of students in further and higher education in Britain are adults. More and more awareness of the importance of adults as learners is being shown by government, the media, employers and trade unions. In a quickly-changing environment it is vital to keep abreast of current issues and initiatives, debates and events.

Adults learning is the only UK-wide journal solely devoted to matters concerning adult learning. It carries the latest news on policy and practice, and is published ten times a year by NIACE. It is a forum for adult educators and trainers to exchange information, share practice, network and engage in dialogue with fellow professionals.

In-depth features, commentaries, reviews and case studies, together with news of courses, conferences and resources, make *Adults learning* essential reading for policy-makers and practitioners, tutors (both full-time and part-time) in universities and further education colleges, staff in voluntary organisations who are developing learning opportunities, and trainers in industry seeking advice on skills development.

Studies in the education of adults
ISSN 0266 0830

Subscription rates:	UK £20 individual;	£30 institutional
Overseas surface mail:	£22/US$40 individual;	£33/US$59 institutional
Overseas airmail:	£25/US$45 individual;	£38/US$67 institutional

An international refereed journal published twice a year (April and October) by NIACE. It is addressed to academic specialists, postgraduate students, practitioners and educational managers who wish to keep abreast of scholarship, theory-building and empirical research in the broad field of education and training for adults.

Studies in the education of adults publishes theroetical, empirical and historical studies from all sectors of post-initial education and training, and aims to provide a forum for debate and development of key concepts in education and training. With feature articles and book reviews, the journal provides indispensable analysis of current developments and thinking.

A full publications catalogue is available from NIACE at 21 De Montfort Street, Leicester, LE1 7GE, England. Alternatively visit our Web site on the Internet: **http://www.niace.org.uk**